THE JUDGEMENT

THE JUDGEMENT

Ian Messiter

MICHAEL JOSEPH • LONDON

First published in Great Britain by Michael Joseph Ltd
44 Bedford Square, London WC1
1981

ISBN 0 7181 2038 8

Typeset in Singapore
Printed and bound in Great Britain by Redwood Burn Ltd.,
Trowbridge and Esher

To Enid

Author's Note

The Judgement is a reconstruction of a true scandal of 1834 which cul-
minated in a trial in Paris, at the Palais de Justice in 1835.

As French legal procedures have changed since then, my thanks and
gratitude go to Mario R. Uziell-Hamilton MA LLB (Cantab), who has
checked and corrected the narrative where necessary so that the repre-
sentation of the French legal system of 1835 is as accurate as possible.

My thanks also to Dr Nicole Marzac for help in translating parts of
some of the speeches given in the Palais de Justice.

In order to confine this tale between the covers of a normal-sized book
I have shortened many of the speeches, but never at the expense of the
evidence, all of which is presented here except where it is repetitious.

Ian Messiter

PROLOGUE

This story, a combination of fact and conjecture, is as near to the truth as research can make it.

In order to provide the setting against which the action takes place, it is necessary to give a summary of French politics from 1830 to 1834 when the story begins.

The inadequacies and unpopular measures of Charles X caused protests by the workers who were joined by students and petty bourgeois citizens, and by 29 July 1830 they had received the encouragement of several army units. Two rival factions emerged. One was made up of workers and students, led by the respected Marquis de Lafayette, who controlled the Paris streets with barricades and used the Town Hall as their headquarters. The other faction embodied constitutional monarchists, who took over the offices of the newspaper *Le National* and proposed Louis-Philippe, Duke of Orleans, as king on the night of 30 July. Adolphe Thiers, a founder of *Le National*, received a message from Lafayette who believed that neither faction was strong enough on its own, but that together they could oust Charles X and crown Louis-Philippe.

Noon the next day saw Louis-Philippe making his way to the Town Hall through a booing, jeering, cat-calling republican crowd. Together, he and Lafayette appeared on the balcony, the proposed king wrapped in a Tricolour. Charles X abdicated. The republicans did not want a king, and many monarchists did not want Louis-Philippe. Discord was a matter of time. Throughout the 1830s rebellions were frequent, mainly in Paris and Lyons, and attempts to assassinate the new king Louis-Philippe were as constant as the republican-inspired rioting by the workers.

King Louis-Philippe's right-hand man was the devious Marshal Soult, whose niece, Solange, was married to Général le Baron Charles Paul de Morell. This most favoured general was instructed by the King and Marshal Soult to silence the insurgents and to anticipate both republican and monarchist attempts on the King's life. He also had the happy task

9

of commanding the military show-piece of France, the Saumur Cavalry School, during the summer months.

De Morell, therefore, had the ears of the two most powerful men in the land, the King and the Marshal. The land ruled by those two men was one in which the death penalty was dealt out for crimes of far less moment than murder.

The story starts on 23 September 1834 in a house belonging to the rich general, in the cavalry town of Saumur on the river Loire, about one hundred and seventy miles south-west of Paris.

CHAPTER ONE

One bright summer evening Monsieur le Général le Baron Charles Paul de Morell was carrying out his duties at the Cavalry School which he commanded at Saumur, where cavalry officers qualified to train cadets from the military schools to the high standards required.

In his summer residence on the banks of the Loire, a short distance from the school, Madame la Baronne de Morell, his wife, was changing into evening dress for a dinner party.

Downstairs, the young, dark footman, Samuel Gilieron, hoped that Marie, the daughter of the house, was in her room with her English governess, Helen Allen. He wanted the opportunity to be alone in the drawing-room.

A domestic disaster was about to take place that would be discussed by all from the highest in the land to the lowest, and become a scandal across Europe.

Across the hall Samuel carried a silver tray set with glasses, a decanter and an unopened box of cigars. He was listening carefully but could hear nothing except for the echo of horses' hooves on the Rue Royale, the cobbled road outside the north-west wall. The south-west wall of the house commanded a view of the Loire slipping past the windows, troubled only by small clouds of gnats and the occasional splash of a fish. Balancing the polished tray skilfully on his left palm, he knocked on the drawing-room door and, hearing no reply, gently lowered the gilded handle of one of the double doors, opening it enough to reassure himself that the room was empty. His large brown eyes noticed the rays of the sun bouncing off the river to play in a corner of the moulded ceiling. Abandoning the subservient attitude he adopted outside the kitchen quarters, Samuel strode across the room, set down the tray on a table, and put the cigar box in a corner cupboard whose bow front, painted by Antoine Caron, depicted the royal entrance of Charles IX to Paris. Samuel had long since ceased to notice the painting. He closed the cupboard door and, holding his head slightly on one side, stood motionless for a few seconds as he listened. He heard nothing, but glanced quickly round before lifting one of

11

the pictures from the wall, looking behind it and replacing it. He continued his examination until he had inspected the backs of all eight paintings in the room. He stood back to make sure he had replaced them correctly. He made a final adjustment to one and then started to search between the books on a small shelf. He peered under the florid Louis XV writing-desk with its intricate pictorial marquetry and elaborate ormolu mounts. All the furniture on the ground floor abounded with fabulous motifs, curious animals and exotic landscapes. Samuel was too preoccupied to dwell on the rare woods of tulip, lemon, violet and king, or the sumptuous effects the richly veined and pink-tinted marble carving round the fireplace.

At last the footman noticed a piece of paper under a baroque statuette on the mantelpiece. He read its contents, and put it back, disappointed, unaware of the figure at the open door.

Marie de Morell's twenty-four-year-old governess, Helen Allen, had come quietly down the stairs, and the way she crossed the hall, almost on tiptoe, reflected her perpetual awe of her employers and of the house itself. As a devout Catholic her constant companion was her missal, which she clutched tightly in her left hand on all occasions. Her hair was parted in the middle and pulled back severely, and she wore drab, well-washed greys and browns. She seldom spoke, was unsure of her social standing, and found it difficult to give an opinion on the rare occasions she was asked for one.

"Good evening, Miss Allen." Samuel had spotted her and was trying to appear as casual as possible.

"Good evening, Samuel." Miss Allen's tone was as subdued as her bearing.

He thought that she probably knew what he had been doing, why he had been doing it, and would possibly do the same after he had left the room.

He moved towards the door. "I was just leaving."

"Not on my account, I hope," Miss Allen replied as she went over to the writing-desk. "I only want to make a few notes for Mademoiselle Marie's geography lesson."

Samuel did not believe her.

"There's a big dinner tonight," he said, hoping such an obvious and useless piece of information might encourage her to say more.

"I know," she said, opening the huge, curved desk top and looking among some papers. "I've been invited. I must make these notes before I change for dinner so that I'm ready for Monday morning. I like to be ahead."

He thought that she wanted him out of the way. He could not help wondering why she kept her tutorial notes in the drawing-room instead of in her own quarters.

Bluntly, and conscious of stepping beyond the strict confines of the world of a servant, he asked, "Where do you keep these geography notes for Marie?"

She sighed impatiently and, without looking up, Miss Allen said, "They're somewhere in here."

His first step over his well-defined boundary had brought no sharp reprimand so he tried again. "Does Madame know you keep them there?"

The reprimand came, and surprisingly sharply from such a nervous girl. She looked up at him in such a way that he suddenly straightened.

"Of course she knows! Madame is curious about her daughter's education." It was a strange way of expressing it, but Helen knew that Madame de Morell's interest was no greater than curiosity. "She asked me to leave the notes with her the other day, and to take them from her desk after she had seen them." She wondered why, after her mild and justified rebuking of Samuel, she was now being so defensive as to explain her actions to a footman. She wanted to ask him what he had been doing in the room, and what was written on the piece of paper she could see poking out from under the statuette.

She wished she were at home in Kent. She found it oppressive in that house on the Loire with its tensions and suspicions. Everyone doubted everyone else from the General to the scullery-maid, and from Madame de Morell to herself. In a determined voice that stemmed from her nervousness she asked, "What are *you* doing in this room?"

It had taken courage to ask, and she watched his handsome face closely. He appeared unmoved as he replied, "I am carrying out my duties. I had to bring in the cognac and see there was a fresh supply of cigars in the cupboard." He smiled suddenly, and with a hint of arrogance because he had noticed her nervousness, said, "You saw me find the paper on the mantelpiece..." He broke off deliberately and put his head on one side again, waiting for her reply.

"Just as I came into the room — I really — " She stopped, embarrassed, but he stared at her in such a way that she went on. "I wasn't spying on you," she explained, "but I did see you put that paper on the mantelpiece." She wished she had not seen him, or better still, that he had not seen her. He laughed, relaxed, took the paper from under the statuette and handed it to her. It was nothing more than a shopping list for the cook. She did not smile as she handed it back. "I'm sorry," she said, "I thought it was to do with those letters."

"It was — indirectly."

13

"Oh?"

Samuel replaced the list carefully beneath the statuette, and wondered if she were really puzzled, or just pretending.

"Yes, Madame asked me to look especially carefully this evening because of the guests coming here. Can you imagine what it would mean if a guest found one of the letters?"

Helen had been given similar instructions. "Look for those letters, and bring them to me." She wondered how many others on the household staff had been told to do the same thing. It was a horrible position to be in because it deepened the suspicion.

She said, "I find it most unpleasant."

"So do I. It means that each one of us is a suspect."

"Have you had a letter yet?"

"No, and I've never found one either. But that doesn't mean that I'm not suspected. You suspected me yourself, you probably still do, or you wouldn't have watched me like that before you came into the room. Have you spoken to cook or any of the others?"

Helen shook her head. She did not trust him. Madame must have asked everyone to look for the letters, but, she reasoned, this would give the writer an excellent excuse to be in any room in the house and so plant a letter anywhere.

He went on. "No one ever says what is in these letters. I hate it. Once or twice I've thought of giving in my notice, but that would only start gossip, and I must have a reference from Madame and the General..."

She interrupted him. "Do they suspect me?" He looked out of the window to avoid her eyes. He watched a couple in a boat gliding down the river. "I asked you if I am suspected," she said.

"Well." He hesitated, and the hesitation was long enough to tell her where she stood. "You're no more suspected than the others. But I want to know what's in the letters. Why will no one tell me?"

The intimacy that he thought was developing between them foundered abruptly as she said, "I'd rather not discuss them. I think this conversation should stop." Samuel returned automatically to his role of footman, and submission showed in the way he stood, head erect, hands at his sides, palms turned deferentially to the rear with fingers slightly curled.

It was a shock to them both when the double doors burst open and sixteen-year-old Marie de Morell, in a vivid scarlet, black and white evening dress, emphasising her shiny, black hair and glowing complexion, almost bounced into the room. She was beautiful and she knew it. She could dominate any company she was in. If she were in mixed com-

14

pany she did it with chatter and bursts of laughter. If she found herself, as often happened, surrounded by army officers, she let them do the talking and appeared subdued. Every man who had met her was aware of her as an exciting girl. She recognised the way they looked at her, and she loved it. When speaking to a man, whether a servant or a general, she would look him straight in the eyes and make him feel that he, at that moment, was singled out for her special favours.

Now, she looked with mock horror at her governess. "Aren't you dressed yet?"

"I've plenty of time," said Helen. "I never join the party until you are about to go in to dine."

She turned to the footman. "Oh Samuel, I hope you're still looking for those letters."

"Yes, ma'mselle." She was staring at him with that half smile that made him oblivious to anything else.

"Have you found any yet?" Her voice had the same effect as her eyes.

"Not yet, ma'mselle."

"I suppose Mama told you to look for them?"

"Naturally, ma'mselle, it would be be most embarrassing, so I've been told, if one of your guests found one this evening."

Marie moved a pace nearer to him and, without taking her eyes off his, increased her smile. Her small, white, even teeth, framed by red lips which she bit to make them brighter, complemented her dark blue eyes. She was making fun of him and he did not know it. "If one of the guests found a letter, it might wake him up a bit. Depends what's in it, really. Have you looked under that tallboy?"

"No, ma'mselle."

"Then do so at once!" Samuel bent down to look under the chest. "That's no way to look," she laughed. "You have to get right down on your hands and knees."

"D'you really think there could be one under there?" complained the footman, thinking of his clean white stockings and the humiliation of his position.

"How should I know? Mama doesn't give *me* three francs every time I find one. If she did," she said, turning to Helen, "it might be worth my while to write a few myself."

"You're not to say such things, even for a joke," Helen reproved her.

Marie raised her eyebrows and asked, "And where have you looked?" She saw the open desk. "I see you've been rummaging through Mama's papers. Did you have any luck?" She did not pause for a reply. "Do *you* get three francs every time you find one, or are you above that sort of thing?" She transferred her attention to Samuel who was still on his

15

hands and knees. "Stay where you are, Samuel, I want to stand on your back so I can see on the top of the tallboy." She stood on his shoulders, so that now he worried about his freshly pressed jacket. Holding the top of the tallboy with both hands she kicked off a shoe and tickled the back of his neck with her toes. Helen did not see, but Samuel enjoyed it.

"There's nothing up here," Marie laughed as she jumped down and let him get to his feet.

"And there's nothing under here," said Samuel, dusting himself down. "It's a mystery to me. If I catch that fellow who's doing it, I'll wring his neck. He's bound to be caught sooner or later."

"Is he? Try the music room. A letter was once found in the strings of the harp. Go on!"

As he left the room Marie giggled. "What a waste!"

"What is?" asked Helen.

"That such a good-looking man should be a footman, and such an ass as well."

"I feel sorry for him. He's just told me that the other servants think he's writing the letters."

"Impossible!" declared Marie. "I once saw him writing an order for the butcher. It was only two or three items, but it took him ages. And what were you doing in here?" she asked suddenly.

"Getting your lessons ready for Monday."

In a flat singsong voice Marie recited, "Geography, exports and imports of Spain, the New Testament, the history of the Vatican City . . . what's that?" She was staring at the missal in Helen's left hand.

"What?"

"That book mark."

Helen quickly tapped the buff-coloured envelope back between the pages so that it no longer showed.

"That's a letter! You've just hidden a letter in your missal."

Helen looked frightened. "It's nothing. It's just an ordinary letter from England. It's private."

"It's not! It's one of those horrid ones. I recognised the paper. It is, isn't it?"

The governess backed away as Marie tried to grab the book. Helen's voice was a hoarse whisper. "No !"

"Show me!"

"No!" she repeated, and held the book in both hands as a shield before her face.

"But if that were a proper letter, you'd have shown me at once."

"Certainly not! It has nothing to do with you. Mind your own business!"

16

"Everything in this house is my business, Miss Allen. You're my governess. My governess!" she emphasised. "Papa pays you to do as you're told."

Helen lowered the book to her side but still held it firmly in both hands. "Another thing Monsieur le Général pays me for is to teach you good manners."

Marie raised her voice. "Show me that letter! Go on! I dare you! If it's from England, I won't read it, I promise. Show me!" She started towards her governess.

"It's none of your business. It's my letter and it was sent to me." Helen was pleading now.

"Even with your missal in your hand you are lying! That's blasphemy!"

Helen's back was against the double doors. She was trapped, and Marie, in a triumphant voice and smiling merrily said, "Good! Now I can just take it from you."

At that moment someone tried to open the doors, pushing Helen against Marie who grabbed her governess's missal.

Madame la Baronne Solange de Morell flung open both doors so violently that the large gilded handles banged noisily against the walls. Solange was a little taller than her daughter, with the same even features and small straight nose. She wore a diamond tiara, an emerald pendant and a brilliant emerald green evening dress with fashionable full sleeves and gloves and shoes to match. One of the few things she and Marie ever agreed upon was that if one wore one colour, the other would contrast. By the authority of her presence alone, she was in command.

None of the three moved. Marie was uncertain and out of breath. Helen, acutely ill at ease, was red in the face. Solange spoke quietly. "What is all this?" Marie and her governess exchanged glances. "What is happening?" Solange tapped the back of her right fingers in the palm of her left hand. "Miss Allen, perhaps you can explain."

Helen swallowed. "I am sorry, Madame . . ." But Marie had taken the opportunity to slip the straw-coloured, lined paper out of the home-made envelope.

Helen repeated herself. "I'm sorry, Madame."

"That is an apology. I asked you for an explanation!"

Marie jumped up excitedly. "Mama! Mama! I thought so! I knew it! Helen's got a letter! It's one of those! It is! Look!"

Solange quickly closed the doors behind her. "Be quiet! Address your governess as Miss Allen, and not by her Christian name. Keep your voice down. Look at your frock! You'll have to go back upstairs again so that Miss Allen can press it."

As Helen's existence was determined by Solange, she was fighting to regain her composure. "Madame," said Helen, "Ma'mselle Marie has taken a letter of mine."

Solange appeared unconcerned as she looked at her excited daughter and said, "If that is so, she will give it back to you."

Marie ran across the room waving the letter. "It's one of the nasty ones! Listen! 'Dear Miss Helen Allen....'" Helen tried to protest, but Marie read on. "'I hear that you are a respectable young lady and that you always have a holy book in your hand. Please tell Mademoiselle Marie de Morell, in quite a Christian spirit, that she is the most unpleasant person in the world. I know of no one more dull and stupid; but her mother is charm itself.'"

Helen appealed to Solange. "Please stop her, please!" But Solange said nothing and made no move to prevent her daughter from reading on.

"'What an adorable woman is La Baronne! What a difference! Dinner last night would have been so delightful had it not been for that girl Marie de Morell who spoiled it by her odious presence.'" Marie hesitated. "I don't understand the next line. It says "When you ...'"

"No! No!" Helen interrupted. "You can't read that part!"

"I've heard enough! Give the letter back to Miss Allen at once!"

Marie pouted. "But, Mama, you said ..."

"Never mind what I said."

"You said that we were to bring such letters straight to you or Papa."

La Baronne was angry. "Give it back! Do as you are told!"

Sulkily Marie handed the letter to Helen who slipped it back into her missal. Solange was about to ask to read it but said instead that she should have been shown it at once.

"I didn't show it to you because it's blasphemy, and some of the words and phrases are so revolting as to be − to be − " Helen could not find the word she wanted. She wanted to escape. She blurted out, "I just couldn't show it to anyone. It's too horrible."

Solange threw back her head and looked down her nose at the governess. "I am most surprised that you saw fit to keep the letter after our instruction that such letters were to be brought straight to me. Miss Allen, I'm sorry that you are now drawn into this. The whole affair is frightening. Perhaps you should go upstairs now and change. It's getting late, and our guests will be arriving." Helen thanked her, and left the room with obvious relief.

Solange turned on her daughter. "That was most unkind of you."

Marie shrugged. "Oh well, what of it? If I hadn't done that, we'd never have known about it. She would never have said anything."

"Because it embarrassed her. Can't you understand that?"

"I wonder how long she's had that letter, Mama?"

"She's had it about two days."

Marie was bewildered, "Oh? And how would you know that?"

"Because of the mention of the dinner party last week."

Marie lowered her voice. "Mama," she said, "listen to me carefully. I think this is important. It was after that dinner that Emile de la Roncière said something so strange." She could see that she had her mother's complete attention. Emile de la Roncière was a young man of consequence to the de Morell family — a good-looking, tall, fair-haired lieutenant in the Lancers. He had a little blond moustache, and he was much sought after by the daughters of Solange's friends. Emile's father was a general in an artillery school north of Paris and because he had had some small troubles with his son, he had asked General de Morell to keep a fatherly eye on him. As a result he had been granted a commission and was now at the Cavalry School. As the son of one of the country's noble families he was socially acceptable and for that reason, under the most careful supervision, Solange always asked him to her dinners and musical soirées, seating him next to Marie who was not unaware of his good looks. Solange privately thought his manners could be improved.

Marie continued. "It was some time after that dinner that Emile said something that was in that letter, the one Miss Allen had."

"What was that?" Solange was interested.

"It was strange," said Marie, "but just as the guests were getting their cloaks in the hall, he stood under your portrait, pointed up at it and said 'What an enchanting mother you have, and what a pity you are so unlike her, being so dull and stupid.'"

Solange raised her eyebrows. "Oh dear," she said flatly, "had he been drinking?"

"I don't think so. Not as much as some of the others."

Her mother, who frequently thought the younger men took too much wine and brandy, said, "If I were you, I would not take any notice of it. He was either drunk or you misunderstood him." She seemed to be about to dismiss it as something of no consequence.

"Mama, wait!" Marie said, sitting on the very edge of the sofa. "What is happening?" She separated the words meticulously to give them emphasis. "What is it? What is going on?"

"What do you mean, dear?"

"Why do we go on pretending that all this is not happening? Why?

You and Papa have had this sort of thing for — oh, easily two months, isn't it? And you still do nothing about it."

"Yes," said Solange in a resigned voice. "It's Papa. I've told him he should have a proper investigation carried out. He just won't, and you know what he's like when his mind's made up."

At that moment Monsieur le Général le Baron Charles Paul de Morell entered the drawing-room. He was tired. Running the summer school at Saumur was a vacation job given to favoured generals, but it was arduous: De Morell, a favourite both of the King and of Marshal Soult, and married to Soult's niece, had been the perfect choice for the task. Soult thought so much of the Cavalry School that he had demolished the original, with Napoleon's permission, and had completed the new building in time for the dictator's exile in 1814. Since 1830 de Morell had been the general in charge of putting down the frequent riots in Paris and Lyons, but for the last two or three weeks his work had been almost entirely social, engaged in showing off the Cadre Noir to visiting politicians, diplomats and generals. He was a sociable man and enjoyed the dinner parties and musical soirées that were so frequent at his house. He loved his uniforms too, and owned six full dress outfits so that he could change several times a day and always appear immaculate. He was in uniform now as he joined his family. He brightened as Marie ran to him, and he picked her up and swung her round, kissing her before setting her down.

"Papa! Papa! I've got to talk to you."

"Have you, my darling? What a beautiful frock!" He took a pace back so that he could admire his enchanting daughter. He scarcely acknowledged his wife.

In a mock mysterious voice the General said to Marie, "Now, leave us. I want to talk to Mama, and it's very private and serious."

"Can't I stay? Please?"

"No. State secrets, and lots of them!"

"Papa, don't joke!"

"I'm not joking. Now run along."

Marie adored her father. He was her hero, he could do no wrong. To her he was the most handsome man in the whole world. But he irritated her when he treated her as a child incapable of serious conversation, and a glint of her temper showed as she said, "I want to talk to you about Helen." The general guided Marie through the doors and closed them after her.

Solange knew from his expression that something was wrong. "What's happened?" she asked.

"Miss Allen ran past me on the stairs just now. She was crying. Is it anything to do with this letter business?"

"Certainly. She's had one. She must have had it for about two days."

"Why was I not told at once?"

Solange wanted to tell him to shut up and stop being so pompous. Instead she said, "I've only this minute found out about it myself. So how could I tell you any earlier?"

The General went over to the corner cupboard, and took out the new box of cigars. "You're supposed to know what's going on in this house. Why didn't you know sooner about this?"

What an absurd question, thought Solange. Am I meant to run around the house all day looking over everyone's shoulder to see if they're reading nasty letters?

"So revolting," repeated the General with a touch of irony, having heard the explanation, "that she could not bring herself to burn it or throw it away? Huh? Well, give it to me now," he said, taking out a silver pocket-knife to slit the seal on the cedar cigar box.

"She still has the letter. She keeps it in her missal."

The General was astounded. He put down the cigar box, walked to the centre of the room, clasped his hands behind his back and, adopting a stance more suited to the parade-ground than his own drawing-room, raised his voice to say, "What is the point of my issuing instructions if everyone goes on doing exactly what he likes? You are in the house all day! You are never alone! There are servants, staff..."

"Please lower your voice. The servants might hear you."

He went back to the cigar box, slit the seal and opened it.

Inside, lying on top of the row of cigars, was a home-made straw-coloured envelope.

His wife did not notice as he used the silver knife to open the envelope. As he read the letter his colour deepened, and a pulse in his right temple throbbed. He pulled in his chin and chewed at his lower lip.

Solange was thinking about the governess. "When you talk to her about it," she said, "I hope you won't bully her."

The General put down the box on the table and went on reading the letter.

"Because," she went on, "if you speak to her as I sometimes hear you speak to the servants, she'll leave us, and she's the best governess we've had. She's more intelligent than most English girls of that background."

De Morell went over to the window to watch the river and think.

CHAPTER TWO

Solange de Morell's marriage to the general when he was thirty-two and she ten years younger, eighteen years ago, was looked upon as a sensible arrangement. Her uncle was the great Marshal Soult, whose loyalty to his country was unquestioned, but whose allegiance to the various heads of state was doubtful. As power was passed on, Soult's fidelity passing with it, he earned the nickname 'The Chameleon' and a reputation for opportunism. Because he had survived while some heads of state had not, Soult had become a man of immense power. This made it simple for him to arrange for his niece, Solange, to be married to a man of status. So Soult had seen to it that de Morell, once a humble lieutenant, became Général le Baron de Morell, complete with land, houses, power and money. And never for a moment did Soult let his niece or her husband forget who was their patron. None but Solange knew that the General's loyalty to Soult was born of fear. De Morell knew that without this lofty patronage, his influence would be less than that of a household cat in a jungle of tigers.

His marriage to Solange was, to outward appearances, perfect. They both knew without prompting which top politicians, which diplomats and which senior military personnel should be entertained during the summer months they were at Saumur. Solange never made seating errors at her dinners and musical soirées. She loved music and was able, with little more than a nod, to command such performers as Franz Liszt to play for her guests in her music-room. She was a capable hostess who, like the General, believed in careful organisation. For instance, they kept a book in which were listed the names of important visitors and possible guests. Against each name they wrote their interests so that conversation at dinner would not falter. They recorded their gastronomic delights so that those of prominence would be offered only what was certain to delight them. They noted their musical preferences, and there were comments on their backgrounds, children and pastimes. They regarded the book as a serious document to be consulted and memorised before any entertaining. Armed with so much information, it was almost impossible to have a dull evening or seat next to each other those who would not have something in common.

It was natural therefore that Solange was a celebrated hostess and a snob quite capable of breaking the rules on purpose. For example, even though she had spent little time in the company of Liszt, she called him Franzie almost at once. She knew he was living with Comtesse Marie d'Agoult before her divorce; nevertheless she asked them both to stay in the Saumur house, knowing that a little scandal would add piquancy to everyone's week-end.

Lesser musicians and their legal wives had to stay at the Hôtel de l'Europe along the road when they played at one of the 'evenings'. Solange excused her behaviour by saying, "But even though Franzie is only a musician, one must never forget that he is also a gentleman."

General de Morell was still standing at the drawing-room window looking blankly down the river. Solange remained silent on the rococo sofa. Neither had spoken for two or three minutes when he took the letter out of his pocket again, went over to the table and tapped the box of cigars with his silver pocket-knife.

"How long have these been in the house?"

She, wondering what was coming next, and worrying about Miss Allen, sounded bored as she said, "Those cigars? I've no idea. You always do the ordering yourself. Why?"

He held up the letter. "This!"

"Oh my God! Another one. Where did you get it?"

"From that box." He tapped the cigar box again. "Had to break the seal and when I opened the lid, there it was, lying on the top."

Solange stood up. "Are you saying that somebody managed to get a letter inside a new, sealed box of cigars?"

"It must have been steamed open," he said "and resealed. I should have thought that that was fairly obvious. Who did it? And why? I know we sometimes say it might be Emile de la Roncière, but is it? Is it?" He slammed his open palm on the table, making the glasses tinkle. "Who did it? Who did it?"

"How should I know? I don't see why you're angry with me!" She sat down again and seemed to shrink into the corner of the sofa. "I find your attitude very tedious."

"Oh, do you!" he said angrily. "I'm at the Cavalry School most of the day, so I think you have something to answer for. Letters delivered mysteriously, and no one knows anything about them! Does everyone in this house walk about wearing blindfolds with ears stuffed with rag? Do they? Do they?"

23

She refused to rise to his mood. She put out her left hand. "May I see the letter?"

"No!" There was no room for compromise in his denial.

"Is it so unpleasant?"

"Only if I took it seriously."

"I assure you that I take it very seriously," she said impatiently. "To know that someone is getting in and out like this makes me feel the house isn't private or clean any more."

"Not what I meant at all," he said, sounding exasperated. "How dare anyone write to his general like this!"

"Oh?" At last he had admitted something, thought Solange. "So you know it's Lieutenant de la Roncière after all. Let me see it."

"No. It's malicious, slanderous and signed with a disgraceful word."

Solange felt there was an unreal, nightmare quality about her husband's attitude in holding back a letter from her which they both knew was a serious assault on their privacy, and doing so because of some silly rude word. She said as much. "You want to protect me from a word which I've probably seen chalked on walls dozens of times? Your behaviour to me is far ruder than any word. Your manner is brusque and unpardonable. Read the letter to me and leave out the vulgar words."

For a few seconds he prevaricated almost like a child who has been told to finish up a nasty pudding. He gave in. "All right! I'll read parts of it. It says something about wanting to ruin Marie, and he says he's written to Lieutenant Octave d'Estouilly about it. . . ." While he silently skimmed another paragraph, she was trying to remember which of the many officers was d'Estouilly. Oh, yes. He was a tall, willowy young man appointed by the War Office to sketch horses and uniforms. He was not what she would call 'a proper soldier' but one in uniform only for convenience as the official artist. She recalled that he had charm and good manners but was a poor conversationalist. There was a seating problem when she asked him to dinner.

"And why," she asked, "should la Roncière send d'Estouilly a letter?"

The General protested. "But we don't know it was written by la Roncière yet."

"It must have been." She was firm. "You've said yourself that you're sure Emile's been writing these."

He ignored her remark as he scanned the letter. "It says here you're having an affair."

She was intrigued. "Indeed? With whom?"

"A very senior officer. He doesn't give a name but says you met him last Wednesday. I was in Angers that day."

24

She was not surprised by his suspicion. She had grown used to his ways so there was no bitterness in her voice when she said, "You sound as if you believe him. At that rate I might equally wonder why you went to Angers. You said it was a military meeting of the top brass."

"It was. The King had ordered a meeting of a few senior officers including myself. We were discussing the possibility of another workers' uprising like the one in April in Lyons. Matters of ordnance had to be attended to so that should the workers get out of line, at least we'd keep a continuous supply of food and arms for defence." She was surprised at the length of his explanation. "A country without military cohesion is at the mercy of the first half-wit who can shout from the top of a cider barrel . . ."

She silenced him by standing up and raising her eyebrows. "I didn't mean you to defend yourself for quite so long." She vaguely wondered why such an important meeting was held in an out-of-the-way town and not closer to Paris or Lyons; but she changed the subject back to the letter.

The General was folding it up to put back in his pocket. "There's no more," he said, "except for a perplexing sentence about forging a letter in Marie's writing, sending it to Lieutenant Octave d'Estouilly, and hoping that he'll show it to us."

"And that's all it says?" She asked, looking across at the paper still in her husband's hand.

"Yes. That's all it says."

"It looks much longer than that. What else does he say? I can see dozens of lines of writing even from here." She stood up and went over to him to prevent his putting it away. "Are you hiding something?"

"No." His voice had risen so that she knew immediately he was lying.

"Then let me see it," she demanded. "This is not the time for secrets from each other. Give it to me."

He relented. "Take the damned thing." He almost threw it at her. She look a long time to read it. She read it twice. The General went back to the window and gazed at the river in silence. She folded the paper, put it back in the envelope, and said that, whatever else, it must be kept from Marie. It would be better burned, and she asked as she handed it back, "Is there any truth in it?"

There was no answer.

"Burn it! It's loathsome. All I expected was a couple of vulgar words. Yes, burn it. The writing's the same as the others. He must be mad, who-ever he is."

She thought he was going to throw it into the cold grate; instead, he

25

jerked the gold-embroidered red silk bell pull beside the mantelpiece. "I must speak to Samuel about this."

"How can he help?"

"My dear wife! What are you saying? Look, the letters are getting into the house! This one turned up in that box which I presume, unless I'm going mad, that Samuel put into that cupboard. I shall see him. I shall see all the servants. I just do not believe that letters can arrive for you, for Marie, for the governess, and for me, yet no one ever sees . . ." He paused and almost shouted ". . . *anything!*"

Solange spoke softly. "Have you forgotten we have a dinner party tonight?"

"What's that to do with it?"

"We are entertaining General Préval and his lady; and his aide-de-camp and his lady too. God only knows who else. I've written eighteen place names myself. If you disturb one of those busy servants tonight I shall go to my room with a headache, and stay there until they've all gone home." She had not used that old threat on him for years.

"Absurd!" he exclaimed. "You must receive our guest of honour with me."

"Then leave the staff alone."

"I've already rung for Samuel."

"Well, just him. He has no kitchen duties, and I think he's already changed into his evening uniform." The General lit a cigar. "I wish you wouldn't smoke in here." There was a knock at the door and Samuel came in.

"Monsieur, madame?"

Solange stood up to leave the room.

"No," said the General to his wife. "Please stay." He turned to Samuel. "Listen carefully. You are in this house all day, are you not?"

Sensing the tension, Samuel was on his guard. "Yes, monsieur."

"And with very minor variations," said the General, "your duties here in Saumur are the same as they are in Paris?"

Wondering what he might be accused of, Samuel answered cautiously. "I – I think so, monsieur."

"So you've not been out of the house all day? Not even into the garden?"

Samuel had guessed. It would be about those letters. "No, monsieur, I have not been out." He wished he *had* been out because he knew he would be asked why he had seen no one or nothing unusual.

"Has anyone called?"

"No, monsieur." Then he remembered. "Only the milk girl from the farm."

"No one else?" The General had filled the question with doubt in order to draw Samuel. "At the front door, perhaps?"

"Not that I know of." He remembered another caller. "Oh, the butcher. I forgot."

"At the front door?"

"No, no." He was getting confused "I mean at the side door, I think." He was hating this. "Or the back door."

"Which?" The General put the question with unnecessary attack.

Samuel was unnerved by the way the questions were being shot at him. "I don't know. Cook let him in."

"You do know," said the General, stating the obvious, "that someone is getting in and out of the house without being seen?"

Samuel's discomfort was increased by the presence of Madame, who was staring at him without blinking. "Yes," he said, "I know someone is getting in and out."

Changing his tone the General asked, "Do you know Lieutenant Emile de la Roncière by sight?"

When Samuel said that he did, he was asked if the lieutenant had been seen near the house recently.

"Well, monsieur, if you mean walking on that bridge there, I've seen a lot of him. Almost every time he's off duty he's on that bridge."

"Twenty or thirty metres from the door?"

"And closer." Samuel's tension was lessening as the General was swinging the burden of questions on to the lieutenant.

"Have you seen him a metre or two from the door?"

"Only, monsieur, when he's been invited to dine or something like that." Samuel felt he was being browbeaten, so with deference he ventured a question himself. "Why, monsieur, if you'll excuse my asking, do you want to know about Lieutenant de la Roncière?" Solange, for reasons she could not even explain to herself, was glad he had asked that.

The General pulled the envelope out of his pocket and held it on the palm of his hand. "It's this," he explained. "It's happened again."

Samuel was not so much surprised as dismayed. "Oh, monsieur! Where did you find it? I have searched and searched. I was in here not long ago looking all around at the . . ."

The General stopped him. "It was in that cigar box. Did someone ask you to put it in there?"

The question shocked the footman. Up to that moment he thought that the General's suspicions of him were over. "Oh no, monsieur! No one asked me to do any such thing. And I put that very box into that cupboard when I was last in here. It was a new one."

27

The General was getting angry. "I broke the seal myself! And there on the top row of cigars was the letter."

Samuel was incredulous. "But monsieur, that is impossible."

"It's possible, Samuel, possible, because I assure you it happened. Now tell me what you know about it!"

"Nothing." He looked at Madame, shrugged and gave a gesture of innocence with his hands. "I know nothing about it." He looked back to the General and was afraid. "Please, I know nothing."

"God help you if you lie!" It was a sharp, merciless retort.

"But why should I lie?"

General de Morell could think of no more questions. It was a mystery and looked like remaining one. He went over to the window leaving the nervous footman standing without purpose in the middle of the room.

Samuel glanced at Madame, but she was looking away. He coughed uncertainly, and the General turned.

"Very well," he said. "Tell the staff that I will see them one by one tomorrow morning at fifteen-minute intervals starting at eight o'clock, beginning with you. I shall expect a report from you about the cigar box. I shall want to know where it came from, when it arrived in this house, where it was kept before you brought it in, what time you collected it and so on. Is that clear?"

"Yes, monsieur."

"Do you know Monsieur Octave d'Estouilly by sight?"

"Yes, monsieur."

"Send him to me the minute he arrives. You may go."

Samuel showed great relief and left the room as fast as possible, trying not to show that he was hurrying.

De Morell went over to the fireplace and set fire to the letter. Then he broke the delicate black ash with the hearth brush and swept the dark mess round to the back of the vase which stood in the hearth with its blazing display of summer flowers.

"I wouldn't be surprised if Samuel looks for another position very soon." Solange was accustomed to her husband's insensitivity but she wished he would keep it for the parade-ground.

"I think he's hiding something."

"I mean because of the way you spoke to him."

"Nonsense!" he said crustily.

"I don't know what to think," she said almost to herself. "Now we have the problem of Octave d'Estouilly. That letter said he'd been written to. What will you say to him?" He looked at her blankly, wondering why she was asking him about how he would deal with one of his own men. It was an intrusion into his generalship. She went on. "But sup-

28

pose he hasn't had a letter, and you ask him about one. He's bound to ask you what's happening. That can only start a lot of gossip. Officers are worse than you say women are. I've seen them gossiping in the cafés."

He did not like this at all. What took place between him and his men was nothing to do with his wife. He said, "Leave him to me."

Now, she thought, he was being deliberately obstructive. This might well be a military matter but it was imposing on her house and her family and she had a right to know how he proposed to deal with d'Estouilly. "Why won't you tell me what you intend saying to Octave d'Estouilly? Is it just because some of the letters are signed with just the letter 'E' that you think he could be writing them?" She might have been talking to a brick wall. "Charles!" she said sharply to gain his attention. "We both think the letters are being written by Emile de la Roncière." His face was expressionless. "If this is so, and the man is under your command," she said, "then what is stopping you asking him?" Still the pale blue eyes were blank. "You'll only confuse everything, dissipate your energies, spread rumours and upset everyone by talking to Octave d'Estouilly. He's not even involved as far as we know."

At last her husband decided to speak. "You don't know that. I don't know it either. He may be involved. That letter" — he pointed to the grate — "says he's had two or three."

"Then speak to Emile de la Roncière first."

"I will not."

"You must. If you don't question la Roncière and it gets out, people will wonder why you didn't send for him at once."

"This won't get out."

"How will you prevent it? How can you stand there having read a letter which says in black and white he has written to someone outside the family, and be so sure this won't get out? People are bound to ask questions."

"What people? It seems that this is confined to my own junior staff, and they're not likely to question their general."

Solange was not satisfied with that argument. "For over two months," she said, "improperly signed letters have been coming to this house, and some were found in the Paris house even earlier. Emile de la Roncière was in Paris and is now not two kilometres away from here."

"If I took a list of men with us in Paris who are at the Cavalry School now it would include many names."

"But the coincidence is too strong. Only this evening Marie told me that la Roncière was overheard saying that while he found me enchanting, he considered Marie dull and stupid. What an absurd thing for a

29

man to say! And in this last letter to Helen, there was a sneering reference to that very remark. For weeks we have endured this humiliation from an officer under your command, and yet you do not question him. Why not? And worse, you go on inviting him to the house, and he's coming here this evening."

"That invitation came from you."

"In my writing, yes; but from the list you gave me."

"Why didn't you query it before?" he demanded angrily.

"Because I felt that if we dropped him, people might start asking questions, knowing of your friendship with his father."

"And that's precisely why I left his name in."

Solange was furious. Her husband was being deliberately obtuse, and over a matter which, as far as she could see, needed drastic and immediate action. Still she did not raise her voice. "All right, then if other people don't start asking you questions, I certainly will! You ask me what is going on in the house while you are at the School! You speak to me as if I were one of your little wooden soldiers! Hasn't it dawned on you that I might well ask you to explain what there is between you and Emile de la Roncière that prevents you from putting him in his place?"

The innuendo was not lost on the General. He flushed and turned his back on her. Solange, her anger mollified, deliberately let the anguished silence grow. The General was appalled that his wife could even think such a thing, let alone mention it. He was hurt. "I can't challenge la Roncière; but he must be stopped. You're quite right; though if I challenge him and he admits writing the letters, do you know what has to happen next?"

"No."

"He will be put before the Council of Honour, the papers would seize on it and it would all be made public. Our lives would become intolerable. If I challenge him and he denies it all, we can do nothing because we have no proof, and I could no longer have him under my command. Follow it through to its conclusion, and you'll see that I would have to arrange his transfer to another command, another regiment . . ."

"But surely . . ."

"No! Hear me out! You're getting into something you do not understand. If I transfer him to another command, I am sure to be asked why I did it, then the matter would no longer be contained."

"Have him transferred. I know he's behind it."

"My dear Solange, have you considered his father, the count, one of France's greatest men? Even the most illiterate peasant can name one or two of the campaigns he's been honoured for."

"What has he to do with it?"

"Everything. If we put the son before the Council of Honour . . ."

"We can prosecute him in a civil court instead. That would settle it."

"Even there his father's popularity might turn everyone against us."

Solange considered. "Write to him. Tell him what's happening. You know him well. After all, he was the one who asked you to keep an eye on Emile. Say what you think Emile's up to and ask his advice."

"He's seventy-eight or -nine, possibly eighty. He's too old to grasp what it's all about. Without proof, such a letter would be difficult. With proof it would be impossible."

There was a knock at the door, and Lieutenant Octave d'Estouilly entered in full dress uniform. Thin and nervous, he was not the sort of man generally associated with the military. He was balding early for his twenty-five years and he had long, tapering, perfectly manicured fingers. He was always sober, never taking cognac, and drinking wine simply because it seemed expected of him. His appetites were reserved for the sensuousness of the arts, especially painting and music. He was not considered a serious soldier.

However, he was industrious, and his output of drawings and paintings of horses, uniforms, artefacts of war and sketches of barracks and military towns was prodigious. He was meticulous in every detail, overseeing the printing, and mixing the paints for use on the prints. Occasionally his superiors would question the time 'wasted' on the making up of the colour pots, but Octave insisted. Having mixed the colours he would decant them into dark wine bottles ready to be shared out among the colourists.

From time to time he would accept a portrait commission; but the continuous pressure from the War Office prevented him from having sufficient time. It was rumoured that if the vain King Louis-Philippe ordered a portrait, he would resign his military commission and leave the army. No such grand order ever came his way.

Now, on entering the room, he bowed to Solange and to his general, who said he would like to speak to him in the garden, so, after making their apologies to Solange, the two men went out.

It was a well-stocked garden, and the side that grew along the bank of the river was a mass of reeds, rushes and tiny white water flowers. A gravelled path ran parallel to the water, and on its other side military precision took over in well-kept lawns, geometrically grown box hedges restrained at nine inches, and a regimented formality of brilliant herbaceous plants in ordered patterns. Octave chose to walk on the river side of the gravel path, from where he could see the stone flies being caught on the wing by darting dragonflies, while smaller bright blue damsel flies caught even smaller creatures in flight. Octave thought there was little difference between their behaviour and that of human beings.

Once out of earshot from the house, the General came to the point. "We've been getting some letters we can't account for."

"Yes, I was afraid you might say that," said Octave feeling ill at ease.

The older man, striding ahead of Octave, turned and faced him, blocking the narrow path. "Well? Haven't you any more than that to say about it?"

"Mon Général, I find this most difficult because I too have had some very strange letters."

"That's what I thought, and that's why I sent for you the minute you arrived."

They resumed their stroll, increasing their distance from the house.

"Did you bring them with you?"

"Yes, mon Général."

"D'you know who wrote them?"

"I'm not sure, but I have an idea. The author says he's written to a lot of people besides you, monsieur."

"Who?"

"I don't know, but I have three."

"What about?"

"Take this one," said Octave, bringing out the now familiar off-white lined paper. "He says . . ."

The General took it from him. " 'I mean to disturb your happiness,' " he read, " 'and that of the de Morell family. Mlle Marie de Morell has listened to me. I have told her that you, Octave d'Estouilly, have no intention of staying in Saumur because your father has plans for you, and he wants you to go home.' "

The General folded the paper and handed it back, observing that it was in the same handwriting as the letter he had just received. "Who do you think wrote it?"

"Monsieur, there is not much room for doubt. When I arrived here this evening I had time to speak to Mlle Marie, and she said . . ."

The General interrupted. "I don't want my daughter involved in this," he said sharply.

"Oh no, monsieur, I was very careful. I asked her quite casually whether anyone had told her I may change my plans and leave Saumur as soon as I have painted the last four horses."

"Yes?"

"She was astonished. She looked down and blushed, and said that she thought my father had sent for me, but it was really of no interest to her."

"So you asked her who had told her that?"

"I did, and she said it was Emile de la Roncière."

"And this happened a few minutes ago?"

"Yes," replied Octave. "You see, the letter didn't arrive until this morning."

"How?"

"How?" repeated Octave.

"Yes, how did you get it? Did you just happen upon it?"

"No, it came through the post, the internal post. I know that because it had the usual date stamp on the envelope showing that it hadn't been posted to me from outside. It had originated in the Cavalry School."

"Let me see the envelope." The General studied it. "The ones we find here never have a postmark."

"How does he get them to you?"

"That's the extraordinary part of it," said the General. "He must have help. One of the servants I suppose. It can't be one of my adjutants who come in every evening with the daily School report. I've only the two and I've known them for years. Have you discussed this with anyone?"

"Yes, monsieur. I asked Lieutenant Joachim Ambert what I should do."

"Did you show him the letters?"

"I had to. He asked to see them and after a most careful examination we both went to the mess book in the dining-hall. As you know, those of us who want to mess in for the evening meal have to sign the book before luncheon on the same day. La Roncière takes his evening meal there regularly and often adds disparaging remarks in the mess book when he signs it. They're designed to annoy the chef. It was comparison with these remarks that led us to see a distinct similarity between the letters and his writing."

"And that is all?"

"No, it's his attitude to life that shows both in the mess book and in the letters. Joachim Ambert and I talked it over for a long time, and of course we can't be sure, but he said I ought to bring the letters to you."

"Don't discuss this with anyone again. I'll speak to Lieutenant Ambert. What are the other two letters about?"

Octave handed a letter to the General who read, " 'She is pure and innocent, of that I cannot rob her; but in the eyes of the world she will appear to be at the centre of a great scandal, and she will appear guilty. As I cannot win her for myself, this will be my revenge!' "

33

The writer boasted he could forge Marie's writing and enclosed a specimen of it as proof.

The General thought it all looked very childish and asked for the forgery of Marie's handwriting. He agreed it was similar but with more slope, although good enough to convince anyone outside the family.

Octave said, "If it's like your daughter's writing then he can make trouble by sending off letters to all sorts of people and signing them with her name."

"And, except for the forgery, these are in exactly the same writing as the ones we've found in the house."

"Have you, mon Général," asked Octave wanting to be helpful, "spoken to Lieutenant de la Roncière about the ones you've found?"

"No."

"Would you like me to call him out?"

"Call him out? Eh? To a duel? About this? Certainly not! You know as well as I do that duelling is illegal. I should have to punish both sides severely."

Octave pulled up a bullrush, made a half-hearted parry and thrust with it, looked sideways at his General and said, "You'd have to catch us before you could punish us."

The General abruptly stopped in his aimless walk. "That is insubordination, monsieur."

"It would teach him a lesson, and stop these letters."

"It would start gossip. You, monsieur, are an idiot!"

"Have you enough evidence to have him arrested?"

"No."

"You could transfer him to Toulon. He has relatives there."

"He could write from Toulon. But why should he? He doesn't make sense; neither his action in writing, nor the words in the letters. I wonder if . . ."

Octave looked up enquiringly at the General but the sentence remained unfinished, and they walked silently back to the house.

Alone in the drawing-room the General said, "Does it make sense that he is the writer?"

"Not entirely, monsieur."

"He's on our list of guests for this evening. I wonder if he'll dare show his face."

Octave frowned. "You've asked him to dinner? Here? This evening?"

"On second thoughts, since seeing those letters of yours, it *would* be unwise. I'd better speak to him in here."

"Would you like me to speak to him first?" asked Octave.

And for the second time that evening the General pulled in his chin, and bit his lower lip. It was a curious mannerism, recognised by his men as a danger signal. He marched over to the mantelpiece and jerked the bell pull. "What could you do by seeing him first?"

"Save you from embarrassment." The General was silent, so Octave continued, "On the other hand he might not have the cheek to turn up this evening."

"Yes, monsieur?" Samuel had knocked and entered.

"When Lieutenant de la Roncière arrives, please let me know at once."

"He's here now, monsieur."

"Where?"

"In the music-room, monsieur. Shall I ask him to come and see you?"

"No, thank you. That will be all."

"Monsieur?"

"Yes, Samuel?"

"Madame says will you please join her, as the guests are arriving."

"Tell Madame that I will be with her shortly. But if I'm not out of here when General and Madame Préval are received, fetch me at once."

"Yes, monsieur," said Samuel and left the room.

The General turned to Octave. "Monsieur d'Estouilly!"

"Monsieur?"

"I will have to see him. As you too are a recipient of the letters, you will stay here with me while I talk to him."

Octave looked unsure, but nodded as the General went on, "I have fought in three major campaigns, and before each battle I've known exactly what to do, how to deploy my forces, where and when to attack the enemy; but this, this has no precedent. I'm not sure I should attack, I'm not sure how to attack and, worse, I'm not sure the man is the enemy."

"If he isn't, who is? Who could it be?"

The General went over to the writing-desk, sat down, changed his mind and pulled up a chair to a small table facing the double doors. "Every soldier," he announced pompously, "has a moment of fear before battle, and it is at that moment he asks God for guidance. I can do no more, and you might well do the same." Both men stood with bowed heads.

The General looked up after a few seconds. "Listen to me carefully. These are your orders. Go to the music-room, and in as few words as possible tell la Roncière sternly that you have been ordered, remember to use the word 'ordered', to escort him to me in here. See that he speaks to no one. On your return he will stand there in front of me at this table, and you will take up your position at attention behind me, to my right. Is that clear?"

35

"Yes, monsieur."

"Except to say that you have been ordered to escort him, you will have no conversation with him of any kind."

"Yes, monsieur. Shall I leave now?"

De Morell nodded and Lieutenant Octave d'Estouilly left the drawing-room.

CHAPTER THREE

Lieutenant Emile de la Roncière, only son of Général le Comte de la Roncière, was boisterous and exceedingly good-looking. He liked girls and they liked him and, as with many young men in his position, some of those girls were attracted as much by his uniform as by Emile himself. His charm was so great that many a cast-off girl forgave him and looked back upon the association with pleasure and sadness, but seldom with anger. Girls too, Emile realised, set out to make conquests, and he was constantly delighted by the joyful arrangement designed by nature for mutual gratification.

His manners, however, did not make him popular among his fellow officers. It was a strict custom never to mention one's romantic triumphs, and certainly not to name names. Emile did both, and worse. He let it be known that he kept a little book of girls' names and addresses which he would lend — at a price. The transaction had to be financial because he was always short of any money. He also boasted of the number of girls he had slept with, which, so he said, sometimes included two or three in the same evening.

Although his father came from one of the most noble families in France, he was relatively poor, seldom able to pay his son's debts. He had once tried giving the boy a small allowance, but that only increased his expenditure. Had Emile been able to pay his way, he might have had a few friends among his brother officers, but they found his absent-minded borrowing irresponsible and his permanent poverty boring. Their other reason for avoiding him was his unorthodox method of securing his commission in the cavalry.

Protocol in the cavalry was more strictly observed than in any other

36

branch of either military or civilian life, and the revolution at the end of the eighteenth century did not alter the procedure by which young men acquired their commissions in a military showpiece, the cavalry. Commissions were still available only to young men from families of substance.

A lieutenant's pay was trivial, the honour of consequence, and the uniform magnificent. So, by granting commissions to young men from the upper classes and the nobility, the cavalry was subsidised by a devious form of taxation on those who appreciated it and were prepared to pay for the privilege. As there were never enough good horses to go round, officers gladly brought their own steeds rather than be seen on inferior government mounts.

Before Napoleon, the sitting of an examination by a prospective officer was often waived. Napoleon, determined to build a great army, insisted on examinations, believing that the art of war was wholly executive. But a man who failed his examination was allowed to gain a commission by working his way up through the ranks.

An investigation of the career of Emile's father, le Comte de la Roncière, reveals another of Napoleon's dicta. "A successful general must have more than his share of good luck." The Comte distinguished himself at the victories of Austerlitz and Jena, and was fortuitously absent from the disgrace of Moscow and the débâcle of Waterloo. This could easily have been reversed. By the 1830s le Comte de la Roncière should have retired but, because he was hard up, he was running an artillery school near Boulogne, the post having been found for him by old friends at the War Office. He would attend meetings whose business he could not hear, inspect troops he could not see, and sign papers he did not understand.

The artillery school was run with an old-fashioned discipline. Emile identified the school with his father and rebelled against both, working his way up without passing any examinations, his debts growing like weeds. His father thought that one way to discipline Emile was to keep him short of money.

The rift between father and son eventually became geographical when the old man, to curb his son's appetite for wine, women and gambling, sent Emile to do service with the Sixteenth Regiment of Light Infantry garrisoned almost on the equator on the north-east coast of South America at Cayenne, a sewer of a town, mosquito-plagued, disease-ridden and humid, built where the insect-infested marshes met the sea.

Traders and military patronised the brothel, efficiently run by a drunken Scottish doctor called Ross McAlister who engaged aging prostitutes to clean the barracks and the church, work in the bar and look after the elderly and sick. This instinctive sociologist said he could cure any form of VD, however rare. Once, discovering a particularly resistant strain, he quadrupled his fee — and the dose — and the patient died. McAlister conducted his own post mortem, gleefully discovering that he had cured the VD in spite of the death of the patient. He also mixed a poison which attracted and killed the Giant Scolopender, a thirty-centimetre long centipede with a vicious, sometimes fatal, bite.

It was from the sophisticated life of Paris and the comforts of home in Boulogne that young Emile was to come with a shock to the coarse realities of this small colonial town. After two years of steamy heat he returned to France, older but no wiser. Le Comte de la Roncière asked le Baron de Morell to keep an eye on his son and so the boy was given a commission by de Morell on the grounds of his experience with the artillery at Boulogne and with the Sixteenth Regiment of Light Infantry at Cayenne. His transfer was arranged to the First Regiment of Lancers, which had brought him to the Cavalry School at Saumur.

So it was that Emile had come to be a regular guest at the de Morells' summer house, and now he was looking forward to meeting General Préval and his wife, a well-known Parisian hostess and friend of his father.

He arrived a little early, resplendent in his dress uniform, and handed his cap to Samuel the footman, who placed it on a marble table in the hall. As it was not yet time to go into the drawing-room, Emile wandered aimlessly down the white steps at the side of the house into the garden, where he spotted Octave d'Estouilly talking urgently with General de Morell near a large evergreen bush.

They did not see him as he went quietly back up the steps and joined some of the other guests in the music-room.

Emile, as we have seen, was not popular with his brother officers, some of whom wished him a polite 'Good evening', but as no conversations seemed forthcoming he pretended to admire the paintings (two of which had been looted from Russia by Napoleon, given to Soult, passed to his niece Solange and so hung at Saumur).

Young Emile was not an admirer of good painting, so he was relieved to see Octave crossing the room to speak to him.

His relief vanished when Octave unsmilingly announced, "General de Morell has ordered me to escort you to him in the drawing-room."

Emile liked neither the words nor the tone. "What on earth do you mean?"

Octave was as uncompromising as he had been ordered. "Follow me," was all he said and led the way out of the by-now crowded room and through the hall. As they passed the marble table, Emile grabbed for his cap, looked inside it for his name and, finding it was not his own, put it back so clumsily as to upset half a dozen others which slid off the polished marble on to the floor. Octave stood watching him as he stooped to retrieve them. Eventually Emile replaced all the caps on the table, found his own and held it under his arm. Octave thought of asking why he wanted his cap, but remembered his orders were to say nothing. They walked on in silence. At the drawing-room door, Emile paused to look carefully down his uniform to be sure that nothing was out of place. Octave knocked, entered, and formally announced him.

Emile followed, and Octave carefully closed the doors before taking up his place by the General as instructed. Emile stood in front of the little table, conscious that he could not control a slight twitching of the right side of his face. He hoped it did not show. That the General was not smiling did not increase his nervousness; he seldom smiled.

"You sent for me, mon Général." Neither spoke so Emile repeated, "You sent for me, mon Général?"

The General's gaze altered. He looked at Emile's boots and slowly up his uniform to meet his eyes. Leaning back in his chair and pulling in his chin he said, "Thank you for being so prompt."

"Yes, monsieur, I came immediately."

Quite unexpectedly the General stood up, the back of his knees knocking over his chair, and said, "Monsieur! I have good reason for asking you not to visit my house again. Will you please leave at once!"

Emile went pale, blinked, put on his cap, drew a deep breath as if about to speak, said nothing, saluted, turned smartly and left the room, closing the doors behind him.

Octave did not know what to do, so he righted the chair. He could think of nothing to say. The General's long silences worried him. Most of the men were cowed by them, but some, not under his direct command, said they were designed to frighten off questions when the General had no idea what to do or say. They were to hide his stupidity, they said.

At last he broke the silence. "Well, I'm damned! Ordered out of my house, and what does he say? Nothing! The man must be guilty, and he knows that I know it, or he would have defended himself."

"Let's hope," said Octave, "he now has the sense to stop writing."

"And keep his mouth shut."

At that moment the doors burst open and Marie rushed in. "Papa!" and then noticing Octave, "Oh I'm sorry, Monsieur d'Estouilly, good evening. Papa, I'm to tell you that Mama is getting anxious you will not be in time to greet General Préval."

39

At the sight of his daughter the General relaxed and smiled. "I'm coming now, my darling. Would you find Samuel please, and ask him to remove Lieutenant de la Roncière's place from the table. I know it will make an odd number at dinner but it can't be helped."

"Why, Papa? What's happened?"

"He won't be dining with us. He won't be here."

"But he *is* here. I've seen him."

"I've told him he is no longer welcome in this house."

"The letters, I suppose?"

"It's the only course possible."

"But, Papa, how dreadful! Is he really the man? Is he?" The General did not reply and Marie, irritated by the silence, asked, "You've spoken to him, haven't you, Papa?"

"Yes."

"What did he say?"

The General looked at her, then at Octave, for some time before replying. As he led the way from the drawing-room he said, "Nothing, my dear. Nothing."

After leaving the drawing-room Emile did his best not to be noticed by the other guests. Nevertheless, some of them saw him wearing his cap in the house, and walking pale-faced out through the front door. They saw the General, looking flushed and withdrawn, leaving the drawing-room with Octave d'Estouilly and his daughter, and knowing Emile's reputation, knew some kind of mischief had happened. They heard Marie whisper loudly to her father in the hall, "Papa, did Emile say he'd done it?"

And they heard the General say, "Never mention that man's name again!"

Moreover, Octave d'Estouilly had not had time to tell Joachim Ambert that the General had ordered that the letters must not be mentioned, so when Joachim saw Emile leaving in a manner which showed there had been trouble, he was in no doubt as to what it was about. He spoke to his immediate circle, and in less than five minutes everyone in the house knew what had happened — or thought they knew. The kitchen staff knew as well, because scraps of information had come from Samuel.

Marie realised she would get nothing from her adoring father however hard she tried. She was bursting with curiosity about what had happened behind those closed doors. Perhaps, she thought, she would be able to persuade Octave d'Estouilly to tell her later, after dinner when he had had a few glasses of wine. Perhaps, she thought, her father would tell her mother. But she dismissed that idea, because even if he did, her mother would never pass it on. Ah, Helen! Yes the governess might find out, and she could get anything out of Helen Allen, a silly, creepy creature.

Miss Allen was in her room changing for dinner. Marie decided to go to see her, and tell her all she knew so far, hoping that Helen would add some details. She did not knock on the door, but walked straight in to find the governess brushing her hair. She gave her frock a disparaging look.

"Is that the sort of thing they wear in England?"

"I bought it in Kent." Helen was still angry with Marie for having read out the letter.

"I suppose you did. I'm sure they'd never make that in London." She changed her tone — if she were going to draw any information from Helen she would have to patronise her a little.

"Sorry about your letter," she started. "I know I should never have snatched it. I was impulsive."

Helen had a forgiving nature. There were eight years between them but the wood of the door between their adjoining bedrooms was only an inch thick. It was impossible for two females at such close proximity not to discover some common ground.

Helen had told Marie of her boyfriends in England and Marie had told Helen of her conquests and hopes, not hiding the pleasure she took in being the daughter of a favoured general. Her opportunities were almost unique, she would say. "I didn't mean that about your frock," she said now. "I think it's most attractive."

"But even if one of the officers does take an interest in me this evening, I can never meet him again anywhere except here. There was one about a month ago. I'm sure he liked me." Helen was ready to confide.

"What was his name?" This was the chance Marie had waited for. She would see that they would meet again.

"I don't know. But he's been here before." Helen's voice drooped with sadness. "I wasn't even introduced to him."

"Well," said Marie brightly "if he's here tonight, just point him out to me and I'll not only see that you are introduced, but I'll make it easy for you to see him privately some time later."

Helen's eyes lit up. "You wouldn't tell Madame, would you?"

Marie laughed, her silvery, bell-like laugh. "Of course I won't tell Mama." She knelt on the floor by Helen's chair and suddenly became serious. "Did you know," she asked, keeping her voice down, "that there's been a bit of a scandal downstairs this evening? Papa has just thrown that delicious Emile de la Roncière out of the house!"

41

"No! What for?" Helen bent close to Marie so she would not miss a syllable.

"Papa won't tell me. He simply said we must never mention him again. I was hoping you'd tell me what it's about."

Helen looked blank. "Me? How would I know what he was thrown out for? I know he drinks quite a lot. He's a — what's the word? Putting it bluntly, he goes after the girls." Helen stopped, put a finger to her teeth as if she had had a second thought on the subject. "Could it be," she ventured, "could it be anything to do with those letters?"

"How do you mean?"

"He might be the one who's been writing them, and now he's been caught."

"Oh, if it's true," said Marie, wide eyed, "I feel so sorry for him. What will happen to him?"

Helen was excited. "If it's true, he'll be court-martialled."

"Then what?" asked Marie.

"I don't know. What do they do after court-martials? Don't they strip him of his rank and just get rid of him?"

Marie was aware that this was all guesswork. She wanted to know exactly what had taken place in that drawing-room. "Now listen, Helen," she said, a touch of command in her voice, "I want you to make up to that Lieutenant Octave d'Estouilly this evening. He was in the room with Papa and Emile. Find out from him."

Helen's face fell. "Must I? What if the man I want to meet is there and I'm making up to that lieutenant?"

Marie had it all set. "Don't worry. If the one you like is there, point him out to me and trust me. But in return you have to find out what happened in the drawing-room."

Next day, the news was to spread round Saumur, through the market, through the cafés, through the shops and the wineries, so that everyone had heard that the General had had to throw a young officer out of his house. The story varied from the General physically hurling Emile down the steps, to a squad of armed men escorting him at gun point to the Cavalry School; and the reason changed from Emile becoming fighting drunk at dinner to being caught *in flagrante delicto* in one of the bedrooms with a kitchen-maid or one of the guests.

Within the Cavalry School the news was to spread more quickly and more accurately. It was said that the General had thrown him out for writing obscene letters.

That evening of 23 September 1834, the night of the dinner party,

Emile de la Roncière walked thoughtfully along the Rue Royale away from the General's house, and turned left into the Rue St Nicholas, the narrow echoing street in which he had his lodgings. It was still possible, by the light of the full moon, and by the glare from a few flares outside cafés and a couple of shops which were still open, to see the gaunt fronts of the shops – grocers, greengrocers, charcuteries, butchers. Weak shafts of light escaped from between ill-fitting shutters behind which the shopkeepers and their families ate, slept, played dominoes, shuffled cards, made love, argued, and got drunk on the heady Saumur wine. One careless couple who had not bothered to close their shutters could be seen undressing for bed. Emile was in no mood to notice any of this as he went down the street and thankfully found the door to his lodging house

La mère Rouault and her two daughters heard their lodger come in quietly and go up to his room. Annette said "That's funny, monsieur is back early. I thought he'd gone to the General's house for dinner."

"Perhaps he's not well," replied Elizabet, who was even prettier than her sister.

La mère Rouault was a woman of elephantine proportions whose bare and fleshy arms contrasted with her black peasant widow's dress. She dripped with sweat from her nose and her chin and her muscular arms bulged as she wielded her huge, pressing iron.

She put the iron back on its trivet in the red-hot grate, picked up a second one, already heated, and said "I'll go up in a minute or two to see if he wants anything. Annette, pass me that sheet." She passed her arm over her forehead to push the hair out of her eyes, and took a long drink from a dirty carafe of white wine. Annette obediently spread the sheet over the blanket-covered table. Elizabet slipped out of the room and ran up to the lodger's door.

She found him lying on his bed, staring at the ceiling.

"What's happened?"

He was fully dressed and had not even taken off his cap.

"Nothing that I can explain."

"I'll understand. Have you been drinking?"

"No."

"Then you're not feeling well, eh?"

"I'm all right." He reached for her hand. He was not smiling. She sat on the edge of the bed and cradled his head in her lap.

"You've not even taken off your boots!"

"I can't be bothered. I can't be bothered with anything. I want to leave the army, but I can't go back to my father's house. Perhaps I should just die."

"What could it be? What has happened to you? You're too much fun to talk like that, so who's upset you? Eh? Tell your Elizabet all about it. I don't care what you've done."

"You're too good to me." He pulled her down and kissed her face. "You can take my boots off, if you like."

She laughed. "Of course I will, but that's all I'll take off. Mama said she might come up to see you."

CHAPTER FOUR

The next day, 24 September 1834, at first light, General de Morell and Solange were awakened by the sound of hysterical sobbing and continuous knocking on the bedroom door. Solange called, "Come in, what is it?"

Helen Allen, her eyes red from crying, dishevelled, but fully dressed, nervously entered the room. The General, dazed from the shock of the sudden end to his sleep, sat up and mumbled, "What's going on? I was asleep."

Solange stared at the girl. "Speak up! What's the matter?"

Helen burst into a renewed flood of tears.

The General was annoyed at being woken. "What on earth's happening? What are you doing in our room? Come on, girl, pull yourself together, stop blubbering and tell me."

Through her sobs she managed to get out a few words. "There's been a — there's been — I think — " and the rest was lost in gulps and sobs.

"Stop that!" commanded the General "Stop that at once! Control yourself and tell me what this is all about."

Helen made a supreme effort. "Somebody has broken in and attacked . . ."

Solange helped her. "A burglar's attacked you?"

"No! No! Not me . . ."

"My God!" said the General. "Marie! It's Marie!" and he was out of bed at once. "Where is she?"

"In her room."

Not waiting to put on dressing gowns, the General and Solange rushed along the corridor towards the narrow staircase, tumbling question on question as they ran. "Is she badly hurt? Who did it? When did this happen?"

Helen had a chance to answer the last question. "About four hours ago."

The General incredulously echoed. "About four hours? Where have you been?"

Solange asked, "What's the time now?"

Helen said she did not know but she thought it was about half past six.

Marie's was a sparsely furnished room with an old truckle bed which had done service on the retreat from Moscow, a corner curtain to conceal Marie's clothes and a plain worktable which was also her dressing-table. The grey paintwork was shoddy, and round the doors and shutters it was chipped.

One pane of the window was broken, and shards of glass were lying on the stone floor with about a metre and a half of white rope.

There was also blood on the floor.

Marie, who had been sitting in her nightdress, struggled to her feet and flung her arms around her father's neck. "Oh, Papa! Papa!"

He kissed her gently and helped her back to her chair. "There, there, it's all right now."

"What's happened?" asked Solange "Who attacked you?"

The General turned to Helen. "Have you told the servants?"

"No, monsieur."

Solange, who seemed to be in an even greater state of agitation than Helen, cried, "Tell them! Tell them! Call out the guard!"

The General held up his hand. "Wait!" he commanded. "How long ago did all this happen?"

"Ages ago," murmured Marie. She seemed to be in pain.

"Why didn't you call us at once?" demanded Solange.

To which the General added the obvious "He's had time to get away!"

"Oh yes," agreed Marie quietly. "He's gone. He went – he went –" She waved in the vague direction of the open window.

"The soldier, of course," answered Marie.

"What soldier?" questioned the General.

"What did he do?" said Solange.

"Never mind that for now," interrupted her husband. "I want to know what soldier."

They all looked hopefully at Marie. They waited some time before she said, "I don't know. They all look alike to me."

"Can you remember if he was dark or fair?" enquired the General softly.

45

There was another long wait. "Fair," she said, and added, "I think."

"What regiment was he in?" asked her father.

"I wouldn't know that. But he had a black handkerchief tied round his face."

Solange turned to Helen. "Did you see who it was?"

"No, I woke up as he was leaving." She went over to the large table, and picked up a piece of paper. "He left this letter here. It wasn't in an envelope so I read it." She handed the General the now familiar straw-coloured lined paper.

" 'You have a way of avoiding the trouble in store for you all. I am willing to marry your daughter, and that will save her from disgrace. It would be stupid of you to refuse this. The solution to your problem is to hand her over to me with a fine dowry. If this is not allowed, your crime will be worse than mine, because no one will want her when all is known. I may have robbed her of her honour, which you can so easily give back to her by the sacrifice of enough money for a really attractive dowry with the house you own in Normandy. Think before you make any of this public. You can be happy and at peace if you command Marie to marry me.' "

The letter was signed "Emile".

The General folded it up and put it in his pocket.

Suddenly Marie moaned. "Oh Mama! Mama! It hurts so. It is so painful." She was rocking from side to side holding her stomach. Solange knelt on the floor by her chair and asked the others to leave.

"I must talk to her alone."

The way from the General's house to the Cavalry School was across the bridge which, on fine days, was used as a meeting place for officers at a loose end. From the bridge one could see the river traffic, such as it was, the road traffic, and the comings and goings of most of the population of Saumur. Near the bridge on the north bank, on the right-hand side of the road if approached from the General's house was a popular and well-appointed café. It was not out-of-bounds to lower ranks but by tacit agreement it was reserved for officers.

That morning Octave d'Estouilly, on his way to see Joachim Ambert, chanced to see his friend taking an early cognac in the café.

"Ambert! Ambert!" he called, threading his way through the little tables, "I was on my way to see you."

"Well, here I am! Join me in a cognac. You always look so serious. Cheer up! Most troubles never happen."

"This is serious."

"It always is, with you. Don't tell me!" Joachim brushed his little fair moustache with a forefinger. "You have a hangover from Madame de Morell's party last night. Those ducks were delicious. And what an orange sauce!"

"No, it's la Roncière again."

Joachim Ambert studied his brandy glass. "Hasn't he had enough? I should have thought that last night would have finished him, and he would be doing his packing this morning and writing his letter of resignation."

"Not at all. As far as I know, the only note he has written is one challenging me to a duel."

Joachim roared with laughter. "My God, what a nerve! I suppose he knows he can be arrested for duelling, and it's a double charge these days. Even sending the challenge is illegal! But naturally you will accept!"

"I don't want to be arrested too." Octave was totally unskilled with a pistol.

"But how can you back down?"

"I shall ignore the note."

Joachim laughed. "Oh come now!" He drained his glass "If you don't rise to the occasion he'll tell everyone. He's like that. You'll be branded a coward. What then?"

"It's against regulations."

"Hiding behind the regulations won't make you the most popular man in the army. Well, I suppose it's up to you. Have you the note with you?"

Octave produced the paper. " 'If you have any spirit at all, you will call me out to a duel after the way you behaved last night.' " It was signed "E de la R". Joachim gave it back, saying in the literary French with a strong Alsatian accent he frequently lapsed into for humorous effect, "It is the gauntlet on the ground! Stoop but once in honour to pick it up and slap his right cheek with the back of it before throwing it at his feet!"

Octave was not amused. Joachim was in one of his rollicking moods — in fact, he was seldom out of them — but he frowned as he added, "He's referring to his humiliation by the General, in front of you."

"Well, there you are! It's plain enough! A challenge is a challenge." Joachim relished the sport that had to be, although he knew he would have to give Octave a shove to get him to fight. "This is something I wouldn't miss for anything."

"Are you serious?" Octave was incredulous.

Joachim ignored the question. "I know just the place for it, where you'll never be seen. If you're not caught, you can't be arrested. There've been lots of duels since Napoleon banned them. I know the wording very well . . ."

Octave stopped him. "So do I. You have to be seen."

"Exactly." He leaned forward so that they could not be heard at the next tables. "Under the north end of the bridge after this dry summer you'll find it's all sand, gravel and rushes. There's no point from which you can be seen except from the river itself. That's the spot. Now, have a cognac."

Octave refused the offer. •

Almost as an afterthought, Joachim said, "It is more important to you than it is to him not to be caught. It could ruin your career, while his is ruined already. So I'll find la Roncière's second, act as yours and tell him that you'll meet him under the north arch at six o'clock tomorrow morning." He paused, looked searchingly at Octave and said "I'm glad you know how to duel."

"Yes. Thank goodness for those few fencing lessons when I was seventeen. What if he chooses pistols? I'm a rotten shot."

"He won't do that."

"I hope I don't kill him."

"Worry about that after the duel. It's most unlikely. La Roncière had quite a reputation as a swordsman when he was stationed at Cayenne. He was usually in trouble with someone or other, mostly to do with cheating at cards."

"Oh dear." Octave was alarmed at what he seemed to be sliding into.

Joachim smiled. "Don't look like that! After all, you've done a little fencing. I'll be your second — I'm better at that than at fencing!"

Out of concern for his family, General de Morell sent one of his aides over to the Cavalry School with a note to say he would not be there until the afternoon, when General Préval was to carry out a formal inspection and presentation.

"Why," Solange asked, and not for the first time, "do you refuse to call in help?" They were sitting in the garden where they could not be overheard.

"I've told you. Had this been a common assault or a theft, I would have summoned the guard at once. But we must consider Marie. If this gets out, what eligible officer in our circle of acquaintances would look at her again? If they were to know of this attack, I doubt if any one of them would ask my permission to call." He was sounding particularly pompous, she thought. "It is my duty to protect her reputation. It is a matter of self-respect. You must take all that into account before you blame me for swearing this household to silence. I must uphold the honour of our name for the sake of France." She was bored with his bombast. What had patriotism to do with it? "I cannot take the action a lesser man would not hesitate to take."

"I think you're confusing duty with pride, and self-respect with ambition," suggested his wife.

Samuel was coming down the gravel path with a silver tray, and on it was a note for the General. As soon as he saw the straw-coloured paper he asked, "Where did you find this?"

"In the hall, monsieur. It had been pushed under the door."

As soon as Samuel had gone, the General read the note. It boasted of the assault the previous evening and said that the writer had challenged Octave d'Estouilly to a duel. It was signed with the letter 'E'. He passed it silently to Solange.

"Why should he want to fight Lieutenant d'Estouilly?" she asked.

"I have no idea. They both risk their commissions."

"I've just remembered a strange coincidence," said Solange slowly. "You mentioned to me, after you had dismissed la Roncière last night, that Lieutenant d'Estouilly had had the effrontery to tell you to your face that he would like to call out la Roncière to a duel. Did he say that?"

"What of it?" he asked lightly.

"The coincidence! Last night d'Estouilly suggested a duel. This morning we get a letter signed 'E' telling of a proposed duel. Lieutenant d'Estouilly could also have signed with an 'E'."

"This is from la Roncière," asserted the General.

"How do we know? What does d'Estouilly do all day?"

"He's an artist. I told you he'd been sent on attachment from the War Office."

"Precisely! He's an artist. Artists reproduce things exactly as they look. Is that so far from forging letters?"

"What an extraordinary thing to say! What would make him do a thing like that?"

"What would make Emile de la Roncière do it?" Solange warmed to her argument. "And I assume that d'Estouilly is skilled at fencing."

"I wouldn't have thought so, but that doesn't make him the man you say he is."

"I'm not saying he *is* the man," she countered, "though I'm beginning to feel less sure it's la Roncière. You'll stop the duelling, of course."

"I don't think so," said de Morell.

"Why not? You'll put your rank in jeopardy if you don't. You must

49

not even be a tacit party to it. You know it's about to happen so you must stop it."

"Officially I know nothing. Only you and I know what's in this letter. And it's probably a complete fabrication anyway."

"You don't really believe that."

"No, I don't," he said, "but if there's a challenge between the two men, let us pray to God that disaster overtakes Lieutenant Emile de la Roncière."

"Why, if you're not sure he's the man?"

"I am sure now. It is you who are not sure. Had you been in the drawing-room last night when I dismissed him, you would have had no doubts at all. He didn't even try to defend himself. Is that the action of an innocent man? Is it?"

Solange made no reply.

"For now, I shall think only of the weapons they might use. Pistols are unlikely — they make too much noise and neither man has any experience with them. So it will be foils, *épées* and sabres."

The significance of the three weapons was not lost on Solange. She knew that the foil was about a metre and a half long, button-tipped, harmless, and used for scoring points only. Officers laughed at it because it was designed for schoolboys who wore the new mesh face guards. The *épée* was triangular-bladed, stronger and heavier, of the length of the foil but with a sharp point that could cut and kill. The sabre was shorter and heavy, with two cutting edges. It was also a killer.

She did not know, and neither did he, that Octave had had little or no experience with any of them. They assumed that both men were reasonably proficient at fencing. A cavalry officer was expected to be able to fence as well as he could ride as well as he could converse.

Joachim Ambert, in his capacity as Octave d'Estouilly's second, went that afternoon to find Emile, but he was nowhere to be seen in the Cavalry School. However, in the equestrian library and trophy room he happened to spot Lieutenant Bérail, who knew Emile better than most.

"Bérail, can you keep your mouth shut?"

"Certainly."

"There may be a duel between la Roncière and d'Estouilly . . ."

"A what? A duel? Good grief, man, there'll be the hell of a row if anyone knows about it. Who's d'Estouilly?"

"That artist."

"Him? Duel? It couldn't be."

"Well," said Ambert, and he couldn't help smiling, "he wouldn't be duelling if I hadn't talked him into it."

"Is it to do with that talk about General de Morell chucking la Ronciére out of his house?"

"Yes. Apparently d'Estouilly was with the General when he reprimanded la Ronciére. La Ronciére's mad about the humiliation, so he's thrown the glove down at d'Estouilly's feet, so to speak."

"And d'Estouilly picked it up."

"I helped him."

Bérail laughed. "I bet you did! You really are a bit of a swine at times. I can't imagine that artist duelling! What'll he use? A paint-brush? What d'you want me to do about it?"

Joachim Ambert showed him the acceptance to the duel. "I'm on duty in twenty minutes. If you come across la Ronciére would you give him this?

"Certainly. It'll give me great pleasure. I'm seeing him in an hour anyway. Who's his second?"

"He hasn't named one. He probably looking for one now or assuming d'Estouilly will funk it."

• "In that case, my dear Ambert, nothing will give me more pleasure than offering my services to la Ronciére. I wouldn't miss this for anything. Who's d'Estouilly's second?"

"Me."

"Fine. Let me see the note."

Bérail read, "'I have been getting anonymous messages from you. I hate to think an officer could be such a coward that he cannot properly sign his name. You are unworthy of the anger of an honest man, but your epaulette makes it impossible for me to hand you over to the Public Prosecutor. General de Morell himself agrees that your shame must not be made public. Illegal though swordplay is, I will not hide behind the law, and will do you the honour of crossing swords. I will stoop to your level for that moment.

"'I choose to meet you at six o'clock tomorrow morning, 25 September 1834, under the north arch on the gravel of the dried river-bed. The Officers' Mess Hall will be empty after eleven tonight, so ask your second to remove the *épées* crossed over the fireplace in there and bring them to our meeting place, where you will, at six o'clock by the church bell. Take the one of your choice by the mounting, and I will take the other.' "

Bèrail folded the letter and put it in his pocket. "How many people know about this?"

"Just the four of us."

"Keep it like that. If this gets out we shall have a crowded river-bed with no room to fight. The others will be mad when they know there's been a duel and they missed it. Where do we stand?"

"In what way?"

"Well, you and I are not duelling but we know it's illegal and we're helping. If it gets out I suppose we'll get transferred or something."

"We might have to resign," said Ambert.

"Nonsense. You're too well in with the General."

"No I'm not. No one is. He keeps himself aloof. Has to, or he'd sacrifice his respect. Well, Bérail, we can always say we were nothing to do with it but had to be there to see fair play. Nobody need know that I wrote that letter."

"You did?"

Ambert explained that Octave had been most unwilling to copy it, and had said he wanted to use foils, face guards and body pads so that no one would get hurt. Bérail thought this so hilarious that he had to hang on to a door lintel to stop himself collapsing with laughter, while tears of merriment ran down Joachim's cheeks.

It was to be an extraordinary duel that took place next morning. At about a quarter to six the duellists and their seconds met on the river-bed under the north arch. Mist over that river in early autumn is fairly common in the morning and occasionally in the evening, but that morning there was thick fog. It was damp and grey, swirling about fifteen metres from the river-bed, so that visibility at times was down to a metre, less than the length of an *épée*. The protagonists sat on boulders, each invisible to the other, waiting for the church bell to sound, while their seconds · discussed whether they should fight in the fog or postpone the duel until a better morning.

Lieutenant Bérail suggested that each fighter should be asked separately, and if one suggested a postponement, the duel should be postponed. The seconds vanished into the fog and brought back the verdict that each man would fight. Lieutenant Bérail offered both *épées* to Octave d'Estouilly who brandished each in turn, finally — and wisely — choosing the lighter.

"Monsieur la Roncière, if you agree, we will not wait for the church clock to strike."

"Monsieur d'Estouilly, I agree."

The rules of fighting demand that the fighters, at the on-guard position, stand at such a distance, the one from the other, that one fighter cannot strike the other simply by extending his *épée* arm, but must make the full lunge first. On this morning, immediately the men had taken up their positions, neither could see the other.

"Fight on!" called Emile, and Octave jumped to his left, terrified that Emile might take advantage of the fog to make the *coup de Jarnac*, a cut at the back of the knee severing the hamstring and crippling the victim for life.

Hoping to make this single and winning strike himself, Octave stood, listening for Emile. He heard the sound of crunching gravel to his right, and whipped round only to see Lieutenant Bérail peering at him through the gloom.

The church bell struck six. As if from nowhere a blow struck and penetrated Octave's uniform. "Octave on the octave," laughed Emile. The pun was not lost on him. The fighter's body has imaginary lines – one from the centre of the neck down to just above the lower stomach, the other from one armpit to the other. Each of the four sections has a name. The lower right quarter is called the octave, and this was where Emile's *épée* had penetrated. Octave was aware of blood but no pain except for the sharp jab. He swung round wildly and found himself up to his ankles in a pool. Emile heard him splashing about, approached the noise and saw Octave standing with his back to him.

"Eh!" he shouted to make Octave turn, gaining ground in the classic style of taking short steps in rapid succession. He lunged, letting his *épée* pass easily under the right shoulder, to emerge about three inches out of Octave's back. Octave fell, breaking Emile's *épée* as he did so. The fog had lifted slightly so that both seconds saw Emile stand back holding less than half an *épée*, and cry, "Honour is satisfied!" Octave, his anger and fear obscuring his pain, leapt to his feet; with his left hand he grabbed what was left of Emile's *épée*, and with his own sliced at Emile, missing him with every stroke.

Emile seized the flailing steel, and Bérail called out, "Stop! This is murder! Stop!" Both seconds went to disarm Octave who had collapsed and rolled into a clump of rushes.

No one spoke to the victor, who walked away into the thick mist. Joachim took out a handkerchief, wrapped it round the *épée* sticking out of Octave's chest, and with the wounded man yelling, he pulled it out as quickly as he could. It was not easy.

They carried him back to his lodgings by the east side of the church on the island. His was a large airy room, poorly furnished. There were two uncomfortable wooden chairs, once white, now mottled brown where the paint had been chipped off. The shutters were grey, one of them lurching threateningly over the large paper-strewn table. The window faced south. Octave had chosen the room for the amount of light it let in but would have preferred a north-facing room which would have been less subject to hourly change. The walls had been given a pale grey wash and were marked with grease, and there was a huge deep red stain which looked as if a wine bottle had been thrown at the wall. The pictures on the walls were all by Octave — sketches and paintings of horses with various harnesses and snaffles, of carriages for officers, of cannon, rifles, pistols, of swords for battle, ceremonial swords, pikes and lances. There were colourful paintings of soldiers in different uniform, each showing Octave's passion for detail. There was a travelling chest of drawers containing a multitude of little pots of colour pervading the room with their distinctive odour. On the top of the chest stood an earthenware jug with two projections from which the handle had been broken. In it, bristling like the quills of a porcupine, were Octave's paint-brushes, pencils and pens. On the opposite side from the big square table was a recess in the wall, curtained off, in which stood Octave's bed.

Bérail and Ambert pulled back the curtain and laid him gently on the bed as his landlord, Monsieur Gotty, in the uncertain stage of a hangover — fat, bald, sweaty and blotchy-faced — watched dazedly as they searched for a cloth with which to stem the flow of flood from Octave's chest and back. He lay still and white-faced.

"Is he hurt?" asked M. Gotty stupidly. "He mentioned the duel to me last night. Did he win?"

Lieutenant Bérail ignored the question and said, "Please watch him for ¹¹s. I have to go, I'm on duty."

They found white cloth, ripped it up and plugged the wounds. Joachim noticed the red patch growing on the right side of his stomach. "You were hit in the stomach?"

Octave nodded and whispered, "Yes."

"He must have some cognac," said M. Gotty, who believed that cognac was the solution to all problems.

"No thank you," muttered the wounded man. "Just water."

Joachim Ambert said they should fetch the doctor quickly, and the two lieutenants left together while M. Gotty almost fell down the stairs to reach the kitchen.

Joachim ran all the way to the Cavalry School, and was lucky to find the doctor there at such an early hour.

"How did Lieutenant d'Estouilly come to be wounded in such a way?" he enquired as he packed gauzes, bandages and instruments into his bag. Joachim admitted it was a duel. The doctor wrote a note reporting the event to the General, asked after the other combatant, and then he and Joachim took the first pair of saddled horses available to ride full gallop back to the sick man.

54

CHAPTER FIVE

After the doctor had treated Octave's wounds there was no choice but to leave him alone as Joachim, his friend and second, had had to go on duty, and the only occupant of the house was Monsieur Gotty.

Gotty had nothing to do beyond collecting the rents from the rooms he let in his three terraced houses and promising his tenants repairs which were seldom carried out. Once dressed, a simple occupation for him except on Sundays when he washed and shaved before going to Mass, M. Gotty would walk round the church to spend the rest of his day drinking and playing dominoes or *boules* in or outside the café.

Having taken the wounded lodger a glass of water, Gotty warmed up the previous day's coffee, drank it, and took one more look at Lieutenant d'Estouilly to reassure himself that the lodger had not died. He was not moved by compassion, but by a month's outstanding rent.

While General de Morell, informed by the doctor of the duel, was doing his best to contain the news within his immediate family circle, M. Gotty was applying his vivid imagination to distort that which was undeniably true. There had been a duel.

He knew of the duel because he had been told, rather foolishly, by Octave the night before. M. Gotty, after his first drink, believed that he had witnessed the fight. He exaggerated the wounds that he had never seen, and told his eager, wide-eyed audience in the café how he had helped hold the patient while Dr Servan stitched the gashes. The serious drinkers were solemn-faced as they gazed into the oblivion at the bottom of their glasses, but those drinking coffee were alert and enjoying the story. Within the hour there was not one café in Saumur in which the duel had not been discussed. The reasons for the duel were becoming as numerous as the cafés. At the Café Royal on the north bank, speculation was rife among the officers. It made interesting gossip but, while Emile was not liked, Octave was hardly known.

Solange knew of the duel by midday because her husband had been told by the doctor. The news made her even more certain that the letter 'E' stood not for Emile but for Estouilly. She did not like Octave

55

d'Estouilly, finding him weak and wanting in the qualities that she considered made a man. His lack of conversation and withdrawal into himself made him, in her opinion, a more likely culprit.

Neither did she like Emile de la Roncière. She thought him arrogant and ill-mannered; he seldom wrote 'thank you' notes for dinner nor brought her the customary presents. But instinct told her there was more to him than to the other lieutenant.

It was this intuition that led her to send a note over to the Cavalry School asking Lieutenant Joachim Ambert to call on her at three that afternoon.

He arrived at the appointed time and was shown into the music-room where Solange, an accomplished musician, was playing the piano.

"Please sit down," she invited, trying to sound casual.

Joachim sat awkwardly. He suspected that la Baronne was also painfully involved with the letters, and guessed that the interview would be about the duel.

Solange produced a strip of paper about fifteen centimetres long and seven centimetres wide. "I have cut this from the bottom of a letter. Have you ever seen anything like it before?"

She passed it to him and he saw that it was pale straw-coloured paper covered with light grey parallel lines.

"Yes, madame. Monsieur d'Estouilly showed me a letter yesterday morning on paper like this. It was from Emile de la Roncière."

"Challenging him to a duel?"

Ambert hesitated until he remembered the doctor's note to the General. "Well, yes, it did."

"Monsieur Ambert, will you give me your word that you will not disclose what I am about to say?"

It was difficult for a young man to refuse la Baronne.

"I think it possible," she said, "only possible though, that these letters do not come from Monsieur de la Roncière."

"But we assumed . . ."

She interrupted him. "We all assumed too easily that it was he."

"If not he, who else could do it?"

"Some that we have received have been signed with the letter 'E'."

"Yes. 'E' for Emile," prompted Joachim Ambert.

"The letter 'E' need not stand for Emile. It could stand for Estouilly."

Joachim was astounded. He knew his friend better than that. "I'm quite sure he would be incapable of such a thing, and I have a good reason to confirm that he could not write them." He was thinking of how he had talked Octave into a duel for which he was entirely unsuited.

56

Joachim had not fully realised how incapable a fighter was Octave until the débâcle under the bridge. He was not going to be so disloyal, however, as to say that his friend was a physical coward and a poor fighter, so he passed on. "What would he gain by writing such letters?"

"That question can be applied to anyone suspected of writing them. Somebody writes them or they would not exist. You can apply that equally well to Emile de la Roncière who comes, you must remember, from a good family. Now, who is d'Estouilly? What do we know of his family? They are of no consequence, are they?"

"I think they're farmers from Chalon-sur-Saône."

"Farmers or land-owners?"

Joachim did not know.

"So what I want you to do for me is to keep that piece of paper, and when you go back to Monsieur d'Estouilly's lodgings, search among his papers to see if you can find more of it. Keep this to yourself, and tell only me what you find."

The treachery of such behaviour shocked Joachim and, while not wanting to refuse his General's wife, he searched for an excuse. "I can't go through his things while he's there."

"Then wait until he goes out." Solange looked at him witheringly.

"He won't be going out for a long time yet. He's badly wounded."

She pulled a sad face, but he could see it was just a formality. "I knew he lost the duel, but I thought the winner just had to draw a little blood. What happened?"

So he told her of his friend's wounds. Solange did not wince at the details, but neither did she show much concern. "Oh, the poor boy! Is he suffering?" Like her daughter she did not wait for an answer. She was simply paying lip-service. "It sounds bad enough to have him moved to the military hospital. Do you agree?"

"Yes. He has a drunken landlord and will be dependent on friends like myself going round to see if he's all right, and get food for him."

"I'll get my husband to make the necessary arrangements to have him moved." She looked away as she came to the point of her suggestion. "It might be a good idea if you go round and help him move. After he's gone, you can go back to tidy up his things and perhaps then you'll be able to have a proper search for that paper?"

On the way to visit his wounded friend that afternoon, Joachim decided not to look for the paper, nor would he worry Octave with the suspicions which the General's wife had asked him to keep to himself. But by the time he reached the door to M. Gotty's house he thought the whole affair so strange that he might just have a casual look. If he found anything he was not sure whether he would tell Madame de Morell. It would hardly be proof of Octave's guilt. What's the point of it all? he asked himself.

M. Gotty was sleeping off his cognac, and staggered bleary-eyed to the door. Joachim hurried up the stairs to Octave's room to find him looking better and sitting up in bed reading a newspaper.

"How do you feel?"

"A lot better. Still hurts."

"Anything you need?"

"No, thank you. Nothing today, but tomorrow I'll probably have some bread and cheese. I'll ask that drunken sot Gotty to fetch some for me."

Joachim wandered over to Octave's table and pulled out some drawing pads.

"You don't want to get bored sitting there in bed. I thought you might like a sketch pad and pencil."

"It'll be some time before I can draw again. My right hand doesn't work too well. The *épée* went through the shoulder."

Joachim put down the pads. He could not recognise any of the paper he was looking for, so he continued his search by pretending to admire one of his friend's unfinished drawing.

"This is a fine horse," he said, flourishing a pen and ink drawing so that he scattered others to the floor. "I'm sorry, I don't think they've come to any harm," he said, picking them up and stacking them neatly on the table to extend his search.

Suddenly, loud voices carried from below and the landlord's slurred protests at being woken a second time that afternoon heralded footsteps ascending the stairs. The door opened, and Lieutenant Emile de la Roncière strode into the room.

"I must speak to you," he said breathlessly.

"You've got a nerve coming here," said Joachim "Go on, clear off!"

"No," pleaded Emile, "I have to speak to Octave."

"There's nothing I want to hear from you," said Octave from his bed.

"You don't understand . . ."

"I think he understands perfectly well," interrupted Joachim.

"Just leave, and close the door, you . . ." Octave started to cough.

Joachim took over. "For God's sake go! Can't you see what you've done to him? He needs to be quiet . . ."

Emile unbuckled his sword and let it fall to the floor with a clatter. "I'll leave my sword on the floor. Draw yours if you like, but I must speak to you. I must!"

58

Octave recovered his voice "What more do you want? To see me die? Go now, if you are a man of any feelings."

"And take your sword with you," added Joachim.

"I want no favours!" demanded Emile. "I just want to ask one question. Nothing else."

"Well?" enquired Octave weakly.

"I've just heard an extraordinary story from Bérail, the man who acted as my second. He told me about some forged letters."

"What about them?" asked Joachim.

"Who are they from?"

"You, above all, should know the answer to that" said Octave.

"Why should I?"

"My acceptance of your challenge to the duel made that perfectly clear."

"I couldn't understand it."

"Then," said Octave feebly, "what were we fighting about?"

Emile looked in disbelief first at Octave, then at Joachim. "I don't know, but your letter gave me no option, so we fought."

"Come now," said Joachim. "No man in his right mind fights a duel risking his life for something he's never heard of! This is ludicrous!"

"But I didn't know. I still don't know."

"You could have asked Joachim when he brought you my acceptance to your challenge," suggested Octave.

"What challenge?"

"You challenged me to come out and fight."

"I most certainly did not!"

"Then why didn't you say so this morning?" asked Joachim.

"How? Before the duel? It would have looked as if I were trying to avoid fighting. I would have been branded a coward."

Octave, struggling for breath, forming his words slowly and with great effort, said, "We fought because you wrote some disgraceful letters. We fought because you wrote calling me a coward. Now do you remember?"

"No."

"You wrote to General de Morell himself. You wrote to Madame de Morell, to Marie de Morell and to the governess."

"That's what Bérail said when he asked me to confess."

"Did you confess?" asked Joachim sharply.

"Why should I? I've never written these letters, and I've never seen them, so how can I know what you're talking about?"

"Who," asked Octave, "do you suggest wrote them? Who else would do such a thing?"

"I don't know. It was certainly not me! I respect the General and his

59

family. I go to his house as his guest and eat at his table, I dance with Madame la Baronne and Ma'mselle Marie, and I enjoy the musical evenings."

"You did," said Octave in a whisper. "You won't any more. Next you'll be saying that you've forgotten that you were asked to leave the house. I was there, remember?"

"Of course I remember. Who could forget a thing like that? Perhaps now you can tell me why I was so humiliated."

The pain in his lung made it difficult for Octave to speak. "For this! For this obscene letter-writing! Are you pretending you don't know?"

"I have no idea why I am in disgrace."

"Ask your general."

"Who, me? A junior lieutenant ask the General why I'm banned from his house?"

"Why not?" demanded Octave, and his vehemence prompted another coughing fit.

"Put yourself in my shoes for a moment!" said Emile, when Octave was quiet. "At the beginning of a very pleasant evening I'm suddenly face to face with my general who's looking very angry. Behind him I see you, also very stern. I am ordered to leave the house. I was completely tongue-tied. In the same position you would have done the same thing."

"Rubbish!" said Octave. "Certainly I would have asked, so would you, except for the one thing that stopped you."

"And that?"

"You knew why you were being ordered out."

"On my honour I did not," protested Emile.

"You not only knew it, you expected it."

"I most certainly did not."

Octave pressed his point. "How long had you been in the house before you were asked by me to see General de Morell?"

"I don't know. Five minutes, perhaps ten."

"Long enough to take off your cap."

"Of course I took off my cap! Do you think I'm some provincial oaf?" Emile was insulted.

"And having taken it off, what did you do with it?"

"Gave it to one of the servants who put it on that marble table in the hall."

"If you didn't expect to be ordered out of the house, why did you go back to the hall to fetch it before you saw the General?"

"But I didn't!" shouted Emile.

"But you did! You couldn't salute bare-headed. You put on your cap and saluted, or can't you remember that either?"

It was the duel all over again in the fog, using words this time, not steel, and Octave parried and thrust.

"Then I must have had my cap with me," Emile said pathetically as he remembered knocking over the others.

"Indeed, you did have it."

"I don't see what all this has to do with some letters."

Octave turned to Joachim. "Show him the one he wrote calling me a coward. It's just inside my jacket there."

Joachim found the letter and handed it to Emile who read it slowly. "Am I supposed to have written this? It's absurd! The handwriting is similar to mine, but I totally deny ever doing such a thing."

"Of course you do," said Octave. "Let me quote you the line just before the challenge itself. 'I shall deny everything, as my only intention is to torment you.' You see, you had to include this duel because you couldn't face me in the mess after I'd seen you disgraced before the General. Handwriting experts have seen the other letters and say that you wrote them."

"I see," replied Emile. "You've had in experts. But, wait a minute! Look! I'll show you something. This writing! To imitate writing to this degree is very easy. Most people can do it if they really want to." Emile searched on the table for a pen, ink, paper. "Have you a sample of your own handwriting?" He found a laundry list. "Did you write this?"

Octave nodded.

"Watch!" said Emile, sitting at the table and clearing a small space in the muddle before him. "This will clear up everything." He wrote laboriously, looking back and forth from the laundry list to his own pen. When he had finished he stood up, smiled and gave the paper to Octave. "There! That's pretty good, isn't it? And it was easy. Just a few seconds to make an imitation of your handwriting. Anyone can do it!"

Joachim went over to the bed and he and Octave compared the two examples of handwriting.

"You understand what you've just done, don't you?" said Joachim.

And Octave added, "And we're both witnesses. Let me read it aloud so that none of us is under any misapprehension." But at that moment he became overwhelmed with weakness and handed the paper to Joachim who read it instead.

"'This is a facsimile of the handwriting of Octave d'Estouilly, written by Emile de la Roncière'."

He read it again, aloud, twice.

"Well," said Emile defensively, "what's wrong with that? It proves my point. Anyone can copy anyone else's handwriting."

"It proves no such thing," said Joachim. "It proves only that you are good at copying handwriting. That is most significant."

"Eh? I was trying to show you . . ." Emile realised what they thought and panicked. "Oh God! I see what you mean. Listen! This is nothing to do with me at all. Tear it up! Tear it up! Give it back. I beg of you give it back!"

Joachim ignored his plea, carefully folded the paper and placed it deliberately in an inner pocket, buttoning his jacket to keep it secure. "We may need this later as proof that you are an expert forger. Thank you for calling. You have cleared up a great deal of the mystery. I don't know whether Monsieur d'Estouilly knows this" – Octave looked up questioningly – "but others were suspected." Joachim sat down on one of the pock-marked chairs, and wagged a finger at Emile. "Do you realise the trouble you've caused? The suspicion that has passed from one person to another? Do you realise the enmity that has sprung up between one person and another because various people have been suspected of this writing? Do you know that poor old Octave there was under suspicion?" At this, Octave tried to heave himself up on one elbow but he was too weak and fell back against his pillows. "You know the trouble you've put others to, because you engineered it. You don't know that Madame de Morell herself asked me to search this room to see if Octave had any of the paper that you've been using." Emile did not seem to be taking in what was being said. "But now, thanks to your consummate skill, I am satisfied as to the source of the trouble. I think we both are."

At that point, Monsieur Gotty's voice could be heard in the hall, even more plaintive than usual at being awakened again from his siesta.

The door was flung back, and General de Morell came into the room. He went straight over to Octave.

"Dr Servan tells me you are badly hurt."

"I shall recover. He's coming back this evening." Octave's head fell back as he said, "You'll expect me to resign my commission after this. I'm sorry."

"No, no, I'll see that it is forgotten. These things happen. I'm having you transferred to the military hospital where you can be properly cared for. This is no place for a sick man." He looked round the room disdainfully, and his glance fell on Emile.

"What's this? What's he doing here?"

"Mon Général," said a frightened Emile, "I have to speak to you."

The General noticed Emile's sword and belt lying on the floor. "Pick those up at once!" He turned to Joachim. "Escort this officer from this house. He has no business here."

"I must speak to you, monsieur!"

"I have nothing to say to him. Lieutenant Ambert, did you hear what I said? Escort this officer from my presence!"

"Yes, monsieur, though you should know we have a paper from him which is as good as a confession. I would like to suggest, monsieur, that first you read this."

While Joachim Ambert unfastened his jacket buttons, General de Morell experienced fear. He was afraid that the confession might be to the assault on Marie and he did not want to see it, much less let anyone else see it. "It's as good as confessing to having written the letters."

"The letters. Yes, the letters." The General's relief was visible. He waved the paper at Emile. "Did you write this?"

"Yes, mon Général, to show how easily I can copy other people's handwriting."

Octave was lying back on his pillows, exhausted by the tensions surrounding him as well as by pain, but he whispered, "It proves he wrote the letters."

The General glared at Emile. "*Did* you write the letters?"

"No, monsieur, I did not."

"I ordered you to leave my house because of the letters, and you went; you fought a duel over the letters; you have written this piece of paper because of the letters."

"But I did not write the letters."

"You are not man enough to admit to them. You are lying."

"No, mon Général, I am not lying. I am telling you the truth and you . . ."

"Silence! You will be stopped. I will call a Council of Honour. You'll see! You'll see!" The General had worked himself into a fury little short of physical violence. Both Joachim and Octave were shocked at his appearance. His face was livid, and he was breathing heavily.

Emile was terrified, and it took courage for him to speak, but he reminded the General, "A Council of Honour would be reported in the newspapers."

This made the General even more angry. "So now you think you can goad me on like this because I might be afraid of the scandal that only you, la Roncière, and I understand." All he could think of was the assault on his daughter. "Very well! You will do what I say. Is that understood?"

Emile's jaw had dropped. "Yes, monsieur."

"If you want this to go before the Council of Honour, I will put you there. If you want to avoid such a disgrace, do as I tell you." He paused. "Make your choice. Make it now!"

"I will do as you tell me."

"You will leave Saumur."

"Leave the Cavalry School?"

"Certainly."

"Resign my commission?"

"No, that would make people ask questions. Exactly what I want to avoid. No questions. I will grant you indefinite leave on full pay, and after a decent interval I will arrange for you to be transferred to another regiment."

"Monsieur . . ."

"After the business of early yesterday morning, the sooner you leave, the better."

"What are you . . .?" Emile was lost.

"I will not have it discussed before these officers."

"I don't . . ."

"Enough! Now find a pen and some paper." Joachim handed Emile the pen with which he had just incriminated himself, and found a blank piece of white paper.

"Sit down," commanded the General, his natural colour beginning to return, "and write this. Are you ready?"

"Yes, monsieur."

"It is a letter you will address to Monsieur Octave d'Estouilly. I have reasons for not wanting it addressed to myself. 'Dear d'Estouilly . . .' Have you got that?"

"Yes, monsieur."

"Carry on. 'I declare that I am the author of the abominable letters and the forged letters . . .' "

Emile had laid down his pen and was staring ahead of him. He pushed the paper away.

"Did you hear me?" asked the General.

"Yes, monsieur."

"Write!"

"I can't. I can't, monsieur."

The General stood, feet apart, hands behind his back, glaring at the blank wall in front of him. It was some time before he spoke.

"In that case," he said slowly, weighing each word with care, "I must summon a board which will include General Préval, Marshal Soult, and your father General le Comte de la Roncière."

Emile rose from his seat. "Not my father, please, monsieur, not my father . . ."

"Sit down!"

"He is an old man. The disgrace will . . ."

"I am not negotiating terms with you. I am dictating them!"

64

"I don't understand!"

"Because there are no other alternatives."

In a frightened whisper, Emile said, "Oh mon Général, I can't confess to the letters..."

De Morell interrupted him. "You have just made it impossible for me to be held responsible for the disgrace which will be publicly brought on you and your name. The Council of Honour will be conducted in public. You will not be the only one dishonoured."

Emile looked from Joachim to Octave and back again. "Please..." Neither lieutenant made a move. Octave was too ill and shocked, Joachim was over-awed.

"Make up your mind!" commanded the General. "Which is it to be? You write at my dictation, or I call the Council of Honour."

"If I write this letter, what will you do with it?"

"Nothing. None of us will ever hear of this terrible business again. I will let you go."

"Will my father be shown it?"

"No one will see it."

"If you transfer me to another regiment, will they have to see it?"

"Certainly not, and I will recommend your promotion with your transfer."

After a few seconds the young man said quietly, "What do you want me to write?"

"Carry on from 'Dear d'Estouilly, I declare I am the author of the forged letters...'" The General waited until the words had been transcribed, and continued slowly "'...sent to Madame de Morell, Mademoiselle de Morell, Miss Allen, and to my general. I also declare that I have written to you, Monsieur d'Estouilly, another signed Marie.' Have you got that?"

Emile did not reply. He handed the letter to the General, who read it and gave it back, ordering, "Now sign it. With your own name." This done, the General took the paper on which Emile had shown how easy was forgery, put both in his pocket, and turned to Joachim Ambert. "Do you know anything about the coach traffic from this town?"

"Yes, monsieur. A coach leaves here at five this afternoon for Tours."

The General faced Emile. "You will oblige me by being on that coach. You will spend the night in Tours, and take the first coach for Toulon tomorrow, where I believe you have relatives."

"Yes, monsieur."

"Have you the fare?"

"I can borrow it."

The General took out his wallet, extracted its contents, including

65

several Louis-d'or, the twenty-franc gold pieces issued shortly after the Revolution. It was a great deal of money that he handed to Emile. "I warn you, la Roncière, that if anything happens to my family which is your doing, these papers will go before that Council of Honour. This money should be enough for your fare and lodgings on your journey to Toulon."

"It's far too much. I can't accept all that."

"Take it, and now go. Go!"

Emile looked unbelievingly at the money in his hands. Doubly humiliated, he pocketed the money, picked up the sword and belt he had flung on the floor, looked no one in the face and walked out without saluting.

The General crossed to the window and stood staring down into the street until he saw Emile come out through the door, cross the road and walk along the path. Not until he had turned the corner and disappeared behind the church did the General turn to address his men. "Gentlemen, you will not discuss this with anyone, or even between yourselves. Is that clear?"

"Yes, monsieur," said Octave and Joachim without looking at each other.

"If any word of this is traceable to either of you, you will both relinquish your commissions." He waited long enough to make sure that his words had had the effect that he intended, and added, relaxing slightly, "It was clever of you both to get him to come here, considering he won the duel."

"But he came of his own free will," protested Joachim.

"I hope you don't really expect me to believe that." The General opened the door. "Good day to you both."

CHAPTER SIX

By the middle of October, General de Morell, Solange, Marie, the domestic and immediate military staff had all returned to Paris. The dramas of September were not mentioned, and the atmosphere had relaxed. There had been no more letters since the banishment of Emile to

Toulon. The cool of October slid gently into the cold of November with its falling leaves, grey skies and rain.

The first floor of the General's Paris house, overlooking the Bois de Boulogne, was large and spacious, and richer than the Saumur house in everything from the ceilings painted with chubby cherubs and big-breasted women draped with diaphanous muslin, to the brocade-covered walls.

Early one mid-November afternoon, Solange was at her bureau — which was even more extravagant than the one in Saumur — writing a letter. The drawing-room, with its islands of Persian and Chinese carpets in a sea of polished parquet, was unusual in that it was on two levels, and from the higher, on which stood the bureau and a harpsicord painted with hunting scenes, she could see through the French windows, across the exterior balcony, through the wrought-iron rail, between the tops of the now almost bare plane trees, and south to a pool in the Bois. Ducks were scurrying back and forth dipping for tiddlers, while the swans looked over the heads of the riff-raff as if they did not exist.

There was a knock at the door and Solange slipped the letter under a book.

"Come in!" The governess came in hesitantly with a dress over each arm and her missal in her left hand. "Well?" asked Solange, irritated by the disturbance and Helen's meek attitude.

"It's these two dresses belonging to Ma'mselle Marie . . ."

"What's the matter with them?

"Ma'mselle Marie is to visit Madame Montesquiou this afternoon, and she wants to wear this one." Helen held up a dress with pleated lapels from the shoulder to the waist and sleeves flounced with pink bows.

"And what do you suggest?"

"For an afternoon visit, I think this would be more suitable." The second dress was of different shades of blue and of simple, clean lines with bishop's sleeves of some tiffany-like material, and wide dark blue lapels stiffened with buckram.

"Tell her she must wear that one. She can't possibly be seen in the afternoon covered in pink bows."

"Ma'mselle Marie says the blue one is for the morning only."

"And the pink one is for informal evenings. I don't expect you to understand that." Helen felt inferior, and could make no reply. Solange went on, unperturbed. "I think my sister would be shocked if she saw her in that one. She will wear the blue."

"That's what I told Ma'mselle Marie."

"If you can't control her, Miss Allen, I may have to find someone who can. After all, you must expect a child of sixteen to be a little wilful." After a pause, her voice softened. "Are you in a hurry to get back upstairs?"

"No, madame."

"Sit down." Nervously, Helen sat on the chair nearest the door. "Not there, girl, sit next to me on the sofa. Leave the dresses on the chair." Helen did as she was told, still clutching her missal. "Is Marie happy?"

"Happier than she was in Saumur a month ago," replied Helen.

"Do you think she's getting over that terrible business?"

"I think so."

"You don't sound sure. Are you?"

Helen did not like the brusque attitude of her employer. "Who can be sure of what goes on in the head of another?" she asked boldly.

"What are you trying to tell me?"

The governess was silent. She wanted to say that Marie repeatedly claimed to be a sensitive person; she wanted to say that from her own limited observations, people who claim to be sensitive are sensitive to themselves, not to the feelings of others; but she could say none of this.

Solange was exasperated, but went on probing. "If Marie shares a confidence with you, you wouldn't betray it, and I would respect that. However, if she had a problem you felt was beyond you, you would come to me, wouldn't you?"

"Of course, naturally; you are my employer."

Helen was bursting with curiosity. She felt certain Solange was about to divulge something important.

Solange was becoming impatient. She was getting nowhere. The stupid girl would go no further than giving simple answers to her questions.

"Has she had any more of those letters?"

"I don't think so."

"You seem uncertain."

"No, she'd probably tell me if she'd had another."

"Probably? D'you mean she might have had some?"

"No, and I think she's almost forgotten the ones she did have. It's such a relief they've stopped."

"They haven't stopped."

If Solange were expecting a look of shock from the governess, she was disappointed.

Helen asked simply, "Is Monsieur de la Roncière still in Toulon?"

"As far as I know. I am sure I would be told if he had come to Paris. He is being watched, but doesn't know it. This last letter forces me to ask you something you must never repeat under any circumstances."

She paused. "May I trust you, Miss Allen, never to repeat this conversation?"

"I never discuss the affairs of this family. I have no time to make friends. I have no one to talk to."

"This latest letter . . ."

"From Monsieur de la Roncière?"

Solange made a gesture of doubt. "Everyone keeps saying that la Roncière wrote the letters. I have found no reason to suppose he did. The writing is the same as the ones he was said to have written, and it forces me to ask you something very private."

The General's secret had been well kept. No one else apart from Octave d'Estouilly and Joachim Ambert knew that Emile had written a confession. Solange came to the point and in a low voice said, "This latest letter claims that Marie is . . ." She looked around the room, drumming her fingers on the sofa hoping for a magic word that would save her from the embarrassment of the question she was compelled to ask: "Is Marie in a certain condition?"

Helen went pale, put her hand to her mouth with shock and blushed deeply.

"Well? Is she? If something were wrong, you would know. You would, wouldn't you? Is something wrong?" Solange had a horrible sinking feeling in the pit of her stomach. There would have to be special arrangements so that she did not have it in Paris. There would have to be lies to explain her absence. Adoption would have to be arranged.

"Oh no, madame, no. She is not in that condition."

"I feel ashamed to have asked you." La Baronne was overwhelmed with relief. "I knew as soon as I read it, that it was a dreadful lie." Her show of antagonism towards Helen had quite passed. "I should never have asked you. Never. It is a shameful thing to have done. I know I should have asked Marie herself. It's just that I find her so remote."

Helen said, "If it makes you feel any better, watch! I will put my right hand on this book. I swear that Marie is not in the condition that you thought she was."

"My God!" exclaimed Solange. "Please don't say that I thought Marie was — well — you know what I mean. I did not think so for a moment. I just had to be certain. I am now perfectly satisfied. I don't know the purpose, though, of this filthy letter I have just received. Why should anyone want to write such a terrible thing?" The horror had passed, the moment of doubt had disappeared, the conversation reverted. "Very well, take the dresses back to Marie and tell her to wear the blue one."

As soon as Helen had left the room, Solange opened a little drawer in her bureau and took out a key. She opened the dictionary lying on the desk and removed the now familiar buff-coloured letter with its sharply sloping script. Holding both close to her, she left the room, crossed the landing, and went downstairs to the General's study, confident that he was safely in Lyons some four hundred and seventy kilometres to the south-east.

She could hardly make out the General's desk until she had pulled back the curtains and opened the shutters. The key opened the desk, and there was the iron box, twice banded with brass, in which she suspected her husband kept all the letters on straw-coloured paper which he had not burned. The catch was stiff and she wondered if it were locked; if so, she would never be able to open it. She took off her shoe and hit the catch a smart blow with the heel. The lid fell back, and proved her guess was right. The box was stuffed with letters written in a sloping hand on the lined straw-coloured paper. Solange put her shoe back on. Anxious lest the servants find her in the General's study, she closed the box and, concealing it in the folds of her skirt with her left hand, she closed the shutters and the curtains with her right hand. Back in the drawing-room, the box out of sight in the bureau, she rang the bell.

Samuel Gilieron answered her summons.

"I do not want to be disturbed," she told him, "by anyone for any purpose whatsoever for the next two hours. Please be sure to tell all the servants of my wishes. Also go up and tell Ma'mselle Marie and Miss Allen."

Samuel bowed and left the room. On the inside of the door was a highly ornate gold-encrusted key. Solange tested it by turning it back and forth a couple of times, noting with satisfaction that the bolt shot out and back each time. Sensibly, she realised that not only would it lock her in, but might embarrass her by not being capable of being unlocked. It squeaked and needed oiling. She did not want to start gossip in the kitchen by asking Samuel to fetch an oil can. She considered. She rang the bell again and went to stand at the top of the stairs. Samuel appeared below. "I'm sorry, madame, I thought you said . . ."

"Yes, yes, Samuel," she dismissed his mild protest, "but before I settle down, I want you to bring me a croissant and a lot of butter."

"A croissant. Yes, madame." Puzzled, he tilted his head to one side.

"And a lot of butter."

"Coffee?" Samuel was used to hiding surprise.

"No, thank you."

Solange waited in the drawing room with the door open and presently Samuel appeared with a tray carefully laid with a lace cloth, a large pot of coffee, a cup and saucer, a plate, a knife, a croissant and a small gold butter dish. "Thank you, Samuel, put it on that table."

Alone at last, she turned the lock so that the bolt protruded, and spread it liberally with butter. She took out the key and buttered that too. She tested her handiwork. It was perfect, the squeak had gone and there was no danger of her being locked in. She poured herself a cup of the coffee she thought she had not wanted. Now she would come across the truth.

She thought carefully about her relationship with her husband. No, she decided, she was not being disloyal to him by looking among his papers. She was no more disloyal than he was to her by hiding them in the first place. Her affection for him was not blind; it was clear that he got his own way by bullying and not by brain power, and held his job by a convincing, but artificial, air of authority and command. She knew she was more practical than he and better capable of making decisions. In spite of his ability to instil fear into his junior ranks, and his appearance of a man of sound judgement, underneath it all she knew him to be a waverer, an indecisive man, a weak man. She had seen him reduced to pulp by a summons from her uncle, Marshal Soult, or from King Louis-Philippe, assuming that such a summons spelled a reprimand. It never was, but she had to share the sleepless nights that preceded such meetings.

All this went through her mind as she opened the brass-bound box and carefully laid out the letters on her desk so that she could study them one by one. A weak man, she thought, is a dangerous man, because he will frequently side-step problems in the hope that they will go away. The General had done it often enough before with lesser events.

Letter after letter she read, all written in a variety of handwriting on the same straw-coloured lined paper. Each letter contained the over-dramatised threats and boasts that were now familiar. There were some, however, that she had never seen. One, written in early September in Saumur to Marie and signed with the letter 'E', read, "You are the only one who knows that I must be avenged because I have loved you, held you sacred; yet you ignore me. We went out together, and since then you lock yourself in your room. My passion eats my very soul, while I suffer the tortures of the damned. I shall mark your father with the sign of villainy from which he will never recover."

Sophisticated and worldy though Solange considered herself, she was frightened by the repressed violence and dangerous hysteria of the messages. She came across the account of the night of 23 September. This letter was also signed with the letter 'E'.

"I must condense all the powers of devilment to write to you. Wretched

71

father that you are, I went to your daughter's room by climbing through the window. The breaking glass woke her, she tried to hide at the foot of the bed and held a chair to defend herself." Marie's mother looked out of the window for a moment, considering what sort of man this could be who would commit a crime and then write in such detail about it. "With a handkerchief and a rope to bind her, I silenced her, for I wanted nothing more than her honour and her blood. I had both, making her a creature of disrepute, and I went away as invisibly as I had arrived, unseen by some stupid girl who hammered on the adjoining door. How, you say, was this entry effected? By waiting until la Baronne, Miss Helen and Marie were out walking." Solange remembered that the afternoon of 23 September was warm and sunny and it had been her idea to go for a walk because she did not like the smell of cooking rising from the kitchen. Yes, the writer was correct, the three of them had gone for a walk that afternoon. "Into the house I went to make all ready for the night. I paid the footman fifteen hundred francs to let me in, and the money was also for the letters he hid round the house. He refused to let me in again that night, so I chose the dangerous way through the window. When you get to Paris it will not be many months before the entire capital will be aware of the shame of your family."

She found and read the challenge to the duel.

Among the collection, she came across a piece of white cartridge paper, startlingly white against the lined straw-coloured paper of the letters she had been reading. On it was written "This is a facsimile of the handwriting of Octave d'Estouilly, written by Emile de la Roncière". She had seen Octave's writing once or twice before in 'thank you' notes he had sent to her after a dinner.

She searched for and found one in her bureau, compared it to the paper signed by Emile de la Roncière, and saw that the writing was the same. It was a good imitation.

She wondered why it was on white paper, artists' drawing paper. She thought it unlikely that Emile would have drawing paper but she realised that Octave would have plenty. This, she thought, could be Octave's real writing followed by Octave's forgery of Emile's signature.

Puzzled, she put it to one side and found another piece of drawing paper. It was the full confession which started "Dear d'Estouilly, I declare I am the author of the abominable letters . . ." and it was signed "Emile de la Roncière."

At last. There was no more mystery, except for the behaviour of her husband who persisted in doing nothing. She knew Emile had been sent to Toulon, and here was the reason safely in writing. Something must be done at once. The latest letter, delivered that very morning, declaring

72

Marie was to be pregnant, was sufficient for Solange to know that Emile had not been silenced.

She remembered angrily that her husband was in Lyons and that it would take too long to get a message to him and wait for a reply. But her temper subsided as she reflected on his odd behaviour in taking no action when he had so much evidence. She knew that had he been in Paris he would put up all kinds of arguments for leaving the whole thing well alone.

She put all the papers back into the iron box and locked it into a secret compartment in her own bureau.

She sat for a full hour gazing out of the French windows at the children playing in the Bois while she considered how the law could be brought in to prevent any more nuisance. La Roncière was obviously mad and in need of restraint.

She badly wanted advice as to how to proceed. She could not confide in her friends, none of whom she could trust not to gossip. She needed good counsel, and a lawyer could surely be trusted to be discreet. A professional man of the law would be bound by a code similar to the doctor's Hippocratic Oath. To find the right man would be a problem.

Then she remembered Monsieur Gisquet, Préfet de Police, whom she had met once with her husband. She recalled a common little man whom she had wanted to snub for addressing her in too familiar a way, but now she was glad that she had not, because this very afternoon she would pay him a visit and charm him into advising her.

"Have my carriage at the front door in ten minutes," she instructed Samuel when he answered her call, and as soon as he had left the room she retrieved the iron box, taking it with her to her bedroom to fetch her coat.

By the time she was ready, Samuel was at the front door which he opened for her while the coachman held the coach door. Before stepping in, she paused to point out some mud on the paintwork, ordering the man never again to bring the coach round in such a state. He said he would bring a damp cloth to wipe if off, but she said this time she was in too much of a hurry. He climbed to his seat, and with a shake of the reins both horses trotted off.

The cobbled streets were lit by flares from the open-fronted shops. The start of the evening was evident from the music billowing out from every café. Young men sitting in the steamed windows had rubbed clear a few square inches to see the girls go by. Old men sat in groups and the laughter from their raucous wives filtered out to Solange as she passed in the padded comfort of her coach. Occasionally she noticed groups of sullen men loitering at street corners. As the coach passed, her expression never changed, but her heart was in her mouth. She had heard how these 'republican workers' as she called them, would sometimes overturn what they considered a monarchist coach. The de Morells owned seven coaches and she cursed her stupidity in not going out in the governess's coach. She wondered mildly why it bore such a name. Miss Allen never used it.

She called to the coachman to use only the wider streets and to stop taking short cuts and he brought the coach to the edge of the Seine where she could see the illuminated boats. Pulled up outside the imposing building of the Préfecture, the coachman climbed down to open the door for her. It was locked from the inside and Solange opened the window. "No, no, you can't expect me to go in there from here. Find the yard and take the coach in there." Obediently, the man climbed back up and drove on until they came to an ornate entrance where the coachman climbed down to open the door for la Baronne. Again she took the precaution of keeping the door locked and instructed the man to go into the Préfecture and bring out a policeman to escort her into the building. This done, she told the coachman to wait, and went inside with her uniformed guide.

The Préfecture was a cold gloomy place. She was forced to wait in an unswept room with bare boards and dirty, stained windows which were shut against the fresh night air, containing within it the unpleasant smell of unwashed bodies. A strange assortment of people was gathered, fidgeting on the hard grimy benches. One man, drunk or ill, moaning on a bench to himself, was violently sick but too feeble to do anything about it. Solange was unable to stand the stench and went into the corridor to be sent straight back by a policeman who told her to sit down. She refused because of the condition of the benches.

"Tell Monsieur Gisquet that Madame la Baronne de Morell is here to see him and that it is urgent." She tapped the back of her right hand in the palm of her left.

The policeman was unimpressed by her title. "He knows. Someone will be down to fetch you as soon as he is free."

"If he's here, why can't he see me at once?"

"That is a question you must ask him yourself. All I know is that he's at a meeting." And he went back into the corridor, not waiting for a response. She thought of writing him a note asking him to call, but abandoned the idea when she speculated on the effect such a call would have on her household.

A fairly well-dressed woman, sitting in a corner, was crying about her lost dog. Opposite were two girls, prostitutes, who were openly discussing how they would treat their next customer — they would either blackmail or rob him, depending on the size of the man and their estimate of his riches. She wondered what two such women could possibly be doing of their own free will in a police station, but by listening carefully she learned that the one with the cupid's bow lips and dyed black hair was convinced that the man they shared for protection had robbed them.

So, she thought, the police offered protection to such women, at a price no doubt, while they could not find time to discuss the terrible affair of Emile de la Roncière. Surely the world was coming to a chaotic end if this was how officialdom was conducted.

The man who had been sick, in his torn clothes and with three or four days' stubble on his face, was now snoring peacefully and she wondered why the police did not come in to drag him to a cell where he rightfully belonged.

From time to time a uniformed man from the corridor put his head round the door, took no notice of the drunk, called out a name from his list and escorted that person to where, it seemed from the conversation, charges were made.

Solange had originally thought she was in a room full of criminals but slowly she realised that they were all people like herself, people with serious complaints about other people, or reports to make about thefts, or, as with the woman who would not stop crying, the loss of a pet.

It was an intolerable room filled with intolerable people, none of whom knew who she was, though they recognised her as a rich woman and so someone to be disliked. It showed on their faces. Many were old enough to remember the energetic guillotine of 1793, and Solange winced as she thought they would probably like to have seen it still in the Palace de la Revolution.

The shabby door with the chipped green paint swung open.

"Madame, the Préfet de Police will see you now. Please follow me." A girl with a baby snorted in disgust; the woman in the expensive coat was jumping the queue after all; and worse, she was going straight to the Préfet while people like herself would have to put up with a semi-literate policeman who would lose their papers and muddle up the charges.

Solange followed the man along the corridor and up some carpeted stairs, noticing that the higher she climbed the better her surroundings became, and the fainter the stench of the public waiting-room. She was shown into a pleasing room where a young policeman was lighting the oil lamps.

Monsieur Gisquet, square faced and moustached, rose from behind his desk to greet her. "Ah ha!" he said meaninglessly, and pulled at his left ear lobe as he pushed back his chair. He stepped briskly round his huge desk that he might welcome so great a lady with propriety. He was flattered that such a person had come to see him, and he was nervous. Solange sensed his disquiet and, assuming cowardice and incompetence, badly under-estimated his importance and power.

As head of the Préfecture, Gisquet held authority in the capital over a multiplicity of duties that in other cities devolved on many officials. In addition to dealing with crime, traffic, and public order, he held the register and so the power to grant licences to drivers of cabs for hire, and he was largely responsible for fire-fighting, although firemen were an army unit. He was also authorised to call out the Garde Royale with their glinting spurs and plumed helmets, breastplates and sabres flourishing. He had cause to do so frequently. She did not know how fortunate she was to be granted this audience.

"A pleasure, madame," he said, bowing her to a chair. "Please sit down." She refused his outstretched hand, and looked carefully at the chair before accepting it, ensuring it was clean. "What is the purpose of your visit?"

She looked at the young policeman adjusting the wicks of the lamps, indicating that she would not speak until he had left the room. He lit the last lamp and left the room while Monsieur Gisquet filled the time by tidying a space on his desk and taking out a pad of paper.

"Now, madame, your problem?"

She was grateful that he had not wasted time asking after the General and her family.

"I know nothing of the law," she said, "and I want to know how to get help from a good counsel. As it must not be known that I need advice I can't ask among my friends for a good lawyer. I am sure that you, Monsieur Gisquet, are in the best possible position to recommend counsel to me."

"I know a great many."

"Who is the best?"

"It depends on what you expect of him."

"This is a matter I will discuss only with the right person."

"In that case there is nothing I can do. I see you are troubled and you want it kept quiet. I am used to such matters. In my position nothing surprises me, so you can confide in me with total confidence." This brusque little red-faced man seemed to be reciting a familiar speech. "May I make the first move by suggesting that you are being blackmailed?"

"I most certainly am not!" La Baronne was indignant.

76

"I beg your pardon, madame, please forgive me. So many conversations have begun this way in this office and have ended with a confession of some indiscretion. We have ways of dealing satisfactorily with the other party, and at the same time keeping it all under wraps."

"I have just told you that I am not being blackmailed."

"So I understand. But I have to know your trouble before I know who to suggest to you."

"I can rely on you not to repeat a word that passes between us during the next few minutes?"

"Naturally! If I were a gossip I would not have remained in the service, and I would not have this position. Nothing we discuss will be repeated to anyone without your express permission."

Solange produced the iron box and put it on the desk between them, hesitantly revealing the problem. Monsieur Gisquet may have been a short man but he had a large chest which gave his voice a resonant depth. "Who," he asked, "are those letters from?"

She looked around her. She had come to this man for the name of a good counsel. She did not want him to start digging into something extremely personal and painful.

"The more I know of the letters, the better I shall be able to advise you."

She still made no reply and rested her hand on the lid of the box as if to prevent him from flipping it open and taking out the letters. He stood up, pulling at his left ear in a mixture of embarrassment at having to insist on seeing the letters and uncertainty as to how to insist upon anything from such an important lady. While he thought, he walked over to the window and made the shutters firm. It was unnecessary but he needed the distraction. Returning to his chair he affected to lose interest. "Of course," he said, "if you don't feel that this business" — he waved casually at the box — "is worth my attention, I will respect your point of view, but I shall not be able to help you."

"What would you like to know?" The logic of the occasion had imposed itself on her mind. She had come all this way. If she did not show the letters to someone she would find herself taking them back to her husband's desk. This funny little man with the deep voice seemed to be behaving like an obstinate mule. She could see that he would tell her nothing unless she told him something. "They are letters," she said, "and my husband and I know who wrote them. I don't know what to do about it."

"From your tone, madame, I suppose they are abusive letters." She did not reply. "Are they abusive? Or are they libellous?" She still would not reply. "Well?" asked the Préfet as sharply as he dared in such company. "Aren't you going to tell me? You must understand that no one can advise you without the information."

Solange relented. "They are both libellous and abusive."

"With threats?"

"Oh, yes. Almost all of them contain threats."

Gisquet felt he was getting somewhere. "What sort of threats? To spread gossip? Threats to life? There are so many threats, how can I guess?" He paused and took a deep breath. "Madame, you can trust me. If you will accept that, please let me read some of the letters so that I can assess your problem for myself." Her hand was still on the box. "Look, madame, I can see now that you are more deeply troubled than I thought when you arrived. I know that this is something very serious indeed. I want to help you. Please, madame, let me help you."

She took her gloved hand from the box and let him pull it across the desk. He opened the lid and saw the quantity of letters inside. "Are they in any order?"

"Yes," she said quietly, nodding. "The earliest that we have kept are on the left, the most recent on the right."

As he sifted the letters Gisquet asked few questions, but enough subtly to extract the whole story. His brevity was classic in its simplicity. When he found the letter about the assault he asked, "To your knowledge, did this assault take place?"

"Yes."

He did not press for details. Arriving at the letter about the duel he asked, "Do you know if there really was such a duel?"

"Yes."

"Who won?"

"La Roncière."

Within the space of half an hour he was ahead of her and doubted that Emile had written the letters. She had became aware of his expertise and realised that he would be a most useful ally.

"There is one man in Paris who can deal with this. He has no equal, and for that reason he may not be free to take the brief. I have one criticism of him."

"And that?"

"His fees."

"I don't want to go to court, so it won't be all that expensive. Who is this man?"

"His name is Maître Berryer."

"I have heard of him. His name is always in the papers."

"And he never loses a case. I suggest you write to him sending him all

78

the papers you have shown me. If he can't help you he will never mention the matter to anyone else. It would be unprofessional. He will simply return your papers and your letter. Ask his advice. Tell him to do nothing until he has seen you. I warn you, madame, he is the best and you must expect to pay for the best. I will give you his address."

That evening she wrote to Maître Berryer, summoned her carriage again, and delivered the letter with the iron box to the lawyer's house, not waiting for a reply, but going straight home for a night of troubled sleep.

CHAPTER SEVEN

Ten minutes after Madame de Morell had left the Préfecture, the Préfet himself departed. He guessed that la Baronne would have gone home to write to Maître Berryer, so he ordered his cab to take him to the lawyer's house. He knew him well enough to call and so presented his card without qualms. He was most courteously received by Maître Berryer whose appearance outside the court room never failed to surprise the Préfet.

He was a mild man of unprepossessing appearance, his high forehead emphasised by receding grey hair, and except for grey side chops he was clean-shaven. It was difficult to remember, thought Gisquet, that he was in the sanctum of the greatest advocate of the century, and possibly the most persuasive orator since Mirabeau. He was in the presence of a man blessed with the most extraordinarily irresistible voice and the power to use it to the best effect.

Gisquet had seen the lawyer in court, and knew that once his conviction and his heart were involved in the plea he was making, his genius was as forceful as a tidal wave in overcoming all obstacles, sometimes, it had to be said, swamping fact and logic. Maître Berryer would say of himself that he had no ability, that he was naturally impressionable, so that when convinced, he could not help do otherwise than speak with passion. He thereby won his cases by an unconscious display of total faith.

There were other points of view. The infamous fence, Georges Metz, who had amassed a fortune handling stolen property, was careless enough on one occasion to be arrested, cheeky enough to ask Berryer to defend him, and lucky enough to get him. The price was astronomical; but Berryer got him off. Metz, a rumbustious, large and noisy man who dressed to be noticed in the cafés he owned, was apt to slap people across the shoulders and tell them, at the top of his voice, "Ah yes! Berryer! A great man! But only when he's on your side! If he's against you, don't waste money on lawyers. Forget it. Jump in the Seine!"

Gisquet told Berryer that he had come to share a professional confidence and warned him to expect a visit from Madame de Morell. His call was essential, he said, because some of the letters he would read were breaking the law by the use of threats.

"And why have you come to tell me that?" asked Maître Berryer, with a faintly cynical smile.

"Because now that I know their contents, I have compromised myself by not taking them straight to the Public Prosecutor," he explained, pulling at his ear with embarrassment.

"From what you've told me, I was already aware of your position. Please go on . . ."

"So I am asking you to agree that the delay has been caused by my first talking to you." Gisquet was still embarrassed, so he was greatly relieved when Maître Berryer laughed, and said that the prosecutor was a common friend, so he saw no difficulty there. He also said that with such a family as the de Morells it would be better to hear it from Madame de Morell before taking any action. No one, he said, could afford to offend friends of Marshal Soult or the King.

When Solange left the iron box, later that evening, with a servant at Berryer's house, the lawyer had already finished dinner, and had given instructions that he was out. This, he thought, would give him time to read the letters without interruption. Only after he had read the papers would he make an appointment to see Madame de Morell.

He took his coffee in his study and read and re-read the letters, making a few notes and replacing them in the iron box together with the letter from Madame de Morell. He stood the box in the centre of his desk, and sat back in his armchair to contemplate its contents. He had never read anything like it before. He could recall no similar case either in his own experience or that of any of his colleagues. He consulted his diary for a convenient date on which to call at the house on the edge of the Bois de Boulogne, at the same time making a note to speak to the Public Prosecutor.

It was to be three days before Solange knew whether or not Maître Berryer would take any interest in the la Roncière matter, and they were three days of anguish. Sometimes at night she would rage with anger at the impertinence, the daring, the stupidity of Emile. Sometimes she would wonder vaguely if it really were of Emile's making. Sometimes she thought that as her husband had not gone to a lawyer about it, he might have doubts too, and his way might after all be the proper course to follow. When she thought of her husband she was terrified at what she might have started, and hoped that the letters would be returned with a polite note of refusal or that the matter could be discussed with Maître Berryer before her husband came back from Lyons. Her feeling of dread was not helped by the delay in the lawyer's reply. It was conceivable, she thought, that he had already spotted something that had escaped her.

A message eventually arrived asking if Maître Berryer might call, and it was about half past three when the lawyer arrived at the house and was shown into the small downstairs library while Samuel went to advise Madame de Morell.

A few seconds later, without warning, General de Morell came home from Lyons, removed his greatcoat and hat, and went up to the drawing-room to greet his wife.

"You're back? I didn't expect you." She had been preparing herself for the lawyer.

"That's not much of a greeting for a husband who has just returned from a mission!"

"I'm sorry. I was expecting someone else."

"Maître Berryer?"

"How do you know?"

"I saw him as I was giving my coat to Samuel. He had been shown into the library."

"Why didn't you bring him up with you?"

"I asked him to wait until I had seen you myself. I told him I'd been away for some days. What's he doing here? Does he know anything of the la Roncière business?"

The one letter that she had kept back from the iron box, although she had referred to it in her letter to the lawyer, was the one saying Marie was pregnant. She went over to her desk, brought it out and showed it to her husband, who read it and examine the envelope.

"I see it's supposed to have come from Toulon, so why is there no postmark?"

"You haven't read it properly. It says it is being brought here by a captain because la Roncière does not know our address."

"What sort of man was he?"

"I don't know. He never called."

The General waved the letter in the air. "So how did this get here?"

"He put it through the front door."

"Am I to assume that Maître Berryer is here to read this letter?"

"No, I could not possibly show a letter of such intimate details to a stranger. I wrote to him asking how to stop them. He has called to advise me." She did not feel she had to make excuses.

"You wrote, on the strength of this letter, to an advocate of his stature asking him to call!" the General was amazed.

"Read it again. Look what it says! Marie is pregnant."

"Is this possible?"

"Of course not!" she snapped. "That's the whole point of it. It says, if you'd taken the trouble to read it, that unless we force her to marry la Roncière he will tell all our friends about her. Now do you understand?" She had still not grown used to his stupidity.

"You should have discussed it with me first."

"How could I? You were in Lyons."

He went to the door. "Where are you going?" asked Solange.

"To compare the writing of this letter with the others."

"I've done that, and it's the same. It's no use looking for the iron box of letters, because I found it and left it at Maître Berryer's house when I wrote asking him for his advice."

If he had been slapped in the face by a servant, the General could not have looked more shocked. He walked up to the harpsichord and struck the lid with both fists so hard that the strings resonated. His face darkened and he bit his lower lip. Then he swung round to Solange and shouted, "Do you know what you have done? Have you any idea what this is going to mean?"

She stood up. "There is no need to shout."

"Was the confession in that box?"

"You know it was."

"I gave that boy my word." His teeth were clenched. "When I swore d'Estouilly and Ambert to eternal secrecy, which they agreed to an oath, I said that no one would ever see that confession. You, you have broken my promise."

In a calculated voice, which even she found difficult to control, Solange said, "You never told me about any oath or confession, and your word, which you make out to be something by which the whole world will stand or fall, will remain intact."

"Impossible! It is already betrayed. I told him that unless any disaster overtook this family which could be traced to him, his confession would never be read."

"So if that was the bargain on which you put your" — and there was a hint of contempt in her voice – "your word, your sacred word, that letter releases you. Do you call that letter harmless?"

"It might be. How can you tell?"

"You have never done anything decisive about this business. I'm glad I have, and I wish I'd made it earlier."

The General gave the bell pull a jerk. "It could be the wrong decision. If we take legal action, the whole city, the whole country will be talking. I've gone to immense trouble to keep this affair quiet; and it's because I took no action that I've managed to keep it within bounds."

"Within bounds!" she echoed. "Have you forgotten the evening with Louis Thiers? Madame Thiers made it perfectly obvious she knew of the assault."

"Good God! This is appalling. I had no idea what the two of you were talking about."

"The way she looked at me when she asked after Marie's health and the words she used plainly implied that she was trying to find out if Marie were pregnant. I didn't know then of the existence of the letter you've just read. And they're important people. Don't forget that he's Minister of the Interior and Commerce."

"I haven't." replied the General as Samuel Gilieron answered the bell.

"Maître Berryer is waiting downstairs. Please ask him to join us." As soon as Samuel had closed the door, the General added, "I'm going to put a stop to this."

"I don't see why."

"I've told you. There's sure to be more gossip if we go to court."

Solange was exasperated. "We don't have to go to court! I've already told you – all I want is to take expert advice. Can't you see the sense in that?"

The General, seeing no point in further discussion, did what he always did when he made up his mind in opposition to others – he took refuge in silence, bit his lower lip and stared out of the window.

He only turned as Samuel announced Maître Berryer.

"Madame, monsieur. It is an honour to be invited to your house."

The General brushed away the pleasantries. "How much do you know about this la Roncière business?"

"Only what la Baronne has written to me. I have read a series of letters including the confession to writing them, but I would like to see the letter saying that your daughter is – er – you know what I mean."

The General interrupted. "No need for that."

"No? If I am to prosecute, I must see it."

Solange joined in. "Surely there's no need to prosecute?"

"I must have misunderstood your letter, madame."

"Yes," said the General. "La Baronne thinks it would be better if you could prevent the man behaving in this way without all the panoply of the law courts."

"How could I do that?"

"I don't know," he said, "unless you can think of a way in which you can frighten him."

"You seem to have done that already, and it has had no effect. This is not an affair to trifle with. One firm blow in the right place will put a stop to him, and the right place is in the Palais de Justice."

"The only people," protested the General, "who go willingly to court are fools and lawyers."

Berryer smiled. "Not necessarily. You have a great name to protect."

"And," said de Morell, "La Roncière's father too has a name to protect, and he will do all he can to do so . . ."

"Le Comte de la Roncière?"

"Just so. The law, maître, is a bottomless pit, and the longer the purse, the lower it will hang in that pit."

The lawyer was insulted. "You must consider your daughter's honour, her name and her prospects, as well as yourself," he rejoined.

The General was aware that he had pricked the lawyer's skin. "Let me be the best judge of how to take care of my family. Meanwhile, I would like you to return la Roncière's confession."'

"Before we go into that, I'd like to ask you some questions."

"You have not been asked here in order to submit me to an examination! I'd be glad if you would return my papers, please."

Solange sat quietly on the sofa, quite detached, almost enjoying the sight of these two protagonists, waiting for the better brain to win.

Berryer said, "I most deeply sympathise with you both; but people of your outstanding rank and ability make tempting targets for gossip. The country, without a war, has never been as unsettled as it is at the moment . . ."

"You don't have to tell *me* that! I seem endlessly to be travelling from one end of the country to the other quelling riots . . ."

"Exactly! There are plenty of people willing to engineer your downfall for political reasons. A successful attack on you would be an attack on Marshal Soult and through him the King himself would be weakened."

"I know my enemies."

"Count yourself fortunate!"

Solange, from the other side of the room, gently reprimanded her husband. "Don't be so uncompromising. Maître Berryer is here to help us, so at least listen to him."

"All right," said the General at last. "But I would remind you that *I* have not retained you. What do you want to know?"

"You must pardon the directness of the first question. Is your daughter, Marie, pregnant?"

"Maître!" The General was taken aback by the blunt use of that offensive word. There were so many . . . other ways of saying it. Berryer had deliberately chosen the most shocking word in order to goad the girl's father. But it was the calm voice of Solange that replied. "No, she is not pregnant." She had chosen the same word. It quite unbalanced the General.

"You are quite certain, madame?"

"Quite."

Berryer turned to the General. "Is the signed confession genuine?"

"Are you suggesting I forged it?"

"Who saw it written?" asked Berryer.

"Three people, including myself."

"Will the other two swear to this on oath?"

"If I ask them to."

Maître Berryer was getting into his stride and had to remind himself that he was in a drawing-room, not a court room. "Was the letter boasting of the assault on your daughter in the same writing as the others?"

The General nodded.

"Is it therefore reasonable to say that the man who committed the assault is the man who wrote the letters?"

"Yes."

"And the man who confessed to writing the letters is undoubtedly Emile de la Roncière?"

"Yes."

"Then why are you afraid of Lieutenant Emile de la Roncière?"

"I am not!" the General was shocked.

"Is he blackmailing you?"

Solange's mind jumped back to Monsieur Gisquet. She wondered why both men, clever men too, had had the same idea.

"I am *not* being blackmailed," said the General.

"Nor any member of your family?"

"I don't know where these irrelevant questions are leading, but I'm sure they have nothing whatsoever to do with that uncontrollable lieutenant."

Berryer pressed on. "How much are you paying him?"

"Who?"

"Lieutenant Emile de la Roncière."

"Nothing."

85

Maître Berryer spoke slowly. He wanted every word to take its toll. "With this history of house-breaking, illegal duelling, abuse, filthy letters, and rape — all you do is . . . what? What did you do? You say you did nothing. This is hard to understand."

"I sent him to Toulon. He has relatives there."

"I cannot imagine anybody thinking that a reasonable thing to do. Is it the behaviour of a powerful father whose daughter has been subjected to unspeakable insults and physical assault?" There was silence. "Are you conscious of the full implications of this? Are you? There must be some explanation."

"I wanted to avoid any scandal."

"How can you say that when there already is a scandal?" countered Berryer. "I don't want to sound callous, but I must tell you that I had actually heard of this before I was asked to call here."

The General was more hurt than horrified. "I didn't know." His voice was flat and tired. "No one has mentioned it to me. People don't talk to me about it."

"Of course they don't. Now tell me why, when you got him to confess to the letters, you did not at the same time get him to confess to the assault? Why not? Come on, why not?"

"Because," explained the General wearily, "the confession was in front of two officers. I did not want to let them know. I was ashamed. I wanted it kept secret. I still do." He gave a sigh of impatience.

"He's written to others about the assault, so where's the secret now?"

"I have to rely on my own judgement." There was a dead look about the General's eyes that Solange had noticed before.

Berryer was puzzled. After a show of anger at the beginning of the interview the General now seemed to be collapsing. The fight was going out of him. Berryer's reminders of Marie's treatment were designed to infuriate him, whip him into a rage, goad him into suggesting the best way of tackling this nauseating young de la Roncière. The lawyer simply could not get the measure of the man.

The General was looking out of the window, his chin pulled tightly into his chest, his shoulders drooping. He repeated in a toneless voice, "I have to rely on my own judgement. I've no choice. D'you hear me? No choice."

The lawyer spoke gently. "This is why you need professional help, from someone not emotionally involved." He forced himself to lie confidently. "At last I think I know where I am."

The General swung round sharply. "Do you?" He squared his shoulders, his military bearing regained. "*Do* you know where you are? I think you're *forgetting* where you are, maître!" He jerked the bell pull for Samuel.

Maître Berryer, persuasively and in a low key, said, "The questions I have been asking you are only a few of the type you may have to face from the defence; in spite of my appearance of attacking you, I was digging for the truth. There was no other way of getting it." He stopped and looked over at Solange, then back at the General. There was something between them that he could not fathom. He could not bring himself to believe that he saw in her face a fleeting expression of pleasure, of excitement. He certainly saw something beyond the expected look of concern. He turned to face the General. "I am now satisfied that if called upon, I can represent the prosecution for you."

"What prosecution?" demanded de Morell as if he had been affronted. "What the devil are you talking about?"

"You have an excellent case. It is indestructible. What more do you want than a witnessed confession, and a sample of how the letters were written?"

"I shall not prosecute. I am too tired from my journey to argue further." Berryer could feel Solange fidgeting with impatience. "So please return the boy's papers to me."

"Why?" interrupted Berryer sharply.

"Because I gave him my word that no one would see them, and I promised his father I would keep an eye on him."

Berryer was unable to restrain himself. "But you're here in Paris, and la Roncière is in Toulon. Is he not?"

At that moment Samuel came in, and the General asked that Maître Berryer's cloak and cane should be brought, and that his carriage should be called to the front door. When Samuel had gone, the General repeated, "Please return the boy's papers to me."

"Monsieur," said Maître Berryer, watching the General's face closely, "I have to tell you that it is an offence to conceal a crime. You have laid yourself open to prosecution by holding these letters and the confession for so long . . ."

"For God's sake!" he exploded. "You don't surely think that you could prosecute me for that!"

Berryer laughed. "No, no, no. You came to me for help. What I am saying is that even as an advocate, I am not permitted by law to hide a crime or a strong suspicion of one."

"Then what are you talking about?"

"As soon as I saw those papers, I knew it was my duty to hand them over to the Public Prosecutor. They now rest in his office."

"And the confession?"

"Especially the confession. It is because of that, a warrant has been issued for the arrest of Emile de la Roncière. You are under no obligation to retain me, but I would be grateful if you would let me know in due course what you intend to do."

The General was trapped. He asked for two or three days to think it over. Maître Berryer agreed most affably. "Take longer, there is no hurry. But whoever handles the matter would like as much notice as possible. Tell me, what is the name of the footman you sent to fetch my carriage and cloak?"

"Samuel Gilieron."

"Has he been long in your employ?"

Solange entered the conversation by replying that he had been with them for a little more than two years, and before that he had spent five years with her mother.

"Why did your mother get rid of him?"

"We couldn't find a suitable man so she lent him to us," she explained. "Her cook has a son who was anxious to go into service, so my mother took the cook's son and Samuel has stayed with us ever since."

There the conversation had to stop because Samuel returned with the lawyer's cloak and cane.

"I'll see you to your coach," offered the General.

"Will that be all, madame?" asked Samuel after the men had departed.

"No. Come back in and shut the door." He did as he was told.

"Is your home address the same as when you first came to us?"

"Yes, madame."

"Wait there." She went over to the bureau and took out some francs which she gave to him. "You will go to your room, change, pack your things and leave this house immediately."

"Yes, madame," he said, opening his large brown eyes very wide, "and when would you like me to come back?"

"Never."

"Am I being dismissed?" he asked falteringly with his head on one side.

"You are. That is more money than is owed to you."

"But what have I done?"

"You know that better than I."

"Madame, the night I went into Julie Genier's room was because she thought she heard a mouse. I was helping to catch it."

"I have no idea what you've been doing with the maid, and I don't care."

"If it was the beef, it was because I had seen a blow-fly on it and

88

thought it safer to eat it with that piece cut off than to let you risk . . ."

"It has nothing to do with the beef, or even the glass of cognac you sometimes take. Goodbye, Samuel."

She stared out over the Bois de Boulogne until she heard the door close softly behind her. Then she went over to the sofa, and sat down to wait for her husband, terribly afraid of what she had started. She consoled herself with the thought that she had got her own way.

Next she had to reassure herself that her own way was what she wanted.

CHAPTER EIGHT

About a week before Samuel was dismissed, he had received a letter from Emile de la Roncière enclosing some money, scarcely more than the fare, asking him to come if possible to Toulon.

"It is not for an officer to ask a favour of a footman, rather he should be given an order. However, it seems that as the English Shakespère (sic) says 'misery acquaints a man with strange bedfellows' and I would deem it an honour if you please accept these few francs, for that is all I can afford, and take the coach to come to see me. I hear all sorts of wild stories going around, even in Toulon, that I have bribed you to distribute some letters round the de Morell houses. I must talk to you about this as there is no truth in it, and I would like you to say so if needs be."

Samuel replied, with difficulty because he was not accustomed to writing, that he could not get the time to see him because of his duties. He wrote that he knew about the letters even though he had found only one which had been pushed under the front door. He wrote, "The madame pays three francs to each person for each letter. Everyone searches. Even Julie Genier, the maid, finds one and gets three francs. They say you are doing it. The madame says it could not be you, but someone else, an officer. I have not found what is in the letters. As I am ignorant of them. What help would there be from me?"

But a couple of days after posting the letter, Samuel was dismissed, and he caught the next coach to Toulon, convinced that his dismissal was to do with the letters.

The warrant for the arrest of Emile had not been issued despite what Maître Berryer had said. There had been a muddle with the name and the warrant had been made out for the arrest of his father, General le Comte de la Roncière. This had no bearing on the outcome, but it was reported in *The Times* in London and elsewhere that the old man, who was in his seventy-ninth year, had been arrested for the rape of the sixteen-year-old daughter of General de Morell.

British breakfasts must have been cheered where that copy was read. British hopes for their dotage were dashed the next day, however, when a correction was printed: "The warrant for the arrest of M. de la Roncière, a lieutenant, (and not a lieutenant-general, as he was erroneously styled in the account of the charges against him, inserted in yesterday's *Times*,) was issued on Monday."

The Public Prosecutor ordered the arrest of almost everyone, of a subservient position, that is, known to the de Morells.

Helen Allen was among them and spent a night in gaol waiting for questioning, which started at six in the morning, and lasted two hours, after which she was released. Quite naturally, she said she had had enough, and would be going home. The police prevented her, and the General prevailed upon her to stay as her evidence would be most valuable at the trial. He trebled her wages.

In Saumur, la mère Rouault and her two pretty daughters, Elizabet and Annette, spent two nights in the local gaol, despite swearing that they had never even seen a member of the de Morell family. They were released after a period of futile interrogation, their questioner alternately insulting and apologising to them. They were ordered not to leave the town in case they should be needed to give evidence for the prosecution.

The same treatment was meted out to the stable hands; and even the Saumur postman and milk delivery maid found themselves embroiled. They contributed nothing to either side and they were released.

In Paris, Julie Genier, the maid, was arrested and thrown into gaol where she remained for seven and a half months, although she could prove that at the time of the curious event for which she was arrested, she was with her mother fifty kilometres away.

The identification of Julie Genier was absurd. It appeared that Solange and Marie were together in a carriage one November night being driven along the Rue de Bellechasse. The window on Marie's side was open and her arm hung outside. A woman in a bonnet appeared alongside, grabbed Marie's hand, thrust a note into it, nearly breaking her arm as she did so. Marie's arm was very severely bruised.

Solange called upon the driver to give chase. All three got out of the carriage to see a woman in a bonnet disappearing up an alley. They could not find her; they all saw her grey bonnet. It was similar to the one worn by Julie Genier when out walking. Such was the identification of the maid which led to her arrest.

The letter which had been delivered so unexpectedly read: "I will now do you a favour. I am a frequent guest of the lady who lives in the Rue Saint-Dominique. The gossip there says that had you been anything of a mother, you would have married off your daughter to the man who broke into her bedroom rather than show up the poor girl in public. More wicked gossip has it that she was seduced by your manservant and not by 'E'. Kinder tongues say that you should see she is married to 'E' within twelve weeks. This will stop the monstrous, grinding wheels of law you have unwittingly put in motion."

The two men who had been despatched to Toulon to arrest Emile and Samuel found them together drinking wine in a café, and this was immediately seen as collusion.

At the time they were not questioned, nor was any charge made against them. But they were brought back to Paris where they were put into a foul and stinking gaol.

In defiance of his considerable infirmity, the old Comte de la Roncière made the journey from Boulogne to Paris. He was a dignified figure with a deeply lined, tanned face, with a mass of white hair and a large white moustache. He had lost his right arm from above the elbow at the battle of Jena on 14 October 1806 and wore his right sleeve tucked into his jacket. He had taught himself to write quite well with his left hand.

The Comte knew of the arrests because his son had written to him from gaol, and he had read the mixture of fact, fiction and speculation in the newspapers.

No official reason was given for the arrests because no charges had been made. His first call on reaching Paris was to the house of his old friend General de Morell, where he was told that le Baron was out and no one knew where he had gone or at what time he would be back. The next day he called again to be told the same story. He called on other old friends discovering that they also would not receive him. For six days in succession he called at the house of the de Morells and each time he was told: "The General is out, and madame has gone visiting."

On the seventh day la Roncière saw de Morell going into his house, so he crossed the road, walked up the short drive, and rang the bell. He was told that the General was out. He never called again.

A week later Emile de la Roncière, Samuel Gilieron and Julie Genier appeared before the Juge d'Instruction, a man comparable to an examining magistrate, whose primary talk was to decide if the case should go to a higher court. The examinations of the three accused took place, according to law, separately, without the benefit of counsel, and secretly, so that the later trial would not be prejudiced. Each of the accused was kept uninformed of the precise charge or charges, and of the evidence on which these charges were based.

Emile was brought into the small court room and told abruptly, "We accuse you of the attempted murder of Ma'mselle Marie de Morell on the night of September . . ."

"Murder?" Emile jumped so violently that he sent a chair spinning across the court room with a clatter. "Why do you accuse me of attempted murder?"

"I have it in various letters signed with the initial 'E', and I have your signed confession that you wrote those letters."

In a very little time the examining magistrate concluded that there was indeed a case to answer. Samuel Gilieron was accused of helping to distribute the letters and also assisting Emile break in through the bedroom window. Julie Genier, frightened, timid, semi-literate girl that she was, was accused of distributing the letters and "of throwing one through the coach window at Mlle de Morell in November in the Rue Bellechasse . . ."

Old General le Comte de la Roncière knew that his son had been wild, irresponsible and at times thoroughly stupid, but he also knew that this charge of attempted murder, subsequently altered to attempted rape and assault, coupled with the outpouring of seemingly senseless letters, were actions of which he was incapable.

He was aware that there had been antagonism between them. Emile had been born when his father was well into middle age and past the point of remembering his own youth. He had forgotten his own escapades and follies, so that he had no sympathy with those of his son. As a harsh disciplinarian in his own artillery school he was conscious, when Emile was under his command, that rules must be applied more forcefully to his own son than to other young men or he might be criticised for favouritism. This had driven a hard wedge between father and son. Other young officers received adequate allowances; Emile had none.

But all bitterness was swept aside at their reunion in that cold, damp, grey gaol. The old man thought his son would be able to clarify some of the mystery, but he could not. Knowing his son's appetite for girls he understandably asked if there had been any sort of liaison, however flippant, with Marie de Morell. Emile said that there most certainly had not, but admitted that she was exceedingly attractive, a beauty in fact, with a a bit of the devil in her laughing eyes. He did say that, the idea of

92

an affair with her had fascinated him. For her part, she had made her feelings very clear by the warm, intimate way she had spoken to and looked at him. There was no doubt, he felt, that he could have, as he put it 'had a fine time of it with her'. She encouraged him as much as was possible under the circumstances. She had even gone so far as saying that she could bribe her governess to go for a walk with her and 'disappear' for an hour or so, so that her mother would not find out that she had had a secret meeting with him.

The old man was rather surprised that, if the girl were as attractive as he was being given to understand, his son had not taken advantage of the offer. Emile explained that with any other girl of equal charms he would have done. But this one was different. She was the daughter of his general and if they were seen together it would create a terrible scandal which might end in his transfer. So he had resisted the temptation. His father asked where these presumably secret conversations had taken place and he was gratified to learn that they had always been conducted in General de Morell's house when Emile had been invited for dinner or a musical evening. It had been quite easy, as Madame de Morell frequently had Emile placed next to Marie at dinner.

Emile's father thought that perhaps his son had given offence in some way to General de Morell, or Madame de Morell or even a member of the senior staff at the Cavalry School. The young lieutenant gave his word that as far as he knew he had not.

After the old man left the gaol he went to see Philippe Dupin, a well-known lawyer who was, also at the time, the Batonnier, chairman of the Paris Bar. General le Comte de la Roncière could have gone no higher now that Maîre Berryer had let it be known that he would be appearing for the prosecution.

The de Morells brought in yet another big gun against the la Roncières and Philippe Dupin − a lawyer to look for possible civil damages. The criminal court had jurisdiction to include in its sentence an award of damages in favour of the civil party − in this case the de Morells.

Enormous legal pressures were being applied to the defendant. First, the President of the Court who, impartial in theory, dealt only through the Act of Accusation, and so appeared to have a bias against the accused; the prosecutor himself, Maître Berryer; and last, the lawyer engaged to pursue the de Morells' *partie civile* interests.

This was Maître Camille Hyacinthe Odilon Barrot, a man noted more for his odd Christian names than his ability in court. He preferred to be known as Odilon Barrot, but, was predictably, called Hyacinthe behind his back. Barrot began his career in 1814 at the bar of the Court of Cassation, the highest court of criminal and civil appeal in France, which had the power to quash the decisions of lower courts, not from the point of pure justice, but when the lower court had not applied the law correctly. Its purpose was also to ensure national uniformity of interpretation of the law.

Barrot had made his name as a defender of liberals and became president of a society whose belief translates easily into "Heaven help those who help themselves".

It was an organisation for promoting legal resistance against the reactionary Bourbon restoration. During the July 1830 revolution, Barrot supported the proclamation of Louis-Philippe as king, and together with two other commissioners of the new government, and some military — which included General de Morell — escorted the former King Charles X to Cherbourg and exile. From 1831 Barrot was an active member of the opposition in the Chamber of Deputies directing the 'dynastic left.'

He was a heavy-jowled man of most solemn countenance, and an air of gravity which lent a sense of importance to any gathering. Those who knew him well said, "No other man can think so long and so deeply of nothing at all."

So Emile had on his side Maître Philippe Dupin, head of his profession; and ranged against him was an army defending the beauty of the youth of Marie and upholding the accusations delivered by the President of the Court represented by the formidably clever Maître Berryer, the grave Odilon Barrot and the de Morell family itself.

The trial was accompanied by an antagonistic, prejudiced and imaginative press. A battle between two of France's greatest families was a frightening array, and all that was known was that one family would triumph, leaving the other destroyed and unable to raise its head in public again.

The appointment of Maître Philippe Dupin was a major triumph for the Comte de la Roncière, and it gave great heart to Emile when the importance of the man had been fully revealed to him. Dupin had a lively mind, he had studied philosophy in addition to law, spoke with wit and elegance, never deviating from the point, and had a quality, rare in lawyers, of being concise and simple. His refinement of speech, in a country aware of the heritage of its language, was a major advantage.

The day after the charges were made known, an injustice was done to Emile by the *Gazette des Tribunes*. They published the Act of Accusation as if it were fact, and they embellished it: "... nephew of a peer of France, son of a general, committed a crime of such audacity that the sixteen-year-old girl on whom this outrage was perpetrated is not yet recovered from the shock..."

It continued as if rumour too were fact. Emile was said to have had three mistresses in Saumur, that he had attacked the wife of the owner of the Hôtel de l'Europe with intent to rape her, that his drunken voice could be heard singing alone in the streets of Saumur when he was supposed to be at the Cavalry School, and that he had served a spell on Devil's Island.

Emile saw this particular edition and wrote to the editor that it was regrettable that the publication of the Act of Accusation so far in advance of the trial allowed no public defence, and that the accused must suffer, without redress, from its dissemination and consequent speculation until the trial, which was not yet on the calendar.

Meanwhile, he emphasised, people's minds were turned against him, making it impossible for the court to choose an unbiased jury when the time came.

The *Gazette* did not publish Emile's letter; other papers did. They also published the Act of Accusation with all its accompanying innuendo.

So much for Emile's first blow. In due course the trial was set for Monday 29 June 1835, but on 8 June, exactly three weeks before, while all France — and several other countries — focussed their attention on the affair, Emile was to suffer a second and far more serious blow.

Maître Philippe Dupin, chairman of the Order of Advocates, did an extraordinary thing.

He gathered up all the papers he held in connection with the defence in the forthcoming trial, and at half past eleven that morning handed them to his office boy with a letter for le Comte de la Roncière which read, "Dear Monsieur le General le Comte de la Roncière, Having made a deep and thorough study of these papers, conducted exhaustive enquiries both here and in Saumur, and employed private investigators to glean all possible material for the defence of your son, I regret to report that I find his behaviour does not admit of defence. I am sorry that I can make no recommendations whatsoever." And as if to rub salt into the wound, he added, "My account will follow in due course."

The office boy with the papers under his arm, coming out into a hot morning and finding it nearly time for his lunch break, took the papers to the nearest park and enjoyed the sunshine until nearly three o' clock before calling on le Comte de la Roncière.

The count was immediately struck by the weakness of his position. He set off at once to find another counsel, conscious that he had slightly less than three weeks to find a top man, and ensure he was properly briefed.

He was turned down by two men of high reputation who did not even bother to read the bundle of papers. They claimed, as tactfully as possible, that having read the case, which was now the subject of public knowledge and gossip, it did not seem likely that an acquittal would be possible, especially since both Marshal Soult and King Louis-Philippe were known to be taking a great interest in the case. One of them mentioned that Maître Berryer never took a brief unless he believed wholeheartedly in it. This in itself was an obstacle for the defence.

A day was thus lost, but such was the charity in the heart of old General de la Roncière that, even under the extreme pressure he suffered, he could understand that a barrister would have to be a brave man indeed to risk his name and reputation against the awesome army which was hourly closing ranks. From time to time he would meet old friends in the street, and they would pretend they did not recognise him.

On the next day the papers were put into the hands of Maître Montrouge, who glanced quickly through them and declared that the defence had more substance than he had been led to believe. He would not make a decision on the spot, but he asked that he might be allowed to retain the papers for twenty-four hours.

The old general went back to the gaol to see his son. Emile was sharing his cell with Samuel, and the Comte worried that the prosecution might seize on this to show that they had had plenty of opportunity to agree on a story.

Samuel was embarrassed by the proximity of such a high-ranking general. He was unshaven, through no fault of his own, as razors were prohibited. His clothes were ragged, while in service he had always taken great pride in his appearance. He also realised that father and son would have liked to have been alone. Samuel stood as they talked because it would have been socially impossible for him to have lain on his bunk in the presence of the Comte.

Discussion between father and son also had to take place in front of the prison guard who remained in the cell, in accordance with the regulations, to be sure that dangerous objects such as pistols, knives or files, could not be passed from visitor to prisoner. The Comte had already suffered the indignity of relinquishing his sword in the prison office.

The prison guard, in his stained and ill-fitting uniform, showed lip service to the Comte by remaining standing during the visit, but that was as far as it went.

Prison discipline was slovenly and this guard was no different from the others. He smelt, he blew his nose without a handkerchief, he shaved once a week, he belched when he felt like it and, having no respect himself, could show no respect for anyone else. He was open to bribes and tips.

The cells contained two wooden bunks, one above the other with one blanket each, sufficient in summer but not augmented in winter. There were no pillows – each prisoner was expected to use his rolled-up jacket. On a stand in the corner, against a wall green with slime, was a wooden wash-stand with a chipped basin. On the floor was a chair – but no table – and two buckets. One was filled with water for drinking and washing, the other was for the two prisoners to relieve themselves. It had not been emptied for two days when the Comte arrived to tell his son the news of Maître Montrouge.

Samuel and the guard stood in the corner by the door, Emile sat on the lower bunk, and the Comte sat on the chair.

The only comforts allowed to the prisoners awaiting trial were those they could pay for themselves, and these were limited to food, laundry and newspapers. The newspapers depressed Emile and Samuel, for without exception the press had already condemned them. Two of Emile's charges – attempted rape and assault – were punishable by death. The press continued to invent colourful stories, and their sales soared as a result.

The Comte made a mental note to visit every one of the Paris-edited newspapers and to make an appeal to each editor.

Emile had a pile of papers on the floor of the cell and had marked those where unfounded assumptions had been made. He had also made careful notes explaining where they were wrong. These he handed over to his father.

"I am sorry, my boy," the Comte unexpectedly burst out, "for having put you in the Sixteenth Regiment in that dreadful garrison."

Emile leaned closer to his father, put a hand on his arm and, embarrassed that he might be overheard, said, "I probably deserved it. I am sorry I've been such a son. I don't deserve you as my father."

Samuel was sensitive to the occasion and started a conversation with the guard in order to distract him. He was told to shut up, the guard reminding him of his duty to see that the prisoner was not plotting to escape.

So the only exchange they could make was for Emile to deny the reasons for his being in gaol, and for his father to unconditionally believe him.

The guard moved closer to them, making the interview even more stilted and awkward, so that both father and son were relieved when the gaoler said that their time was up.

On leaving the gaol, General de la Roncière went to see the editor of the

Gazette de Tribune, and was ushered respectfully into a little office. That everyone on the staff had heard of him was made obvious by the number of excuses they made to get into the room and have a look at him. After three-quarters of an hour of such treatment he again asked if he might see the editor. It was getting late. Ten minutes after his second request, a nervous young man came in and said that he was sorry but, due to a misunderstanding, Monsieur Rideau had gone to a meeting in another part of Paris, after which he would almost certainly go home.

The Comte ascertained that the office was quite close to the chambers of Maître Montrouge; so he called. He was told that the barrister was in court and not expected back until tomorrow morning.

The next morning the Comte was told by Maître Montrouge that he had not been able to devote sufficient time to the brief to decide whether or not to accept it.

It was not until the evening of the following day, and after the Comte had been refused access to editors of several other newspapers, that he again called on Montrouge only to be told that the barrister felt that just over two weeks was not sufficient time for him to give the case the preparation it needed.

The Comte left with the papers in a leather case under his arm.

He bought a newspaper in the Champs-Elysées and settled down to read it at an outside café table, having ordered a carafe of red wine. It was a pleasant scene: the wide avenue – two hundred and thirty feet of it – was bordered with chestnut trees behind which were gardens full of laughing children, accompanied by their nannies, some having donkey rides, some being drawn along in goat carts. Two Punch and Judy shows competed for the children's attention.

The Comte was aware of none of this. He was reading an article on the front page of his newspaper; "General le Comte de la Roncière is having to swallow bitter medicine. It seems that after a careful and meticulous study of the case for the defence of his son, the reprehensible Emile, an ex-lieutenant in the Lancers, no less a personage than Maître Philippe Dupin, chairman of the Order of Advocates, has declared the case indefensible. Maître Dupin has studied the whole affair from the transparent forgeries of vile letters by la Roncière, to his rape of the daughter of General de Morell. This rape took place on the very day that the governess, an English girl, declared herself pregnant by la Roncière, and two days after a kitchen-maid in the General's household was dismissed after being found in a compromising situation with that same disgraceful lieutenant."

The article attacked General de la Roncière himself. "It appears that the distraught father of this debased creature is himself not without taint. We do not blame him for touting the brief round the barristers of Paris, but he should have had more decorum than to try to interfere with the freedom of the press.

"It was with that intention that he had the audacity to call upon our editor and ask him to stop printing any news of the case.

"Justice depends partly on the freedom of the press in which journalists may tell the truth without fear. In this way we are a shield against interference with liberty, for which so much young French blood has already been spilled."

The Comte left his wine untouched, and got up from the table. As he set off towards the Place de l'Etoile, the waiter ran after him; in his distraction he had forgotten to pay. After paying and tipping copiously to make up for the oversight, he walked on. There were no more than two cafés in the Champs-Elysées, a grand thoroughfare lined with stately homes for rich Parisians.

He walked until exhausted, the stump of his right arm aching and the arthritis in his left hip forcing him to limp, which made him ashamed. He sat down dismally on a bench to look again at the terrible newspaper article and its totally fictitious story.

His eyes caught another paragraph about a trial of a man, who had been accused of murdering his mother. The report stated that a young barrister acting for the prosecution had created a sensation by standing in the centre of the court facing the accused, and describing in detail the condition of the body. The cold and powerful way in which the barrister had behaved had made the accused cower in the dock, and finally jump up and bring the trial to a swift conclusion by shouting, "Enough! Enough! I killed my mother. I am prepared to die." The report went on to say that the case had been expected to last another three weeks. Not one witness had been called, although an elaborate procession of them had been arranged.

It was not too late in the afternoon for General de la Roncière to call a cab and have himself driven to the Île de la Cité, the island in the Seine in the middle of Paris, on which stands the imposing edifice of the Palais de Justice. There he soon found the address of the lawyer who had, thought the Comte, deprived himself of some three weeks of work by his feat of brilliance.

The man might well be casting about for another brief, thought the Comte, so he took a cab to the address of Maître Chaix d'Est Ange.

He was much younger than the Comte expected, and he was received with courtesy into the man's comfortable but sparsely furnished bachelor rooms.

The introductions and the Comte's explanation of his presence over, the young man said, "I know of the impending trial only from the papers. I know that the largest court room has been reserved from 29 June onwards. I know the papers are inaccurate. They usually are about most things. Perhaps you will tell me where you say they deviate from the truth?"

It took about an hour for Emile's father to do this, and to explain briefly the accusation and the impossibility of his son's involvement.

What was going on in Chaix d'Est Ange's head was most understandable. He knew he had created a legal ripple by being the first barrister to have driven a man to confess from the dock, and by doing so had carved himself a unique reputation. He saw the possibility of increasing that reputation by taking a case, popularly supposed to be a lost cause, and winning it. He believed that the Comte was sincere in that he thought that all he said about the papers and the accusation was accurate. He liked the old man because he did not hide his son's shortcomings and make him out to be a misunderstood second Messiah. He listened to tales of women, gambling and debts; to the story of his father sending him to Cayenne to try to straighten him out; to how the boy was put under the command of General de Morell.

All this he accepted as the behaviour of a high-spirited boy who in all probability would not prove himself to be very bright.

Maître Chaix d'Est Ange was young enough both to remember similar, if lesser, escapades of his own, and at the same time to be something of an idealist. He knew the reports in the newspapers were biased and unjust. He had also noticed that they were inconsistent, thus supporting the Comte's statement that they lied.

"Have you any of the defence papers with you?"

The Comte produced the leather case and handed it over.

The young man looked at the large quantity of papers.

"This is what I am going to do. I will sit here with my bread and cheese, and read these all night until I am familiar with the case. Early tomorrow morning I will visit your son in gaol, and speak to him alone. I will then speak separately to Samuel, the footman. After that, but only if I think it still worth while, I shall see the maid in her gaol. This will probably take until lunch-time. Perhaps you will be kind enough to call on me, here, at about two and we can discuss the matter further."

"Then you accept the case! Oh, thank God! Bless you, Maître...." The old man nearly wept. He was tired.

The barrister raised his hand in protest. "No, no, please. I have not said I will accept. This is something I alone can decide after seeing the accused. The press may be biased — it is their business to sell copies.

You may also be biased – it is your instinct to protect your son. My reason for spending the whole night and all tomorrow working on the case is simple. If, but only if, I take it, there is damned little time left for preparation and finding witnesses. Just over two weeks. If I reject the brief it will leave you even less time to hand it over to someone else. Please do not misunderstand me when I say that I know you think you are telling me the truth; but as a barrister I have to have more than that. I have to prove to my own satisfaction that your son is innocent, or in the final stand discover some good reason that will mitigate the offence and allow me some defence against the ultimate penalty." The young man wished bitterly he had not said the last two words as he looked at the broken, brave old man before him. "You, monsieur, must get some rest; I can see you are nearly at the end of your tether. I will get you a cab."

When the young man was alone again he took a long loaf, some butter and some cheese from his kitchen, and he put coffee on the stove, preparing himself for a night's vigil.

By three in the morning he had read all the relevant papers, and after making some fresh coffee, he sat down again, this time with pen and paper, so that he could make notes as he re-read.

He was one of those lucky people to whom missing a night's sleep seemed to make no difference. He called on Emile at half past seven in the morning, knowing that prison regulations would mean that he was up and dressed.

He had a fierce argument with one of the guards about interviewing his potential client in a private room. The guard knew nothing about such prison rules and told the barrister to wait until after nine when one of the governors would be on duty.

Swiftly, the barrister made the guard aware that he was exposing himself to a charge of obstructing the course of the law if a room were not made available in less than three minutes. He got his room. He saw Emile alone, instructing the guard to remain outside the door. Later he saw Samuel alone under the same conditions.

He resumed his cab to the women's prison, and after solving the problem of privacy in the same way, he saw pretty Julie Genier who wasted a great deal of valuable time crying, not realising that he was trying to defend her. In order to defend Emile he must first satisfy himself that neither Samuel nor Julie Genier had had any connection with his client. If he felt that these two servants were guilty he knew which way to point the evidence so that his client would be acquitted. If they were innocent, he knew it would be to the advantage of his client to show their innocence. Both Samuel Gilieron and Julie Genier had been accused of helping to distribute the letters. If it could be proved that

Samuel Gilieron had not been involved, nor had helped Emile into the house at any time unknown to the de Morells, and if Julie Genier could also be shown equally innocent of being an accomplice, then the case for the acquittal of Emile would be that much stronger.

The barrister went back to his rooms with his notes, compared them with those he had made during the night, and made up his mind that when the Comte returned at two o'clock he would accept the case.

Every one of the four accusations levelled at his client would fall under close examination, and all he needed was the chance to stand up in court and prove them false.

CHAPTER NINE

On the morning of 29 June 1835, Lieutenant Emile de la Roncière faced four charges at the Palais de Justice. He was accused of writing obscene letters, of causing severe injury, of assault and attempted rape. To be found guilty of either of the last two would make inevitable the death penalty.

The trial was to start at nine o'clock. Everyone in the public seats was to be in his place half an hour before because of the enormous interest aroused. None but the very rich could afford seats in the court room. These seats were sold by corrupt officials to the highest bidder and then changed hands several times for even more money. The drama had not escaped the press, nor anyone in France. The press gallery was ominously swelled with those who had never seen a press at work, nor smelled the curious aroma of printers' ink. Unfamiliar faces appeared in court-room officials' ill-fitting uniforms, unsure where to stand or what to do. The public sector overflowed into the aisles where chairs appeared as if by magic.

Society leaders were there; politicians; soldiers of rank; artists such as France's greatest moral and social satirist, cartoonist Honoré Daumier, who left to posterity a few drawings of the affair; there were writers – Victor Hugo, whose *Angelo* and *Chants de Crépuscule* had emerged together the previous week; the prolific Théophile Gautier, whose best-selling book, *Mademoiselle de Maupin* had just come out; Lucy

Dudevant, better known as Georges Sand, with her special favourite, Frédéric Chopin; there were notable judges rubbing shoulders with cardinals of the Church of Rome. All had paid heavily, and contrary to the laws of liberty, in order to see this spectacle which promised to be greater than any gladiatorial contest mounted at the Colosseum by the Romans two thousand years before.

A delighted and excited jury of twelve had been duly empanelled and sworn, and given the best seats from which to see reputations ripped, hearts broken, and blood flow. What was going on in the outside world at that moment mattered no more to the fashionable than to the unfashionable. There was only one focus for attention, and that was the drama about to take place in that sombre, large, dusty, hot room.

At a quarter to nine a hush came over the crowded court-room as General de Morell made a dignified entrance and took his place next to his wife.

On that very morning he had found time to write in his diary: "One of the most nauseating results of going to law is the newspapers. They harry, pry, state and mis-state. All this I was anxious to avoid for Marie's sake. It is quite impossible now to stop the wheels of the law. I wish I could. The Juge d'Instruction has examined us all, and our statements will be used in the prosecution of la Roncière together with our verbal statements.

"Our case is strong. I have seen to it with the help of Marshal Soult. Everyone agrees that the cause of a serving general must not be discredited. It must be seen by all thinking people that I, who represent stability and the establishment, must be upheld by that same establishment.

"If we at the top are not united, France could be brought to her knees again. History has shown how often this has happened before. Visible gaps in our armour can let in anarchy, so there will be no gaps. There must be no gaps. There can be no gaps.

"The la Roncière family is reduced to the services of the unknown Maître Chaix d'Est Ange. Little did they know when they retained Philippe Dupin that he is a friend to both Soult and the King.

"Because Dupin had the clever idea of retaining the papers for so long, my own counsel assures me that the trial will be short and little more than a routine exercise. For that reason we shall be able to keep my darling child out of the witness box where she would be subjected to public gaze. It is unthinkable in this modern age that a young girl such as she could be exposed to any form of public questioning!"

The babble rose and then abated for a second time as General le Comte de la Roncière, tall, distinguished and painfully upright took his place

103

at a table under the dock. There was a small disturbance when it was realised that a fashionably dressed woman had taken his chair and moved it into the more public area. The first usher approached did not know what to do as he had paid for the hire of an off-duty usher's uniform. It was some moments before the muddle was resolved.

Just as the clock over the Palais de Justice was striking nine, the President of the Court, President Férey, took his place, a judge on either side of him. Nobody outside legal circles knew much about him. He was one of those people shaped by events they set out to master. He was gentle, grey-haired, and rather flabby, with a drooping moustache concealing his receding chin. But his moustache, for all its size, was not sufficient to cover his habit — which he had developed over the last two years — of letting his lower jaw sag open whenever his attention wandered. It quite gave his age away. Maître Berryer was aware of this deficiency in the President and was ready for it. If he saw it during a vital prosecution moment he would be prepared for his evidence to be repeated. He hoped that this weakness was not known to the defence because he knew that the moment the great jaw dropped, the President was no longer listening. Berryer also knew that President Férey could charm but not reassure. He had concluded that this President, on whom so much of the result of the trial would depend, was a strange soup of stubbornness, timidity, boldness and feebleness. One minute he would be a forceful, didactic man, delighting in his own authority. The next minute some inescapable logic would be imposed upon him in such a way that he would be over-ruled and in consequence appalled at his own inadequacy.

There was no need for him to ring his bell to call the room to order. Not a sound came from the expectant multitude as he asked, "Is Monsieur le Général le Baron Charles-Paul de Morell here?"

The General rose to his feet and started towards the witness box.

"There is no need for you to come up here. You are the plaintiff, so you must be here throughout the entire hearing. You must have no contact with the witnesses except where I specifically allow it." He turned to the jury. "You, gentlemen of the jury, will give the arguments your full attention, and you will not discuss what you have seen or heard when you are outside these precincts."

He turned to the press. "Gentlemen of the press, the columns of some of the less responsible journals have been full of accusation, counter-accusation and irresponsible speculation which is damaging to the course of justice. Through you, I appeal to your editors to see that all mention of this case is restricted to direct reporting of facts until we have reached a verdict. Please bring up the prisoners." He paused and looked round the court room. "Wait! I see that some members of the public are standing. Will they either leave the court room or sit down at once, please."

No one left the court but everyone managed to be seated. Again the hubbub died down, and President Férey called, "Bring up the prisoners!"

The appearance of the three accused was a shock to all. Julie Genier, red-eyed from crying, stumbled into the dock, her chestnut hair unkempt and matted because she had no comb. Her dress appeared to be a washed-out, dirty blue shapeless sack with a hole for her head and two more for her arms. Samuel Gilieron had several days' growth on his chin and wore trousers tied with string and a shirt torn at the elbows.

Emile was smartly dressed in his neatly pressed uniform, and clean-shaven, because d'Est Ange had insisted on his client appearing well-dressed. The authorities had wanted him to appear in civilian clothes in order not to disgrace the noble uniform of France. D'Est Ange argued that at this stage his client had not been found guilty and was still on full pay. He demanded either to see the written regulation that prevented an accused officer wearing his uniform, or that a uniform should be provided, freshly pressed, for each day of the trial. He won his argument.

While the Act of Accusation was read to the accused, who were all seated, the two men stared straight ahead while Julie Genier cried and sniffed and wiped her nose on her skirt. She had not been provided with a handkerchief.

There were murmurs from the public at the mention of attempted rape, and the catalogue of accusations ended with a muddle when the President asked to see Marie de Morell.

Maître Berryer for the prosecution jumped to his feet to say that Ma'mselle Marie de Morell was so shocked from her terrible ordeals that she could not be present.

The President said he would like some proof of this as it would be very difficult to continue with the case with the primary witness absent. Maître Berryer said he was prepared for this and had already asked the family doctor to be at the court.

The clerk of the court asked the doctor to give his full name.

"Charles Edouard Olivier. I am a doctor of medicine in general practice, and I live..."

The President interrupted him impatiently. "Yes, yes, yes, thank you. We know you're a doctor. That's why you're here. How long have you known Marie de Morell?"

"Since she was five or six years old."

"And what has her general health been like up to but not including last year?"

"Quite normal. When she was about ten, she had chicken-pox and two years later, mumps."

"Was there," asked President Férey, uncertain of himself because he did not know he would have to take this line of enquiry, "any marked change in her during 1834?"

"Yes. After the assault in September she was perfectly normal for a few weeks. Later she started having fits."

"I don't know the precise meaning of the word 'fit'. Will you please describe one in relation to Ma'mselle Marie de Morell?"

"The fits are heralded by a state of excitement in which she becomes more active than usual. This is followed by a quietness when she sits perfectly still and appears not to see or hear anything."

Maître Berryer could see that President Fèrey was out of his depth, so he pressed the doctor to be more explicit.

"In what way? What does she do?"

"She sits on a chair or lies on her bed with her eyes open or shut, and seems unaware of her surroundings."

Berryer wanted to make the point quite clear. "Is this the result of the assault?"

"From my many years' experience as a doctor . . ."

"Please answer 'yes' or 'no'."

"Yes."

"Thank you." Berryer sat down.

President Férey asked, "How often do these attacks occur?"

"Four times a day," replied the doctor promptly.

"Do these fits occur every day?"

"Yes, and at certain, almost precise times."

"When?"

"The first is at eight in the morning, and lasts until six in the evening. The second is from eight until a quarter past ten. The third is from eleven until just before midnight. The last is at two a.m. and I don't know when that ends because she usually sleeps naturally until daybreak." Somewhere in the middle of the doctor's summary of the times of the fits, the President's jaw had fallen open. He had stopped listening.

"Monsieur le Président," said Berryer, jumping to his feet. "Monsieur le Président," he said more loudly, and the President closed his mouth. "Would you care for me to repeat that?"

"Oh, yes," said the President. "I don't believe it. You'd better tell me again." He sat up straight and inclined his head to Berryer.

"The learned doctor has said something that I am already aware of.

106

Mademoiselle Marie de Morell has four fits a day. The first is at eight o'clock, and it goes on without respite until six in the evening. The next one is from eight until just after ten. The third starts at eleven and stops just before midnight."

"Poor child!" said the President. "When does that one stop?"

"Just before midnight, and from then on she's quite clear until two o'clock."

"Thank you, maître. I find that very strange indeed." The President looked to the witness box and had forgotten the name of the doctor. "Doctor, er, is this true?"

"Yes, Monsieur le Président."

"Umm. And it's always the same?"

"Yes." The doctor was upset that his evidence should be questioned.

The President thanked the doctor and asked him to wait a moment in the witness box while he conferred with the two judges. After a long interval he addressed the doctor. "We are agreed that we must hear Ma'mselle de Morell's evidence. If she has a fit while in this court room, a room just outside will have been prepared for her, and you may be in attendance. When do you suggest would be the time when her mind is clearest — between six and eight in the evening?"

"No, monsieur le Président, she is usually rather muddled then."

"She must be clear sometimes. We have sworn statements signed by her which are perfectly sound."

"They were made during her best time which is from midnight until two in the morning."

The President spoke to each of the judges in turn. He looked up. "Very well, it seems most extraordinary to me, but if there is not another time, we shall have to hear her evidence at midnight."

The President looked over to Maître d'Est Ange who indicated that he had no questions. He thanked the doctor and dismissed him from the witness box.

"Will the girl Genier and the man Gilieron remain seated while the prisoner Emile de la Roncière stands?"'

Emile stood. A muscle in his left leg twitched and he hoped it would not show. He felt ill. He wanted to avoid the sight of his father sitting below him and whom he loved and felt he had disgraced. All the old animosity was gone.

Somewhere in the distance he heard the President's voice asking, "When you were garrisoned at Pont-à-Mousson were you heavily in debt?"

It was odd how far away the voice sounded and he wondered if that was what it felt like to faint. The front of the dock was moving towards him. He put his hand out to stop it and realised that he was about to fall. He checked himself as the distant voice became clearer.

"When you were garrisoned at Pont-à-Mousson," repeated the President, "were you heavily in debt?"

"I had debts. They weren't much."

"I see your father had you sent to Cayenne because of your debts, and you served in a disciplinary battalion."

"No, monsieur, that is not right. My father sent me to Cayenne because he felt I was getting into bad company. I had a few debts; but I served in the Sixteenth Regiment of Light Infantry which was garrisoned at Cayenne. You do not have to take my word for this, it is in the military records."

"When you left Cayenne in South Africa . . ."

Emile corrected the President. "South America. I was on the northeast coast."

"When did you go to South America?"

"When I was with the Sixteenth Regiment. They were stationed at Cayenne."

"It says here that Cayenne is in South Africa."

"Monsieur le Président, the papers you have before you are full of mistakes. If they were not, I would not be standing here."

"That is a most improper way to address the court."

"I am sorry, monsieur."

"I will not waste the court's time with arguments about geography." He took a breath to hide embarrassment and asked, "When you arrived at the Cavalry School in Saumur did you dine often at the Hôtel de l'Europe?"

"Yes, and before I found cheaper rooms I stayed there for a month."

"Did the proprietor's wife receive unwanted attentions from you?"

Emile was indignant. "No, monsieur!"

"And did she and her husband receive anonymous, abusive and disgusting letters?

"If they did, they were certainly not from me!"

"And these letters, combined with your appalling behaviour, caused the couple to leave the area?"

"As far as I know, they sold the hotel because they found it was continuous hard work for little profit. Madame told me they had bought a shop in Angers."

"So you were on fairly intimate terms."

"Please, monsieur! I don't think discussing the sale of a hotel and the buying of a shop could be regarded as an intimate conversation." Emile was frightened at the slant the questioning was taking, and he looked over to Maître Chaix d'Est Ange for help. The barrister held his tongue. He was waiting for an opportunity when he could have a far more devastating effect than confirming that Cayenne is in South America, or that a couple of hoteliers had bought a shop.

The President changed his direction slightly. "Now, in 1834, because your behaviour had improved, Monsieur le Général de Morell started to invite you to his house."

"I had always been received there."

"Did you know that large numbers of anonymous letters had been received by the de Morell family?"

"I have been told so since."

"They reveal among other things that you were in debt. They reveal aspects of your character, too. Do you still persist in saying that you didn't write them?"

"These letters were not written nor delivered by me."

The President picked up a paper. "The first exhibit is a letter to Madame de Morell starting, 'I tremble with desire . . .' Members of the jury have copies . . . it's the one which includes the line, 'I shall be close to your house today . . .' "

The jury found the letter to which the President referred, but not all the copies were identical. A certain amount of disturbance was caused by their comparison of the letters.

The President repeated the line he had chosen to quote. " 'I shall be close to your house today.' Note that line well," he said, "because as Monsieur le Général de Morell read this, he walked over to the window of the house in Saumur and" — he addressed Emile directly — "saw you on the bridge just outside his house. You appeared to be waiting. What were you doing?"

"I don't know when this was supposed to have happened. But I *can* tell you that on fine evenings it was quite normal for many of us from the Cavalry School to get together on the bridge and watch people go by. We couldn't afford the cafés all the time, and I certainly would not want to go back to my room alone. The bridge offered company and a fine view of the river."

"This happened at the very moment Madame de Morell showed the General the letter which had just been discovered."

"I can't explain the coincidence, except that it could have been written by anyone who know the habits of the junior officers."

"And in your hand writing! As is the next, written to Ma'mselle Marie de Morell. 'Your life will always be miserable and tormented.' Do you know the one I mean?"

"Yes."

"Ah! You admit it!"

"No. Of course I don't. I've been shown it. It's not from me."

"At the same time, letters containing *le mot de Cambronne** were addressed to Monsieur d'Estouilly."

"I have never used *le mot de Cambronne* in writing."

"Have you used this word in conversation?"

"What young officer has not?" protested Emile. "But never in mixed company, and not in writing."

The President looked up from his papers and continued the questioning. "On 23 September in front of Monsieur Octave d'Estouilly, a brother officer, General de Morell asked you to leave his house. Is this true?"

"Yes."

"You asked him what you had done to deserve this?"

"No."

"Are you telling me that you did not ask why?"

"No, monsieur, I couldn't ask him."

"What restrained you?"

"My rank. The General did not ask me to leave his house. He ordered me to do so."

"You were not on duty, nor were you on service. You were a guest, so you could have asked him politely."

"It was in front of Monsieur d'Estouilly. I thought I might ask the General quietly next day."

"This was a private occasion, and the next day you might have met him under different circumstances. It was surely easier to bring the whole thing into the open in his private house than at the Cavalry School?"

"I didn't think so."

"What did you do after you left the General's house?"

"I went back to my room in the Rue St Nicholas."

"What were you wearing?"

"My dress uniform."

"You have no doubts about that?"

"No, monsieur. Nothing else would have been appropriate. Had I been wearing anything else it would have attracted a great deal of attention in the de Morell household."

The questioning continued. Occasionally Maître Berryer interrupted

---

* *Le mot de Cambronne* was a euphemism for the word used with great force at the height of the battle of Waterloo when General Cambronne yelled "Merde!"

to hammer home a point; sometimes Maître Odilon Barrot stood and made a ponderous observation with such verbal complexity and pomposity that its point was lost before it was finished. Maître d'Est Ange continued to listen, to observe, to make notes and to exchange slips of paper with old General de la Roncière; but he never spoke.

After two hours, and still before the case against Emile was completed, the prisoner was allowed to sit down and there was an abrupt change of direction.

The maid, Julie Genier, was told to stand.

So terrified was she that, had she been in front of a firing squad, her expression would have been no different.

First, it was established that she could write her name and nothing else. This was a strategem to prevent the defence suggesting that the maid herself might have been writing the letters.

Second, it was shown that the girl had not been made pregnant by Emile, or anyone else for that matter. Her eight months in gaol would have produced irrefutable evidence.

Third, it was established that before the trial she and Emile had never met.

Fourth, those acting for the *partie civile* admitted that she was not in Paris at the time the note was introduced to the carriage in the Rue Bellechasse. Odilon Barrot solemnly blamed the girl for not bothering to establish her alibi, forgetting the eight months she had spent in gaol.

Fifth, she was dismissed from the case by President Férey who reprimanded her for wasting the court's time.

The court adjourned for lunch.

Julie Genier was so simple that it did not occur to her that she would not go back to gaol, and it took a great deal of persuasion by court officials that she should leave the precincts and make her way home to her mother. She protested that "they will come after me on their horses and drag me back" as punishment for having run away.

A kindly official led her, still protesting, over to the Nôtre Dame and left her talking to a nun.

CHAPTER TEN

Maître Chaix d'Est Ange had lunch for two sent in: a bottle of red wine, a chicken, a tomato salad sprinkled with parsley and garlic, a loaf of bread, still hot. He had had trouble insisting that he took lunch with his client in his cell under the court, and was disconcerted to find Samuel there also; he offered to share the meal, but Samuel accepted only a glass of wine and was content to eat his own bread and cheese.

Emile asked why d'Est Ange had not spoken. His lawyer answered that he was waiting for the whole of the case against Emile to be presented before taking it apart piece by piece in his final speech to show there was no case against him. He also thought that it might fall apart on its own. There was now a precedent for this in the dismissal of Julie Genier — another irregularity in the procedure — who should have been sent to the witness room in case she were needed again. Asked why he had not pointed this out to the President, d'Est Ange said that to criticise the President might prejudice the result. As the prosecution had talked themselves into her removal, the same would surely happen to Samuel during the next few days, and by the same token to Emile. The wine cheered them and the two accused resumed their places in the dock in far better spirits.

Many members of the public had not dared leave their seats in case they were taken. Only those with friends in the court had been able to step out for a little fresh air. Those who stayed behind had brought food, so that when the President returned, the public came to its feet scattering breadcrumbs and paper wrappings in all directions.

Emile was asked again to stand, and the President ordered him to "Just think back to what you did when you left the General's house on the evening of 23 September."

"Yes. I walked home to my room in the Rue St Nicholas in the boarding house run by la mère Rouault and her two daughters, Elizabet and Annette."

"And then?"

"I went up to my room to think about what had just happened. I could not think why I had been asked to leave the General's house and I was very unhappy."

"Were you intimate with the two girls there?"

"No, monsieur. I said good night to both of them and went to bed."

"Was la mère Rouault in at the time?"

"Yes, monsieur, I could hear her singing in the kitchen."

"But not having the charms of her daughters you left her out of your good night wishes."

"What are you getting me to say?"

"Nothing. I am just making sure of one aspect of your character."

"I have just said I did not see the girls alone."

The President shifted his ground of questioning. "Now, either late at night on 23 September or in the early morning of the next day, the accusation states that you climbed into Ma'mselle Marie's bedroom, threw yourself on her, bound her hands behind her back, took off her nightdress, stuffed a handkerchief into her mouth and attempted to rape her. What have you to say to that?"

"As I have said all along, this man was not me."

"Ma'mselle Marie has positively identified you. This man kept talking of revenge. You wanted revenge because you had been thrown out of her father's house."

"It was not me, monsieur. I was in my room."

"And next day you wrote to Monsieur d'Estouilly talking of revenge. How can you explain this coincidence?"

"As I don't know what it's all about, I cannot explain it."

"You left letters boasting of the assault on Marie and saying you would meet Monsieur d'Estouilly on the field of honour."

"I don't know about that either."

"But the duel forecast in the letter, which Samuel found in the hall and took to the General in the garden, did take place! You were there, you fought! You also left Saumur as you said you would!"

"I left after the duel. Before the duel I didn't know I was going to leave. How could I know? My general had not then ordered me to leave."

At his client's protestation, Maître Chaix d'Est Ange, whose silence had been noticed, stood up and, with permission, said, "Monsieur le Président, I am puzzled about the letter you mentioned, forecasting the duel and stating that my client would leave Saumur. Do you have the original in front of you?"

"Indeed, maître."

"And is the envelope there?"

The President held up both for the court to see.

Maître d'Est Ange asked if the letter was dated.

"No."

"Is the envelope date-stamped?"

"No."

"The letter, therefore, could have been written after the events it sets out to pretend to forecast."

President Férey made no comment and returned to the night of the assault. "You claim you went straight back to your lodgings and to bed."

"Although I went to bed early I was the last one in. The house door was shut at night by a lock and two bolts."

"Did any of the Rouault family go round to make sure all the lodgers were in before this?"

"Yes. Elizabet Rouault herself came to my room to make sure I was there."

"You've just said you saw neither of the two girls alone. Now you say you saw Elizabet alone. Could the explanation of your inconsistency be that you did not go to your room that night, but that you skulked about from café to café working yourself up into a drunken and towering rage at the de Morell family, because you had been found out in your disgraceful letter-writing?"

"No, monsieur le Président."

"It was this rage that made you break into Ma'mselle Marie's room. How else could she give the very words used by the person she said was you?"

"It seems impossible."

"At the preliminary investigation she stated that without question she recognised you. She used your full name."

"That's easily explained. She had seen me often at her father's house."

"She was told of the seriousness of her allegations, and that if proved against you, they would result in your death, so how could it be that she could persist if you are not the man?"

"I don't know. I swear before God my Maker that I am not that man."

"Let us move on to the next day. You wrote to Monsieur Octave d'Estouilly and challenged him to a duel, because he had seen you disgraced by the General the day before. Is this right?"

"No, monsieur le Président. I never wrote such a letter. Duelling is illegal."

"Don't teach the law to me! It seems that Monsieur d'Estouilly, being a man of honour, felt he had no option but to take up your challenge. Seconds were appointed and the time, day and place were agreed. This would have been impossible if you had not written the letter of challenge."

"But I did *not* write it. Why should I challenge him to a duel?"

"You already had a reputation with the *épée*. I'm not going back over all that now. Was this duel properly conducted?"

"Yes, monsieur le Président, except that it was conducted in a fog, but there are no rules against that."

"You carried on in the fog! Did you hear someone call out 'Stop it! This is murder!'?"

"Yes, monsieur le Président! When my sword went through his shoulder it broke off, leaving me with a few centimetres beyond the mounting. D'Estouilly tried to go on fighting so I had to hold his sword. Those are the rules."

114

"You had already broken the rules. You scored a point on the octave position drawing blood. That should have brought the fight to a finish."

"I didn't see the blood. He did not say he was wounded. Neither of the seconds saw the blood or they would have called a halt. We were fighting in a fog. No one could see properly. I do not cheat, monsieur!"

"You consider yourself a gentleman, do you? So when d'Estouilly was on the ground, twice wounded and you daring to hold his *épée*, did you then shake hands?"

"No."

President Férey repeated the word "No", looking at the jury in a theatrical fashion. "It is another example of the kind of man with whom we are dealing. An honourable man always shakes hands after such an event."

Emile protested, overwhelmed with emotion. "How could I shake hands with him? If I had let go of his *épée* he would have struck me when mine was broken. When I finally let go he was almost unconscious!" Tears started down his cheeks, his voice broke. His father got to his feet and embraced his son.

The President suggested an adjournment while the prisoner composed himself. Emile held up his hand in protest and the Comte sat down as his son asked that the case go on. A glass of water was provided, and the President took command again.

"It seems," he said, "that the report of this duel upsets you more than being on trial for your life."

"I don't want people to think I am a cheat!"

"Don't you think rape is a form of cheating? Now, after the duel you were shown the letter that provoked it."

"Yes. At the time it was the only one of those letters I had ever seen."

"Then the logical course was to suggest that they were all sent to the Public Prosecutor. Why didn't you suggest that?" asked the President.

"Because I had been told they had been seen by several hand-writing experts who agreed that I'd written them. I've since found out that no expert had seen them."

"If you insist you were innocent, why did you write a full confession?"

There was a long silence. President Férey looked around the jury, and back at Emile, saying, "The jury are very curious to know how you will answer that. What is your answer?"

"I imagined," he said at last, after another gulp of water, "that as experts had said the letters were by me, that I was done for." He addressed the jury, his voice giving way every few seconds to a rush of tears. "Gentlemen, consider my father, whom you have already seen, the peace of the evening of his life destroyed by these charges against me. I thought of his sorrow if the police were made aware, and of the subsequent publicity. I had already caused him a great deal of trouble." For a few seconds more he was again incapable of speech. Then he said, "I did not write the letters."

"Your father's peace of mind," stressed the President, conscious of the proximity of General de la Roncière, "would have been best served if you had gone straight to him to tell him of your innocence. It is impossible that you went to such lengths to show your guilt if you are truly innocent."

"My general told me that my signature to the confession would be the seal against more trouble. He swore he would show it to no one. I trusted him as an officer and a man of honour, and for some reason I believed that the real authorship of the letters would be known in a short space of time. I also had no idea of the serious content of the letters. I imagined them to be trifling, and not horrible as I now know them to be. If I had known what was in them I would never have confessed."

"Come now! You must have known they were significant or you would not have been thrown out of the General's house." The President gave a sigh of exasperation. "Did you at any time write to your general saying that no one in his household had ever been compromised by you, but if everything were known, the de Morell family must expect to suffer?"

"Yes. I wrote that letter from Toulon."

"You admit it. It's time you admitted something!"

"I will admit only the truth."

"Later, when you were in gaol, did you write to Monsieur Joachim Ambert throwing the gravest doubts on the morality of Ma'mselle Marie de Morell?"

"Yes, I did."

President Férey looked over to the jury. "At last! We make progress. The accused admits this too. Although you have copies of the letter, I think it so important that I will read to you from the very paper written on by the accused." He picked up a letter from the papers in front of him. "'You will see'," he read, "'that Marie is just a silly girl with a passion for someone. There is proof of this too, because one of the servants has told me that Marie is pregnant, and she has admitted it to her father who hopes to save her honour by accusing me of criminal rape.'"

The President looked up from the letter and addressed Emile. "And how would that save her honour?"

Emile spoke quietly. "If she became pregnant because of an affair,

116

she would receive no sympathy; if it were the result of rape, everyone would be sorry for her."

"This argument is ridiculous!" remarked the President, leaning back in his chair and spreading his arms wide in an expression of hopelessness.

"Monsieur?"

"You are not accused of rape! You are accused, among other things, of *attempted* rape. Who said the girl was pregnant?"

"The servant girl, Julie Genier. She told Samuel of quarrels between the girl and her mother."

"All this is kitchen gossip. I don't want to hear what someone is supposed to have said to someone else. It is not evidence!"

The President ordered the maid to be brought back. As tactfully as possible he was reminded that he himself had dismissed her. An instruction was given that the maid be found and brought back as quickly as possible.

It was known that Julie Genier had a mother some fifty kilometres outside Paris and it was believed that that was there the maid would go. But it was not known in which direction. The prison records were produced and showed that she had given her address as the de Morell house. Solange, who had employed her, said she had no trace of the wanted address. It was impossible to find her. Advertisements were to be placed in the papers asking for her to come forward. Of course, she would not have been able to read them but it was to be supposed that the notices would be read to her.

Her treatment in prison before the trial was sufficient, however, for her to decide not to come forward.

This was a pity because her evidence of quarrels between Marie and Solange would have been valuable. It was also noted by d'Est Ange that it could have been to the advantage of the de Morell family to lose the maid's address. But conjecture was not enough.

Meanwhile, as the futile search for Julie Genier was being set in motion, Emile stood down and Samuel Gilieron was brought forward for examination by the President.

"Did you know about the letters found in the General's house in 1834?"

In spite of his demoralised appearance, Samuel was quite composed, and showed an unsuspected strength to his character. He answered quietly and firmly.

"Yes, I knew about the letters. I never found any myself, except for one which I thought had come through the front door."

"Was that because you were hiding them?"

117

"No, monsieur. It would have been to my advantage to find some as Madame de Morell was offering us money to bring them to her."

"No letter was ever delivered to the house on a day or at a time when you were not there. Can you explain this?"

"Yes, monsieur. We are not talking of a shower of letters, but of a few. I was almost always at the house. My time off was limited to every other Tuesday afternoon, and one Mass on Sunday."

"You did no shopping for the household?"

"No, monsieur. Madame de Morell herself visited the shops in Saumur, and the cook was responsible for buying all the food. Most of it was brought to the back door by the tradesmen."

"Nevertheless, letters arrived and you, who were about the house most of the time, saw nothing. Have you formed any opinion as to where the letters came from?"

"I have no reason to suspect anyone. In fact, I have good reason to suspect no one in case I am wrong. I have the misfortune of being suspected myself, and I know what it feels like. I would not wish it upon anyone. I want no one to suffer such injustice as I have suffered."

"I have it on record that you said that if you should meet Ma'mselle Marie de Morell face to face, you would tell her that she should confess, and more, you said that you know a way to make her confess. Are you now saying this report is false?"

"No, monsieur. I said that. I realise now how easy it is to jump to the wrong conclusion."

The President questioned Samuel about the cigar-box, and then moved on to the assault.

"During the early morning of 24 September last year, a man climbed into Ma'mselle Marie's room, and was helped in this by someone above with a rope ladder. Where was your room in relation to Ma'mselle Marie's room?"

"Above."

"Directly above?"

"Yes, monsieur, in the attic."

"I want this absolutely clear so that the jury can visualise it. If, for instance, you had let a rope ladder out of your window would it pass immediately by the window of Ma'mselle Marie's room?"

"It would, monsieur."

"Did you let such a ladder out of your window?"

"No, monsieur."

The President had a disconcerting habit of switching his questioning. "Did you meet the prisoner in Toulon?"

"Yes, monsieur. He had asked me to meet him there before, but my duties would not allow it. After I had been dismissed from the de Morell household, I went straight there."

"What reason was given for your dismissal?"

"None. I have found out since."

"When you met la Roncière what did he say to you?"

"He offered me twelve hundred francs to tell him who wrote the letters. I said that I was hoping *he* would be able to tell *me*."

"Did he give you anything?"

"No, monsieur."

At this, Maître Berryer interrupted. "Didn't you know he had no money?"

"But he did, maître. He showed me twelve hundred francs."

"Address me, please," President Férey said crossly.

"I'm sorry, monsieur. He showed me the money and said he valued his honour more than his money."

"When you were in prison did you have a visit from a relative of la Roncière?"

"An uncle, I think, monsieur. He asked me if I thought Ma'mselle Marie was pregnant at any time."

"You didn't put the idea into his head, did you?"

"No, monsieur. In fact it was only after this man had left that I remembered times when Ma'mselle Marie often refused her breakfast because she felt sick. Also her skin, which frequently had a little spot or blemish here and there, cleared up completely, and she could often be found in the kitchen helping herself from the pickle jar. That was something she had never done before."

The President smiled. "How is it you know the classic outward signs of pregnancy so well?"

"I was the eldest of fourteen children and five of my sisters are married with children."

Maître Berryer stood again. "I think the prisoner reeled off these symptoms rather too well. Did someone put you up to this?"

"No, maître."

Maître Berryer was irritated by the footman's calm, collected manner, and spent a fruitless twenty minutes trying to unnerve him.

"Do you know how serious are the charges against you?"

"Yes, maître."

"And yet you take this all in your stride! I must ask you if you have been in a court before."

Maître d'Est Ange swiftly rose to advise Samuel not to answer.

"But I would like to answer," said Samuel totally relaxed. "I have been in this very room before."

Berryer could not stop himself triumphantly saying, "You see!"

"Yes, maître," went on Samuel. "When I was fourteen years old my father brought me here. He wanted to show me where the law is dispensed to rich and poor alike. He told me that the swearing of the oath under the gaze of God assures us all of absolute justice. It is another way of understanding the words from the Club des Cordeliers — Liberty! Equality! Fraternity! This is why I am not afraid. I have nothing to be afraid of."

Berryer was getting angry. He took the accused through the whole rigmarole again, trying to make him answer differently. It seemed the footman's memory was flawless. "Too flawless?" suggested Berryer to the jury, sowing doubt in their minds.

The President was more kindly disposed to Samuel, and thanked him for being so clear. This sparked immediate optimism in the hearts of Emile and Maître d'Est Ange.

Their confidence grew as the President announced, "I am afraid, gentlemen, that we will be sitting well into the night. Arrangements have been made to examine Ma'mselle Marie de Morell in this court in the presence of the jury. She will be brought here tomorrow for examination at midnight. This will mean we shall adjourn tomorrow morning's session at midday, and sit again tomorrow evening much later than usual. The precise times will be announced when I have agreement from those most directly concerned."

Maître Berryer jumped to his feet. "Monsieur le Président, this is most irregular."

"What is?"

"Having to sit in the middle of the night! There is no precedent."

President Férey smiled for the second time that day. "After tomorrow night, you needn't worry about finding a precedent. One will have been established. After that, we can do it as often as we like."

It was the turn of General le Baron Charles Paul de Morell.

"Will you please tell the jury why you think the prisoner wrote the letters which form part of the Act of Accusation?"

The General was quite at ease in the witness box. He was accustomed to addressing large numbers of people.

"Yes. I hardly understand the point of your question when you have it as evidence that Monsieur Joachim Ambert and Monsieur Octave d'Estouilly, both competent and efficient serving officers, agreed that the writing is similar to that of the prisoner. It is known that the prisoner fought a duel because of the letters, that he showed how he could forge the letters, and that he wrote a confession saying that he had written the letters. I think we are wasting time."

With tolerance and forebearing, fully aware of the implication behind his question, President Férey asked, "Do you think, General de Morell, that it is possible for the letters to have originated in your house?"

This thought Berryer, was going too far. Vague as the President could be at times, surely he could not go so far as to depart from the Act of Accusation. He wondered if the President was beginning to think la Roncière innocent. Muddle-headed old fool, thought Berryer.

The question caught the General off his guard. No one noticed it except Solange who wondered why it had come as such a shock to him, and noticed him pulling himself together to reply, "That is a most, extraordinary and ill-considered suggestion."

The reply from the bench was nearly an apology. "I am trying to discover the truth. Please answer my question."

"Very well," said the General raising his eyebrows and looking defensive. "It is impossible for the letters to have been written by any member of my household because one letter to me, and several to Monsieur Octave d'Estouilly, carried the Cavalry School postmark."

"What does that signify?"

"No one but an officer, or man in uniform, has access to the post boxes there. Not even the tradesmen who deliver there."

"You are telling the jury to believe that it would be impossible for anyone not belonging to the Cavalry School to post a letter so that the stamp of origination is on it?"

"Exactly."

"Do any members of your family have admission to the school?"

"No."

"No one sent from your house, in say, an emergency, with a message for you, if you were in the school, could get to you?"

"No."

"May I suppose, for a moment, that Madame de Morell has fallen and hurt herself. Someone would be despatched from your house to tell you. How would the message reach you?"

"Such a person would be stopped by the guard and the message would reach me from there."

"So if an outsider wanted to post a letter from inside the school it could be handed to a guard who would then post it."

"No. It would not be posted. Such a practice would allow all and sundry to take their letters to the Cavalry School, or for that matter any other military establishment, and get them posted for nothing. Such a ban is rigid military practice throughout France. Does that convince you that no one from my household could post a letter from the Cavalry School?"

"Other than yourself. Yes."

The General started to chew his lower lip. Maître Chaix d'Est Ange got to his feet and asked, "Will you tell the President if you had any of these letters before 1834?"

"No, of course I hadn't."

"You are quite sure of this?"

"I am. You must take my word for it."

D'Est Ange remained on his feet to prevent interruption and prayed for the indulgence of the President as he looked significantly at each of the jury and back to the General. It was a consummate piece of theatrical timing. He was aware of the effect it was having on the General's nerves. Slowly he asked, "So if I were to produce evidence to show that there were some strange letters found in your house in November 1833 would you say this was forged evidence?"

"What do you mean by 'strange' letters?"

D'Est Ange timed his moment of minor drama with care. He looked at the jury and raised his voice. "Threatening letters!" He looked at the President and at the two judges "Abusive letters!" He walked over to the witness box and said quietly to the General, but making sure everyone in court could hear him, "Sexually deviant letters!"

The General appealed to the President. "Do I have to answer this?"

"I can't advise you."

Maître Berryer, spoke from his seat. "Where did you get this kind of information?"

President Férey said, "Please address the bench. This is highly irregular, but I cannot leave it. Monsieur le Général, please answer."

The General's normally high colour left his cheeks. "There might have been five or six of them."

D'Est Ange said to the bench, "Please ask the General if they were in November 1833."

The General answered without prompting. "About then," he nodded.

President Férey consulted his papers. "But la Roncière was in Cayenne during November 1833. Did you keep these letters?"

The General said he had not. He had thought them such nonsense that he had thrown them away.

D'Est Ange was pleased with himself. His bluff had worked. There was no 'evidence', only hearsay from Samuel Gilieron who had told him of the letters. It had been a risk to play that card, but he had turned it into an ace.

D'Est Ange addressed the President. "If my client had written those

122

letters they would have had the distinctive Cayenne postmark. There was no postmark and they were received here, in Paris."

The General was nodding in agreement, anxious to change the subject.

The President picked up the reins of the trial again, having almost absent-mindedly allowed it to proceed unchecked. "On the morning of 24 September last, you heard of an assault on your daughter. We don't know the exact time this took place but can we agree it was at about two in the morning?"

The General nodded.

"And the governess, Miss Helen Allen, came to your room to tell you of this?"

"Yes."

"At about six in the morning?"

"Yes."

"This leaves an extraordinary gap of four hours. The delay must have seemed to you to be unaccountable. Did you ask for an explanation?"

"I did. I reprimanded Miss Allen for having taken so long to report the assault, and she said she did not like to leave Marie alone because of the terrible experience she had had."

"What sort of experience?"

"What are you asking?" The General was indignant.

"I want you to tell the court whether your daughter was subjected to attempted murder, attempted rape or a violation of some other kind."

"This was established at the outset of this case. You cannot ask me such questions!"

The President was becoming impatient at the General's prevarication. "Answer my question at once! What kind of violation was it?"

"Are you suggesting that I should have asked my daughter about the intimate details of the attack?"

"Any other behaviour would not be in keeping with your duties as a parent."

The General, red in the face, struck the rail on top of the witness box to emphasise his words. "I am not here to be abused!"

The more violent the General became in his speech and manner, the more gently the President persisted with his questions.

"But surely you must have asked precisely what this attack was?"

"I don't think you understand! My daughter was only just sixteen at the time. After her most careful education and circumspect upbringing . . ."

The President interrupted him. "Very well. If you won't answer, I shall ask Madame de Morell."

"I don't want her called."

"That is not your decision."

After delivering his rebuke, the President seemed temporarily to lose interest and his jaw dropped open. By now Maître Chaix d'Est Ange had noticed this strange deficiency in the President and had been waiting for it to happen again. He seized the opportunity to question the General.

"Was your daughter very shocked, monsieur?"

"She was." The General was worried by the apparent innocence of the questions that came from this young barrister. They always seemed to lead him into saying things he did not want said.

"Did she complain to you that she was in some pain?"

"Yes, maître, and she complained to her mother." The shorter his answers, the less likelihood there was of the young barrister embarrassing him.

"The exact cause of the pain was unknown to you, as was the cause of the shock?"

"I had formed an opinion."

"That morning?"

"Later that day, after discussing it with my wife."

"But it is not an opinion you want discussed in this court."

"It is not."

"You took her seriously? You never thought that your daughter could be inventing this?"

"What are you trying to suggest?"

"Do you know what happened on the evening of 28 September?"

"How should I know? I have no diary with me. I cannot remember."

"I will remind you, monsieur. There was an important social occasion — a glittering ball held at the Château de Saumur. I would not expect you to remember who the guests were, but one was Madame de Morell, another was you, monsieur" — he paused and dropped his voice — "and yet another was this poor, sixteen-year-old, sick girl, shocked and in pain, none other than your daughter, Ma'mselle Marie de Morell. Can this be true?"

"I find your manner offensive. A personal attack on me is hardly the purpose of this trial."

"Was your daughter at that ball four days later? Yes or no?"

"It was essential to us as a family to preserve the outward appearance expected of us. I don't think you have yet understood that for people to know about this attack is damaging my daughter's opportunities in marriage. By going to that ball she was carrying out my orders. She was doing her duty. But, she was in great pain."

"So you admit she was there. Thank you, monsieur."

124

The President asked the accused if he had any questions, and Emile shook his head hopelessly.

There was an outbreak of such muttering and mumbling in the court that the President was obliged to ring his bell for order.

At five o'clock the President reminded the court that as Ma'mselle de Morell was to be seen at midnight the following night, there would be only a morning session on that day. The evening session would begin at eight o'clock.

The morning of Tuesday 30 June was taken up with the routine examinations of three of the four hand-writing experts. They agreed that Emile had not written the letters, but that Marie had written them herself. The President was not aware of most of the evidence, sitting throughout with his mouth open. But the first mention from an 'expert' of Marie as the author of the letters did catch his attention and caused such excitement among the jury and the public that he had to ring his bell again to restore order.

Berryer dispensed with each 'expert' by the same method. "Have you," he asked, "ever proved the forgery of a letter to have been committed by one person from an examination of the writing alone, and without the assistance of other evidence?" To this disarming question each had replied "No". The fourth expert was to appear later.

Elizabet Rouault gave evidence that on the night of 23 September she had checked quite early to see that all the lodgers at their house in Rue St Nicholas were in, and she was surprised to see Emile at home as she had thought he was to have dined with the General. After sliding the bolts on the street door, she had taken the key with her to her bedroom. To the accusation that she had acted as a go-between with Samuel, she denied that she even knew Samuel.

"I never saw Samuel, and would not have recognised him if I passed him on the street. The newspapers have been horrible in suggesting that he and I were intimate, and the Monsieur de la Roncière and I were lovers. Just because we are poor women there is no reason for people to be able to say anything they like about us." This summoned no wave of sympathy from the public in the court: she was just another ant scuttling under the magnifying glass of public gaze. The President heard her speech but mumbled that it was of no consequence to the court.

There were no outbursts from Emile, nor from General de Morell, at any of the evidence that morning. There was a great deal of fidgeting among the public and press, and one member of the jury was reprimanded for going to sleep during the evidence of an architect who swore that examination of the roof and the window above Marie's Saumur bedroom revealed no traces of rope-ladder hook marks, and that it would be impossible for anyone to carry a forty-foot long ladder outside the house on a bright moonlit night without being seen by the guards stationed at each end of the bridge. He also gave evidence that all the outside doors carried firm locks and bolts.

The court adjourned and a reminder was given that it would reconvene at eight that evening.

CHAPTER ELEVEN

The spectators, cramped and uncomfortable in crumpled clothes tinged grey with dust and sweat, emerged from the court room and poured down the steps of the Palais de Justice. Most crossed the bridge over the Seine, some settled in the nearest café. The air was hot and still.

Old General de la Roncière went slowly down the wide steps, left foot first, too proud to carry a stick. Just as he reached the bottom a figure emerged from the crowd and took his arm. It was Maître Chaix d'Est Ange.

"Monsieur," he said breathlessly, "will you do me the honour of having lunch with me? I know a little café not ten minutes from here."

"That is most thoughtful of you, maître, but I was going round to see my son."

D'Est Ange simply said, "It is important that I see you alone. I'll explain why when we are seated out of earshot. Our worries may well be over."

The café held only four tables inside, and two outside on the pavement. The two men took an outside table and ordered a light meal and a carafe of red wine.

"Tell me," said the Comte, "what has happened that seems to have given you so much confidence?"

"We're not out of the maze yet, but the position has improved with President Férey insisting on seeing Marie de Morell. I'd never heard of someone being so conveniently ill that they cannot be questioned during the normal hours of the court. And yet, just when no court has ever been known to sit, she is pronounced well enough to be examined. I think the prosecution know very well she wrote the letters, and faced with an examination she cannot do otherwise than break down. Your son has some questions for her too. It will be difficult for her to lie when questioned by two people who know the truth."

The old man, untouched by the barrister's enthusiasm, reminded d'Est Ange that the King was taking a keen interest in the matter and was anxious that the de Morells did not lose face. Both the King and Marshal Soult were indebted to General de Morell for his services since 1830.

"You see," said the old Comte patiently, "when I showed my loyalty to Charles X, I had no idea that one of the people to see him off into exile would be General de Morell, my old friend. I've no time for this so-called People's King, Louis-Philippe."

D'Est Ange tried to interrupt but the Comte was into his stride. "They call him the Liberal King, too. Rubbish! He shouts for freedom of the press, but the minute they use it against him he throws the editors into gaol. People's King, Liberal King! Rubbish!"

D'Est Ange was aware that political influence would make the unseating of the de Morell family difficult, but not impossible. "If," he said, "they are so anxious to keep Marie out of court, there can be one reason only. Marie wrote those letters. But more important than that, it means that Emile did *not* write them."

"Of course she wrote them. The experts said so!"

"Yes, yes, yes!" said d'Est Ange. "An expert opinion increases the probability but it is not in itself proof. There has to be something else, and that's what I'm looking for. A very large piece of this problem is missing."

"I don't understand."

"Motive. Reason. Cause. There has to be one. Tell me, General de la Roncière, think back, have you or your son ever offended the de Morell family?" He paused. "Or Marshal Soult. Or the King. Have you? Either of you?"

The old man frowned. "What are you driving at?"

"Remember René Descartes. You know his philosophy, how he always liked to work things out for himself, rejecting the accepted ideas of his day. What an excellent philosophy! Everything, he claimed, could be reduced to cause and effect."

"What's that to do with my son?"

"The effect of this blast from the de Morell family is that your son stands in the dock for something he has not done. We must find the cause. You say you have not offended any of the interested parties. It is just possible that the de Morells are afraid of you or your son."

"How is that possible? Afraid of me? I'm seventy-nine. I must have been forgiven my loyalty to Charles X or I wouldn't still be an active

127

general at my age. There's plenty of excuses to retire me. My son can have done nothing serious, or de Morell would not have taken him on and acted almost as a guardian to him at my request. He was a guest many times at their house. No, no, no," repeated the old man obtusely, "that silly little girl Marie wrote those letters and you can damned well make her admit it tonight."

"Monsieur, you have not followed my reasoning. I am not interested in whether the girl wrote the letters. She may have done. She may not have done. I am trying to find out why the de Morells want to destroy you and your son. Once I know why, we can disgrace the de Morells." The young man thumped the table with such vigour that he spilled his wine.

General de la Roncière said, "You say I don't follow you. You, maître, cannot follow me if you are too young to understand the excesses of politics."

"In what way?"

"It will be impossible for us to get the jury to accept that the de Morells are wrong. There is too much at stake for a man of such importance to the country. Such things have happened before, and will happen again. I can't understand why de Morell took this to court when it is so clear that my son could not be guilty."

"And it might not be Marie either. She would not have been able to post those letters from the Cavalry School.

"How well did you know General de Morell?"

"Very well indeed," said the old man. "And if you're going to ask me if I think he posted them, the answer is certainly not. He could never do such a thing."

"Somebody did, and it couldn't have been Marie unless the story of security at the School is untrue."

"I can vouch for the security. In these times of riots there can be no slackness. Even members of my own regiment can't get in without a special pass."

"We might be wrong," suggested d'Est Ange, "in assuming that Marie wrote them."

At that moment a group of young officers and their girlfriends passed the café. One of them recognised General de la Roncière and said to his companions in a loud voice, "Look! There's the father of that lecher in court. They should both be guillotined."

Luckily the old man was so deaf that he did not hear it. But d'Est Ange did and muttered under his breath, "They'll have changed their minds tomorrow."

Meanwhile, inside the café a rich man and his over-dressed wife were

128

sipping chocolate, a luxury only found in the more expensive cafés. They, like many others in the cafés nearby, had come from the Palais de Justice and were glad of the break before they would return to savour the evening's excitement. The woman glanced through the window. "Look!" she said, nodding towards General de la Roncière. "Don't stare, but see those two men at that table out there?"

"Oh yes," said her husband. "That's the defending counsel talking to la Roncière's father. I'm sorry for him."

"He should have brought up his son decently. That boy's a depraved monster," retorted his wife.

"I don't understand it all, but there does seem something to be said for the boy," mused the man.

"Something to be said for him!" she echoed as if he had insulted her. "Haven't you seen the papers?"

"Yes, but that's not what's coming out in court."

She wrinkled her nose and sniffed as if she thought her husband a fool. "You don't understand anything. That la Roncière family has influence. They'll have paid someone to keep that newspaper stuff out of the court. You can be sure of that. Those sort of people are like that. Listen" — she lowered her voice and looked around her to be sure no one was listening — "that Julie Genier, and the footman and that young la Roncière got up to all sorts of things back in Saumur."

"What sort of things?"

"Well," she said, sitting up straight again, "you know, bed and all that nasty stuff."

"What!" The man opened his eyes wide. "All three at once? Together?"

His wife nodded knowingly.

"And another thing . . ." She leaned forward again. "They organised that the maid should disappear. She knows too much."

"Oh no, surely, if you saw how it happened . . ." her husband protested.

"It had to look right. She'll be found some time next week." The woman paused for effect. "She'll be found all right! In the Seine with her throat cut. And that'll be too good for her. Mark my words, she probably slept with all the soldiers in Saumur." She was now out to embellish her story. "It's common knowledge that she couldn't get enough of" — she dropped her voice to a whisper — "you know what I mean. So she was la Roncière's mistress along with several others including the footman."

"Is that the truth?" asked her scandalised husband.

"I got it part from the papers and part from the midinette who does my hats."

"What would she know about it?"

"Her brother has a friend who works at the Palais de Justice."

"Never!"

"Certainly. How else do you think I arranged for us to get in?" Her expression told him that that clinched the argument.

At the table outside, a newspaper boy had just sold a copy of the *Le Mercure de France* to d'Est Ange, who apologised to the Comte for reading it in his company. The whole of the front page was taken up with an inaccurate report of the trial. The defence was getting a very rough ride. D'Est Ange decided not to worry the old man with it. On the next page there was a scanty reference to uprisings in the capital and in Lyons, and a mention of a young man firing a pistol from a hundred metres at King Louis-Philippe. It was a silly gesture of defiance from such a great distance and it had only resulted in a basket of broken eggs. The man had been arrrested and the King sent for him to find out why anyone should want to assassinate him. The young man refused to answer and was flung into gaol knowing that his future would be further curtailed. There was the usual collection of anonymous letters from futile organisations with strange names such as "The Society of Five Fingers", "The Society of Bared Arms", "The Society of the Guillotine" and so on. It was impossible to know if they were genuine or whether the letters were the work of one or two cranks. News of scientific discoveries, exploration or the arts was nowhere to be found, the remainder of the paper being taken up with items giving the background of almost anyone who was connected with the case. What they did not know, they invented.

The General offered Maître d'Est Ange a cognac, which he refused. As they drank their coffee he explained that, although he was now certain that Marie would be questioned and that they would therefore win, it would be a long day, running into the early hours of the next, so he must keep a clear head.

General de la Roncière said he wanted to spend the afternoon with his son. He said it in a matter-of-fact way, concealing his dread that there might only be a few hours left in the boy's life for such meetings.

D'Est Ange was aware of the old man's sadness, but had to demand a little time alone with his client. "We have seen the effect that the de Morell family is having. I must try to discover the cause. With that, we can be sure of victory."

The old man grunted. "There may not be a cause. She may just be mad. Quite mad. It's as simple as that."

CHAPTER TWELVE

By the time the bell of the clock over the Palais de Justice had stopped chiming eight, the two accused were in the dock and, after taking his seat between the two judges, President Férey asked to see Solange, Madame la Baronne de Morell.

She had changed her clothes since the morning session and was now in black from head to foot with several black veils covering her face so that her features were not visible.

After she had taken the oath, the crowd straining to catch every word, the clerk asked, "Your full name?"

"Solange de Morell," she said quietly.

The President asked her to repeat her name in a louder voice, making a pleasantry of it by remarking that some of those on the jury and on the bench were not as young as they were, so had a little difficulty in hearing. Solange did as she was asked.

"Thank you," said the President. "When your daughter was assaulted . . ." There was an interruption.

Maître Chaix d'Est Ange was on his feet. "May I ask this witness to identify herself?"

"I don't understand, maître," replied the President. "She has done that twice. Once for the young ears in the court, and a second time for the older ears. What more can you want?"

"Madame is well-known in society here and her face is familiar to many in this court. How do we know that it is she who stands in the witness box?"

"How can you doubt it?"

"It is not a question of doubt, it is a question of proof. I for one have never met her and have no reason to be sure she stands there. I would like to see her face while she answers your questions, and later I must see her face while she answers mine."

President Férey conferred with the two judges. Maître Odilon Barrot also got to his feet.

"I represent the *partie civile*," he said, "and I know that la Baronne is

131

a most sensitive person. It has taken her great courage to submit to this court. Please allow her a little privacy."

The young barrister was tenacious. "I don't want to hold up the court for half an hour while we look up the precise reference, but I know it is written that witnesses must be seen. Neither I, nor anyone else in this court room, can see this witness. It is on that ruling I ask that she should remove her veil. In fact it looks as if she's wearing several veils — she must be suffocating under all that in this heat."

President Férey was doing his best to let her remain unseen, but it was evident that the two judges wanted the veils removed. Solange raised her hands in silent protest and prayed that she would be allowed to stay hidden. There was a muttering among the jury and whispering in the court room. Férey was over-ruled and asked Solange to remove her hat. This she refused to do but compromised by turning her veils over the hat so that her pale face was framed dramatically by the black of the many layers of muslin. The jury were struck by her beauty; some even thought her face had a Madonna-like quality about it. She was suffering and it showed. This, she thought, would be the start of her most dreadful nightmare. She stared at the floor to avoid the gimlet gaze of the public, the heartbroken expressions on the faces of General de la Roncière and his bewildered son, and the cold, analytical stare of Maître Chaix d'Est Ange.

D'Est Ange thanked her courteously, as did the President.

"When your daughter was assaulted in September last year, what kind of assault was this?" asked the President.

Solange looked at Berryer, at Barrot and then at the President. She avoided the two accused and ignored Chaix d'Est Ange.

"I don't know what kind of assault, Monsieur le Président."

"Didn't your daughter tell you about the attack?"

She looked to Barrot for help, which was not forthcoming. "No, monsieur le Président, she talked about bruises, bites and cuts, though."

"Have you seen them?"

"Some of them."

"Where?"

"I didn't like to ask her, and she didn't think it proper to show me."

Maître d'Est Ange was on his feet at once. "Forgive me, madame, isn't this carrying modesty a little too far? This is your own daughter, your own flesh and blood, and you've just said that you saw some of her injuries. Where?"

"On her arm." She refused to look at him.

"And what did you see there?"

"A bite."

The President did not seem to mind d'Est Ange taking over the questioning so he went on. "Did the bite bleed?"

"No."

Maître d'Est Ange suddenly threw off his gown, pulled up his sleeve and bit hard on his forearm. He held it up so that all could see the red mark.

"Was the bite about here?"

She was forced to look at him now. "Yes."

"Roughly ten centimetres back from the wrist?"

"Yes."

"And on this side of her forearm?"

"Yes."

"Madame, with the court's permission, I ask you to indulge in a little play-acting with me. I won't move from this spot, but just pretend I am coming over to bite or kiss you, and you want to defend yourself; please put up your arm to protect your face."

Very slowly Solange raised her right forearm across the lower part of her face. "Like that?" she asked.

"Yes, just like that. Now, if I were to rush across this court room and attack you by biting your arm, the bite would be on the opposite side, it would be on the part we can all see. The bite you talk of on Marie's arm was on the part against her own mouth. I will not ask you to account for that. That is the business of the jury."

He sat down with a nod of acknowledgement to the President, who damped the moment by saying drily, "After that exhibition of the dramatic art, madame, I would like you to think back to being roused that morning by Miss Allen. Did you say something to her about the delay between the assault and her appearing in your room?"

"That question was answered by le Baron de Morell earlier."

"Did you think it strange that Miss Allen, who sleeps in the room with the adjoining door, should hear nothing of the break-in, nothing of the assault and nothing of Marie defending herself?"

"Miss Allen sleeps soundly."

"Indeed!" said the President and, almost as an afterthought, added, "There are no more questions. I would like to see Miss Helen Allen."

But Maître d'Est Ange was not finished with la Baronne. "Please excuse me, Monsieur le Président, but before Madame de Morell leaves the box I have two more questions for her. Madame, I sympathise with your having to give evidence at such a trial, but I can't pass by your answers so easily. You mentioned that you had only seen the bite on her arm, so how did you know there were other injuries if she didn't show you?"

"I called a doctor."

"Very sensible. At once?"

"No, not at once. It could have been two days later."

Maître d'Est Ange addressed the President. "Monsieur le Président, I would draw your attention to that answer. The child, we gather, had been seriously assaulted, and there was blood, which her mother says did not come from her arm, on the floor. Yet her mother admits she waited two days before calling the doctor. The witness is obviously deeply shocked by all this and in an acute state of tension, and I do not wish to make any imputation against her. This assault took place many months ago and memories can be faulty, but I have seen the doctor's diary. It shows no evidence of a call two, three, or even four days later. He was not called until 15 October, three weeks later! The family was back in Paris. Am I telling the truth, madame?"

Solange made no reply but stared straight at the President as if appealing for help. D'Est Ange did not press on immediately, knowing the destructive effect of silence at the right moment. At times like these he would count slowly to himself. Then he asked, abruptly, "Will it be necessary for me to call the doctor to give evidence about his visit to your house?"

By now her head was bowed and she did not look up as she replied, "No. It was three weeks before we called the doctor."

"As it was so long after the event, what made you call him at all?"

"Marie started to cry that morning."

"Three weeks later! What made her cry?"

"She asked to be forgiven for not telling me about the other violence. She said she had been stabbed on the inside of her thigh which was the reason for the blood on the floor of her room three weeks before."

"What?" asked President Férey as if he had just woken up. "What was that about blood on the floor of her room? This is the first I have heard of that! Perhaps we should see the doctor after all."

D'Est Ange answered "One more question, monsieur, and I think you'll find it would be pointless. May I ask it?" President Férey nodded his approval. "As the doctor left your house on 15 October 1834, what did he tell you about your daughter?"

"Nothing."

"Why not?"

"Because Marie's natural modesty made her too shy for him to examine her."

The President thanked her for her evidence and apologised for allowing her to go through such an ordeal in public. He was about to let her go when d'Est Ange, still on his feet, asked to be allowed to continue questioning.

There was a shout from the back of the court, and General de Morell called out in a stentorian voice, "I think, Monsieur le Président, that you have forgotten we are the plaintiffs."

"No, monsieur," said the President. "Please sit down. I will not tolerate a disturbance. And you, maître, will be seated too. This witness has already suffered a great deal. Between us we have covered all the questions necessary. More questions would be merely repetition and would draw the same answers."

The young barrister did not sit down. "What answers?" he demanded angrily. "So far we have had no real answers at all! You know that, and I know that, and the prosecution knows that, and the jury know it too!"

"No useful purpose will be served by addressing me in that way. Sit down, maître. I will hear the evidence of Miss Allen."

Helen's evidence was straightforward and largely coincided with that given by both General and Madame de Morell. Asked if she had seen a rope ladder outside the window she replied that she had not looked. She had been too concerned with Marie who had blood on her face and nightdress, as well as being gagged with a handkerchief with her hands tied behind her back.

Asked what happened between this discovery and the calling of the girl's parents four hours later, she said she had washed Marie, tidied up the room, and put the girl back to bed.

The President asked, "Was there enough light to see the bruises and bites?"

"Not until sunrise."

"Did Ma'mselle Marie give you any details?"

"She said the man had taken off her nightdress, thrown himself on her, beating her on the arms and . . . er . . ." She stopped, her face bright red.

"Where?"

"Lower."

"Yes, but where? Thighs? Legs? Buttocks?"

She was embarrassed at the mention of such places. "Oh! Monsieur le Président!"

"Where then? I can understand your modesty but I must have an answer!"

She mumbled.

"Speak up!"

Another mumble.

The clerk, who was nearer to the witness, spoke up. "If you'll pardon

135

me, monsieur le Président, the witness said . . ." and he coughed politely
". . . thighs."

"Thank you. What time did you put Ma'mselle Marie back to bed?"

"About ten minutes later."

Maître d'Est Ange interrupted. "Didn't you call for help? I cannot
imagine why you did not when you are responsible for, and in charge of,
a girl who was little more than a child at the time."

Helen shook her head meaninglessly so d'Est Ange continued, "You
didn't call through the window to the military guard just below you on
the bridge?"

Again she shook her head, this time in the negative.

"And if this man didn't escape out of the window, it is possible he
went through the other door and was still in the house."

"I didn't think of it."

President Férey asked, "Did Ma'mselle Marie say who was the man
who attacked her?"

"She said it was the prisoner, Emile de la Roncière."

"Did she tell you this before you went to fetch her father and mother?"

"Oh yes, Monsieur le Président, there was a full moon that night."

"In your written statement you say that Ma'mselle Marie only *thought*
it might have been la Roncière, and his name was not mentioned until
the afternoon. Have you changed your mind?"

"I must have explained it badly," was the governess's reply.

She recounted how Marie had been at the ball some four days later
from the beginning right through until daybreak, laughing and singing
and dancing with friends. The President made sure she was not confusing it with another ball; later it seemed to d'Est Ange he was giving the
girl a chance to change her mind. Helen stuck to her story, saying that
Marie was brave to have attended.

D'Est Ange asked two questions. "Was there a carpet in Ma'mselle's
room?"

"A carpet? No, maître, the floor is a whitish grey stone."

"Did you hear the broken glass from the window fall inside the
room?"

"No, maître."

Maître Berryer asked but one question. "Did you sweep up the glass
the next day?"

"Madame de Morell id the room was not to be touched for two days.
After that time I put the glass in the fireplace."

The President asked each judge if he had any questions for the witness. They said they had none, but one leaned forward to point to a note
made by the President. Those closest to the bench could hear him say,

"No, no, Monsieur le Président, the witness said she had *not* seen a rope ladder." The President turned to the other judge for confirmation, and looked embarrassed as he too said that Miss Allen had said she had not seen a rope ladder. The President dipped his pen in the large pewter ink-pot and scratched out his error.

The next witness was to have been a glazier from Saumur, Monsieur Jorry. Maître d'Est Ange had ensured that he arrive in Paris two days early, had talked to him carefully, telling him to speak up and tell the truth about what he had seen, and had found him lodgings. Jorry had been quite excited about appearing in court and had been looking forward to his short-lived fame, making his wife promise to buy the newspapers every day in Saumur, while he would buy as many of the Paris papers as mentioned the trial. He had been to the tailor and bought himself a new suit so that he would appear in court properly dressed. He had estimated the cost of the expensive new suit in the number of windows that would have to be repaired to pay for it. But with all this preparation he now failed to respond when his name was called and the proceedings were held up while every room was searched. He had been seen during the afternoon and, as he was to have been a witness for the defence, the young barrister was suspicious. During his talks with Jorry he had found him to be honest and simple, but not stupid.

D'Est Ange pleaded with the President for more time to find the missing glazier, but the plea was rejected. He knew something was badly wrong because every time he looked over to Maîtres Berryer and Barrot they avoided his eyes and seemed solemnly engaged in putting their papers in order.

Time was short, said the President, summoning the cavalry artist, Lieutenant Octave d'Estouilly who, noticeably balder than in the previous September, stepped neatly into the witness box and went quickly through the swearing and identification. He described his occupation while Maîtres Berryer and Barrot seemed to relax again. This was a witness of some consequence for the prosecution.

President Férey looked at his list of questions anticipating, wrongly, that this would be a routine witness who could be disposed of happily in ten or fifteen minutes. All his statements from the preliminary examination would be repeated to the damnation of Emile. There could not possibly be any awkwardness here, he thought, and for the first five minutes he was right.

Octave told concisely how General de Morell had, just before a dinner party, "ordered him to escort" Emile to the drawing-room. He told how Emile had been dismissed, how he had received a challenge from him to a duel which, he shamefully admitted, he had accepted in spite of its

137

illegality. The evidence was going predictably well. From this moment it seemed that Emile's position as defendant was, as so many men of law had said prior to the trial, untenable.

"And," said the President, wanting to get to the evidence of forgery and confession, "you lost the duel."

"Yes," said Octave. "La Roncière came to me later and went down on his knees to me confessing the whole thing."

"I have the papers in front of me."

A cry rang out and echoed even in the muffled, crowded, hot court room. It was Emile from the dock. "Stop!" he shouted. "D'Estouilly is saying that I went down on my knees to him."

"You did!" replied Octave. "Joachim Ambert, my second, will verify it."

The President rang his bell and called for silence.

Emile paid no attention. "No! I was unjustly accused. I may have cried, I cry easily; but I have never gone down on knees to anyone but God himself!"

"Silence!" called the President, standing up and ringing his bell again.

"What's more," Emile went on, "Ambert had to push d'Estouilly to fight at all! He told him he would be accused of cowardice if he didn't fight."

The President tried again. "That's enough! This witness is above suspicion. There will be no more interruption from the dock unless it is a relevant question."

Emile was not to be stopped. "No — and they said I was a coward to grasp my opponent's *épée* during the duel!"

The President was still on his feet.

He rang his bell again. At the mention of the *épée*, however, he sat down suddenly. This had a greater effect than the call for silence. The court was still and expectant. The President looked directly at Octave and asked, "What is the truth of this? We heard earlier from the prisoner's statement that he only grasped your *épée* after his own was broken, because it was embedded in your shoulder."

Looking very sure of himself, Octave struck back after the humiliation of losing the duel. "Ambert and Bérail were both there. Let them answer. I have nothing to say."

Emile was crying again. "What is the conspiracy for? How can he stand there and imply such cowardice on my part. Oh, Monsieur le Président, please, I beg of you, find Ambert, he will tell the truth. What can I say?"

Maître Berryer replied sharply. "You could say that Monsieur d'Estouilly wrote the letters!"

D'Est Ange faced Berryer squarely. He had waited for such a moment. He knew that to show that Marie had engineered the whole affair would be difficult to prove and would lose him the case because of the power of General de Morell. He hoped that proving that his client had *not* written the letters would be sufficient to get him off. He did not care what conclusions people drew outside the court, after the case was over. He wanted to let the de Morell side know that he would settle for proving his client innocent of the letter-writing and all else would follow.

The de Morell side, he thought, might have the foresight to understand the sense of calling a halt to a case which, even if they won, would from the very considerable doubts already raised, rub off most unfavourably not only on the General, Solange and Marie, but on those higher in the land.

"That remark," he said, "coming from a distinguished man such as the prosecuting counsel, is quite incomprehensible. Accusation is a matter for discretion, and we are not going to accuse lightly. My client is innocent, and this hearing may reveal the real culprit. Let us, therefore, wait for the truth. When we see the truth, and only if the defence demands it, then I will make that accusation myself. I know who wrote the letters, and it was not Emile de la Roncière."

Maître Berryer had obviously not seen the point of this short speech, for he asked, "If it was not your client, who was it?"

Maître d'Est Ange tried again. "This trial is being held to discover not who wrote the letters, but whether my client wrote them. Let us stay with that goal." He was not sure, but he was hopeful, that he had at last made contact with the prosecution. To hammer it home, he added, "We do not seek revenge, we do not want names, we do not throw mud. We merely want justice shown by the immediate release of Lieutenant Emile de la Roncière. He is an innocent man!"

These were the words he should have saved for his closing speech and President Férey knew it, and showed it by asking if there were any questions for the witness to answer. When there were none he dismisssed Octave, turned to Emile and said, "Your behaviour may have had an adverse effect on the jury. I must, although it is not for me to do so, advise you for your own sake to be more circumspect. You called for Lieutenant Joachim Ambert to support your statement that you did not grasp your opponent's *épée* until your own was broken. This lieutenant" – he stopped and ran a finger down a piece of paper—"doesn't seem to be on the list of witnesses." He looked up. "I really don't know why his name isn't here. It should be. I want a reason for the omission by this time tomorrow." Then, to no one in particular, he said, "By chance is Monsieur Joachim Ambert in court?"

A voice in the crowd answered, "Yes, Monsieur le Président," and all turned to look at a young officer disentangling himself from two pretty girls, one on each knee. He stood up, dusted himself and stepped carefully over people sitting on the floor.

"Are you Joachim Ambert?" asked the President. Joachim said he was, and the President asked him to go to the witness box.

After he had been sworn and formally identified, the President said, "To clear this accusation of cowardice, which has no place in the Act of Accusation, but is nevertheless a serious imputation on the prisoner's character, I would like you to tell the court about the duel."

Joachim confirmed that it was properly conducted and it was only after la Roncière had broken his own *épée* that he had grasped the blade of his opponent. This was the correct behaviour and both men had fought bravely.

"Did you see the accused on his knees before Monsieur d'Estouilly?"

"No, monsieur, but he did mention something about bending the knee before him."

"No!" shouted Emile from the dock again. "No! No! No! I never said such a thing."

Joachim continued, "I remembered thinking at the time that such a remark was unworthy of an officer."

"That will do!" ordered the President, and the court became an uproar as d'Est Ange tried to subdue his client, Berryer asserted that Emile was a coward, and the President rang his bell unheard. Odilon Barrot looked unbearably pompous by ignoring the outbursts, and the spectators enjoyed themselves immensely.

As the storm abated, Joachim Ambert could be heard saying, "I can't answer these questions properly when that man is in the dock."

"What you're saying is worse!" shouted Emile.

"Wait!" called the President.

"If you were outside," went on Joachim Ambert to Emile, "then I'd answer."

"This," said the President, slamming a book down so hard that it went off like a gun, "must stop! Immediately!"

"Am I a coward?" asked Emile.

"It would be cowardly of me to answer that," said Joachim Ambert, "while you are at such a disadvantage."

General de Morell's voice could be heard above the hubbub. "Only a coward would attack a girl. That man is not only a coward, he is a liar and a cheat!"

The President called out, "General de Morell, please! I appreciate your feelings in view of the evidence we have heard . . ."

Maître Chaix d'Est Ange was furious. "Monsieur le Président! You cannot make such a comment until all the evidence has been heard!"

"I will say what I think fit," retorted the President, "and not what is decided by the defence. Unless this stops at once, we will adjourn."

There was another uproar.

The President stood with his hands above his head, and stayed in that position until there was silence.

"Maître Berryer, be seated. Maître d'Est Ange, be seated. Thank you. Now, Monsieur Ambert, did you ever hear la Roncière say he had a way of forcing a rich family to give him their daughter?"

"Yes."

"Can you remember the words he used?"

"No, I didn't hear him say it myself, but it was freely discussed in the mess . . ."

"In that case it is tittle-tattle. Did you know if the accused had a rope ladder?"

The President and most of the others in the court room appeared to have forgotten about Samuel, the other accused.

"I don't know. He could have had one. He made one for me when I needed it."

"When you needed it?" echoed the President. "What would you need with a rope ladder?"

Joachim Ambert went very red in the face and looked all around him. He had a girlfriend in Saumur with an upstairs window through which he would climb on his rope ladder. He was now in the highest court in the land, surrounded by reporters, about to reveal a little affair he was enjoying with the pretty daughter of a local vintner. He looked for an escape.

The President offered him one. "What would you need with a rope ladder? Was it for military exercises?"

What a gift! thought Joachim, and dared himself to agree. He thought better of it, however, when he remembered that many present would know that lancers did not climb rope ladders on their exercises. He was engaged to one of the two pretty girls on his knee at the time the President had called him. He felt trapped.

President Férey's curiosity had grown with the delay in answering such a simple question.

"Come along, why did you need a rope ladder?"

Joachim hesitated. "I needed it to climb into a house – er – when I couldn't use the door – so I got in through the window. To see someone."

"Who? Is he to do with the case?"

Joachim thought it was going from bad to worse. "It was not a man. She has nothing to do with this case."

It was the President's turn to be embarrassed. "Oh. Ah. Um. Yes. Eh? Well. Very well then. Now let me see. Yes. Where was this ladder on the night of the assault?"

"At my home in Tours."

"But the prisoner, having made one, was quite capable of making another. Thank you. You may stand down."

Joachim returned to his place to find a most uncertain fiancée had planted herself firmly in his seat which she shared with her girlfriend, so that Joachim had to sit on the dusty floor.

The President talked for a few seconds to the judge on his left and then, after all, asked to see the glazier, Jorry.

Because Jorry was to give valuable evidence for the defence, Maître d'Est Ange had arranged for no one to know where he was lodging. He had good reason not to trust the prosecution, and did not want his witness approached, or influenced in any way. By a stroke of fortune, one of his clerks lived on the Ile de la Cité in a part not yet affected by Louis-Philippe's 'sanitisation' of the island, which consisted of pulling down antique structures and replacing them with ponderous new government offices. Monsieur Jorry was to stay with that clerk, conveniently close to the court room. He had been instructed to wait in a room reserved for witnesses until he was called. D'Est Ange would have liked to have had him guarded, but it had not been practical.

The President had Jorry called twice more. D'Est Ange asked leave to go to look for him but it was not granted. The President emphasised that as the court had a lot of business to get through, he must therefore pass over the statements made by Jorry and call the next witness. The young barrister now had no doubt that his witness had been spirited away.

He quietly instructed one of his clerks to go over to the house where Jorry was staying. The clerk came back to say there was no sign of the missing glazier.

CHAPTER THIRTEEN

The method used to spirit away the plump, sixty-five-year-old glazier was ingenious in its simplicity.

About an hour before the court was due to sit that evening, a man with an official air about him went into the witness room where good-natured

Jorry, proudly dressed in his new and only suit, sat humbly eating some bread and cheese, and pondering the high price of wine in Paris. The 'official' told him that he would not be required to give evidence until the morning. He asked him where he was staying and, discovering that it was so close, offered to show him some of the sights of Paris to help him pass the evening. Jorry had little money and when he demurred, the official, guessing the reason, said it would all be paid for out of court funds as was the custom with witnesses subjected to a delay through no fault of their own. It all sounded to the glazier a most plausible idea, and he was delighted by this offer from such a thoughful and important-looking person, so the two set off together. The man, Monsieur Lescot, his pockets lined with francs from the prosecution fund, thought he too might just as well enjoy himself as he was being paid to entertain the glazier, with whom, he realised at once, he had nothing in common. Had the prosecution had any insight into the character of Lescot, they would never have trusted him with their money. Lescot was, as with most legal clerks, badly paid and still inexperienced. Barrot, who had instigated this unpardonable trick, was unaware of the risk of giving such a junior clerk what amounted to a blank expenses sheet.

Lescot and Jorry crossed the Pont Neuf to the Left Bank and started to walk among the confusion of houses, cafés and alleyways. Jorry wanted to see the Ecole Militaire, where he had heard that the fifteen-year-old cadet Napoleon had been enrolled in 1784. Lescot suggested that they should have a drink on the way—it was only just over two kilometres to the Ecole, less than twenty minutes' walk.

They found a café, and Jorry sat at a table in the evening sun, shaded by leafy plane trees.

"Let's go inside," said Lescot. "If we stay at this table we'll get smothered in dust from the horses and carriages."

As Jorry was the guest he agreed and they went into the stuffy café. This seemed a shame, he thought. The cobbled street had not been dusty. The proprietor and his wife knew Lescot and treated him with respect. They also treated Jorry with deference, which he enjoyed, never having enjoyed such regard in Saumur.

Absinthe and water were provided, and two glasses into which the proprietor poured large measures of the most vicious of all alcoholic drinks.

Lescot said, "Pour your own water."

The one factor the prosecution had left out of their reckoning was that, in spite of being a true Frenchman, Jorry was teetotal. With many apologies he owned up to what he considered an inadequacy.

"I tried it years ago," he confessed, "and it made me very sick. I can't even drink wine."

"Never mind," smiled Lescot, signalling to the proprietor. "Fetch my friend a cup of coffee." A cup was immediately placed in front of him and he was offered cold sausage and pastries. Normally he would have accepted but he had just eaten his bread and cheese, and was not hungry.

"Have what you like," said Lescot expansively, as he sipped his absinthe. "The court is paying for everything. You must pay for nothing."

Jorry was disappointed that he had not been told of this unexpected treat earlier. No one had been as gracious to him before.

For hundreds of years, for reasons never properly understood, Paris had basked in its own light of enchantment that millions could not resist. In 1835 the city had a greater magic than ever before. Jorry's anticipation of renown at appearing in the court room was increasing under the spell of the wonderful city and the pleasant behaviour of this nice young man.

"Pleasant," reflected Jorry, as he watched the elegant gentlemen and their ladies passing the window on foot and in rich carriages. "Pleasant," thought Jorry as young men and women mounted on well-groomed horses rode with impeccable manners past street hawkers pushing their barrows home after a day's trading under the sun. He was not in the mood to notice an old, crippled, one-eyed woman in black pleading with passers-by on the other side of the narrow road to put a few sous in her hand, distorted with arthritis; blessing them when they responded, cursing them and spitting after them when they ignored her. He was not in the mood to see the barefoot urchins of seven and eight chased out of the café when they looked round the door to beg for a few old crusts.

He had no idea how long he had been listening to the sophisticated talk of his young host, nodding and smiling when he could not follow the conversation. He started to get a little concerned when he saw how much absinthe Monsieur Lescot was drinking and he was beginning to detect its effects in his voice; but he was not being treated like a provincial and he did not want to sound like one. Now the man was starting on his fifth or even sixth glass of absinthe, each with less water than the one before, and his eyes were beginning to have a glazed stare about them. Ah well, Monsieur was a man of the city, probably an intellectual, and certainly wise and clever or he would never have such an important job. Jorry wondered what precisely he did there. Perhaps his job was to entertain witnesses at the court's expense. A happy way to make a living.

His reverie was interrupted by a marked change in Lescot's voice. The nice young man seemed to be having difficulty in speaking.

"I think," said Lescot thickly, and pausing so long before going on that Jorry imagined he had forgotten what it was he thought. "I think," he repeated, "that the Ecole Militaire is a silly place."

"Oh, monsieur, why is that?" asked Jorry innocently.

"Because it's very boring and full of a lot of . . . and lots of very stupid people. D'you know what those soldiers do? I've seen them. They march across the parade-ground and when they get to the other side — and this is where they're brainless — why, they turn round and march back again. It doesn't get them anywhere. Back where they started. And what d'you say to that? Eh?"

"Oh," said Jorry, aware that his host had suddenly become drunk.

"Yes, I suppose that's the sort of thing you would say. Dunno what it means. Oh. That's what you said. Oh."

Jorry did not know what to say or do.

"I don't suppose," went on the drunken voice, "that you know anything about soldiers, d'you?"

"I come from Saumur. We have a magnificent Cavalry School there, the finest in Europe, the home of the Cadre Noir, founded the year before Napoleon Bonaparte was born." He sounded like a guide-book, but he was trying to stop his host being overheard by the other people who were now filling the café and who, he noticed, were mostly soldiers with their girls. "And," went on the glazier desparately, "whether you're a Bonapartist or a Bourboniste or for the House of Orléans, there's no denying that Napoleon had a great and good influence on the military discipline there."

"Soldiers are bloody silly." An unwise remark in the circumstances, thought Jorry, even from a drunk. "Anyway, what d'you do in Saumur? Swill out the pigs?"

"I'm a glazier."

"A what?"

"Glazier. I'm a glazier. I put glass in window-frames, and when one gets broken I put it in again, and so on. Very good trade. Very profitable trade in a military town. The young gentlemen get rowdy sometimes, especially in the evenings, and shove things through windows all the time. There's three of us in Saumur and we're never without work."

"What's that to do with the girl?" asked Lescot, finishing another glass of absinthe with even less water in it than before.

"What girl?" asked Jorry. He had been most carefully instructed by d'Est Ange not to discuss the case with anyone.

"Oh shit!" said the nice gentleman from the court. "You're not going to be bloody awkward, are you? I only asked. What the hell can putting windows in have to do with that girl who was raped?"

"I've been called to give evidence, and that's all I'm allowed to say."

"Your name is Jorry, isn't it?"

"Yes. Albert Henri Jorry. Why?"

"That's somewhat of a great relief. To think that for a moment I thought I was spending all this money on the wrong man. Maître would have sacked me tomorrow if I'd got the wrong man. Can't think why your evidence is so important that I was told to keep you out of court."

The significance of this was lost on Jorry, so he asked, "Who is the maître, you mention?"

"Oh, Jesus Christ! Don't you country people know anything? He's the top, no, not the top, he's the best, brilliant man! Brilliant! He's a walking brain. He's the counsel for the some of the prosecution and his job is to represent the de Morell family."

None of that meant anything to Jorry, who was more preoccupied in hoping that Lescot would not topple from his chair.

"Why did you have to get me out of court?"

Lescot looked around drunkenly. He held up his glass and flicked it with his finger. The proprietor heard the ping and came over with more absinthe and another cup of coffee. Then he scribbled the bill on the marble-topped table. Lescot dropped a handful of francs and centimes on the table, not bothering to rescue the few that fell to the floor.

"Help yourself," he said to the proprietor who was sensible enough to collect his money while he could, taking a few extra centimes for his tip.

Jorry was curious and repeated his question. "Why did you have to get me out of the court?"

Lescot looked at him in a way that showed his problem was twofold. One, to get Jorry into focus; and two, to understand him. "I should have thought that bloody obvious. You've got some evidence for the defence that the prosecution doesn't want the jury to hear."

"They'll hear it tomorrow. You said so."

"No. Tomorrow'll be too late." There was still a pile of money on the table. Lescot tapped the table three times with his forefinger. "See this money? That's what they gave me to spend on you, taking you round Paris in a cab. I have to get you drunk. How was I to know you don't bloody drink? That's not my fault. They can't blame me for your silly habits."

Jorry was beginning to understand. He was a simple man and did not follow the court-room jargon of evidence for the defence or for the prosecution. He did not know the meaning of the phrase 'counsel for the prosecution' or the phrase 'represent the de Morell family'; but he knew he was meant to be back in court to tell them about the glass in Ma'mselle Marie's bedroom. He was aware of the significance of what

146

he had seen, and he knew that his words would probably mean the release of the high-spirited but harmless young la Roncière.

He got up from the table. "Thank you, monsieur," he said, offering his hand to his host who was intent on trying to drip a single drop of water from the carafe on to the centre of a franc. "I must go immediately."

"Where d'you think you're going?"

"Back to the court room."

Lescot grabbed Jorry's hand, and would not let go. "Sit down!" he ordered, temporarily sobering. "You're staying with me!"

"I can't! I have to go!" With a jerk Jorry snatched his hand away and Lescot overbalanced and sprawled to the floor, knocking over the wrought-iron-legged table and scattering the coins across the floor with broken glass, water, absinthe and coffee.

Jorry had always had trouble hurrying because of his bulk; but now he hurried. He shot through the café door and into the street. All he could remember was that they had gone into the café by turning left, so he turned right and ran up the street, hoping that Lescot was too drunk to give chase. But he heard Lescot's drunken voice shouting, "Come back! Come back, you bastard! I'll lose my job if you get back to the court room."

Jorry ran and ran, but the younger man, drunk as he was, was catching up.

That part of the city was a muddle of little streets, alleys and cul-de-sacs. Some alleyways were so narrow that a man could stand in the centre of one and by stretching out his arms could touch the houses each side of him. Lines of drying clothes were strung between the houses, and the occupants could talk to each other with ease as the sound was confined by the close walls.

It was down one of these alleys that Jorry, lungs at bursting point, dodged and stood panting in a doorway, his heart pounding like a steam engine and sweat pouring down his face.

He could hear footsteps pause at the entrance to the alley. He pushed himself hard against the door and prayed that he would not be seen. The drunk ran past him. Jorry gave a sigh of relief and, slipping out of the doorway, he walked quickly back into the street.

He thought he had escaped; but the alley, as the drunk soon found out, was a cul-de-sac. Jorry heard him shouting behind him, and slipped into another narrow alley. He pressed his heavy frame into a doorway, leaning solidly against the flimsy door so that it gave way and he found himself in a narrow passage.

Breathing hard, he was thankful for this temporary sanctuary as he heard Lescot run by.

This time, thought Jorry, he would wait a while to give Lescot time to get well away. Just as he was thinking it was safe to go out, a door in the passage opened and a girl, about twenty-five years old, appeared.

"Good evening, monsieur. Are you an old friend? Was I expecting you?" It was obvious she was a prostitute, from her voice, the way she moved, her dyed red hair and her flimsy dress, which made it desirably obvious to the glazier that she wore no underclothes.

He had heard of such people — he knew there were three or four in business in Saumur — but he had never seen one like this before. This was how they were always described to him.

"Oh, my goodness!" was all he could think of saying.

"Let me have the money first," she cooed, holding out her hand.

"Sssh! I'm hiding."

"Of course you are. Hiding from your wife, no doubt, or has your mistress been sleeping around and you're cross with her? Never mind, I can help you forget all that." She walked back through the doorway into the room and he followed her to explain. She misunderstood him, and in one time-saving move, born of experience, she pulled her dress over her head. "Give me the money first," she repeated, as she lay naked on the bed, her hand outstretched.

Jorry saw that she was in fine physical condition, with beautiful legs and a perfect body. He wondered vaguely why life could be so cruel as to reduce such a wonderful-looking girl to this. Her body did not show her trade; but her face did. The powder, the paint and the dye repelled him.

"I have no money," he said truthfully. "I was being followed by someone I wanted to avoid."

The girl swung her legs to the floor. "You bleeding liar! You followed me in here and thought you'd get away with it! Let me open the door."

It was a very small room and there was nowhere else for Jorry to stand except with his back to the door. The rest of the space was taken up by a large bed and a chair. He could not help but bar her way.

"Come on!" she shouted "None of that stuff. Get your fat arse out of the way." She pushed him over on to the bed, squeezed into the passage and at the top of her voice yelled, "Pierre! Pierre!"

"Yes, love," replied a man's voice. "I'm coming."

There was a thunderous noise as a heavy man's boots could be heard upstairs and then banging quickly down the wooden staircase.

"I've got another bleeder in here!" She looked round at Jorry cowering on the bed. "You're the third sod in five days. We have ways of dealing with you lot!"

148

Pierre appeared in the doorway. He was about six feet two inches tall and the contrast with frightened tubby Jorry would have been comic under any other circumstances.

"Come on, let's have the money." He looked at the girl. "Has he had you?"

"I'm not silly," she said. "You know I always get the money first. He comes in, gets me to undress and lay on the bed, and then says he's got no money. By the look of him I shouldn't think he's got anything else either."

Jorry protested at last. "No, I came in here to hide. I was being chased by a drunk."

"Balls!" said the big man belligerently. "Balls! Them things you probably haven't got."

"Come on," said the girl, "give him the treatment."

Jorry was shaking and wondering what 'the treatment' would be. "Please," he said, "please just let me go."

The big man ignored him. "Sit on the bed." Jorry sat up. "Now take your trousers off!" Obediently and meekly Jorry removed his new trousers. "Give them to me!" He handed them over. The big man looked in them for cash but found nothing. "Give me your jacket!" The new jacket was passed and again searched for money. There was none. "Now get into the passage!"

"What!" said Jorry. "Just in my shirt and boots?"

"My mistake," said Pierre. "Gimme your boots."

Passively, Jorry removed and handed over his best boots, new for the journey to Paris, and went in stockinged feet into the passage.

"I'm not keeping your clothes," said Pierre. "You can get them back from the second-hand market next week. So you'll know where to come for them." He told Jorry to open the door to the alley, and as he obeyed, he got a hard kick in the bottom, so hard that it sent him sprawling right across the alley, banging his head on the wall of the house opposite. He got up, relieved to find no broken bones.

"And don't come back!" shouted Pierre, slamming the door.

It was still broad daylight as Jorry stood there considering whether by stooping he could make the front of his shirt cover his essentials. He found that it did, but the back of the shirt was too high to cover his behind.

With a little experimenting, he soon found a compromise by crouching and pulling his shirt down at each side. In this position he could not run, but he could trot through the streets of Paris, while onlookers on foot, in carriages and on horse back laughed aloud at the spectacle of the little fat man bouncing along with tiny footsteps, dodging the women who sat knitting in the warm evening light outside their doors, and occasionally sticking out a foot to try to trip him up.

It seemed a thousand kilometres before he found the Pont Neuf and, still doing his odd little trot, Jorry crossed the bridge, staring straight ahead, finally disappearing into his lodgings. He silently thanked God he had kept his working clothes.

It was after ten o'clock when he reached the court and, mercifully, they were still in session. He passed a message to Maître d'Est Ange that he had arrived, and settled into the witness room to nurse his bruised knees, his sprained right wrist and the gash over his right eye.

CHAPTER FOURTEEN

Back in the candle-lit court room, later that evening, Georges Montgolfier, paper manufacturer, son of Joseph Montgolfier, one of the pioneers of hot-air ballooning, was in the witness box giving evidence for the defence. He was the fourth hand-writing expert, deliberately saved to the last because of the weight his name would lend to the defence.

President Férey was speaking. "Forgive me, Monsieur Montgolfier, but I had always understood you to be a famous balloonist like your father, so how is it that you're here as a hand-writing expert?"

The wiry little man lacked the charm and dignity of his illustrious father. He spoke rapidly, with a disconcertingly high-pitched voice which had a mean nasal tone. He sniffed between sentences and fiddled with his greasy moustache.

"I own many paper factories in different parts of the country," he sniffed, "and good paper-making is bound up inextricably with an understanding of calligraphy and graphology."

With the momentous task of condensing months of preparation for the defence into a few days, Chaix d'Est Ange's contact with Montgolfier had been limited to the post and third parties. He knew that a really presentable and likeable witness was an asset, and he suspected this man would not be liked. However, he hoped that his evidence would be almost irrefutable and that the great name of Montgolfier would carry it.

Maître Berryer stood up, anticipating the merry mangling he would push Férey into giving Montgolfier. "So you're not a full-time professional hand-writing expert!" The cadence in his voice made the sentence by a statement and not a question.

"If by 'professional' you mean that I earn my living by studying hand-writing, then I am not." He sniffed again. "It is very much a part of my business; the texture of . . ."

Berryer cut him short. "Have you ever been presented with a series of specimens of writing and been successful in selecting the forgeries from the real? I am not referring to this case."

"I have collections of various forms of hand-writing at my . . ."

Berryer cut him short again. "Have you been successful in selecting forgeries from real? Answer yes or no."

"No." he sniffed.

"Thank you." Maître Berryer sat down and yawned ostentatiously. In Berryer's opinion the witness was already discredited.

President Férey asked, "What do you make of the letters you have examined?"

"My colleagues and I have given them a thorough and searching examination, and we conclude they were not written by the prisoner, la Roncière. All the letters were written by the same person who is intelligent and writes well. La Roncière's writing does not show the same intellect and is not so neat. There are other differences as well; the letter V for instance is in the English style . . ."

Odilon Barrot remembered his duty. "I don't think it is necessary to try to implicate the English governess."

The President looked puzzled. "And how would that happen?"

"Did you not hear?" asked Barrot. "This self-styled writing expert says the letter V is in the English style. The only English person in the vicinity was Miss Helen Allen. The defence earlier admitted that they don't care who get the blame for the letters as long as it is not la Roncière. Mud is now being thrown at Miss Allen. An irresponsible attitude by the defence."

The President nodded that he understood and looked over to Montgolfier. "Monsieur, please continue."

"I was saying that the English style V, no doubt taught to Ma'mselle Marie de Morell by the English governess, is a constant feature of her writing. The capital letters, too, are also in Marie de Morell's style."

There was an embarrassed silence. The President did not seem to be paying attention. Maître d'Est Ange took the opportunity to stress the point for the sake of the jury and to bring the President's attention back to the evidence. "Monsieur le Président, may I please ask the witness to enlarge on the word 'style'?"

President Férey closed his mouth, hid his inattention as best as he

151

could and said, "Yes, maître, I was about to ask the witness what he means by the word 'style'?"

Montgolfier sniffed. "I mean that they're the same shape . . ."

"What are?"

"The letters, Monsieur le Président, the letters are the same shape as those by Marie de Morell; and it doesn't end there. The direction of the stroke, the pressure on the pen is the same, so is the spacing between the words."

The President did not seem to know what question to ask next. He was out of his depth. Maître d'Est Ange prompted the witness. "Did you find any spelling mistakes?"

"Yes, maître . . ."

Férey looked up sharply. "Address the bench please, monsieur."

Montgolfier turned to the bench. "Yes, there were some spelling mistakes, but the grammer and spelling are vastly better than that of the accused." He sniffed.

The President was pleased with himself. He had thought of a good question. "Monsieur Montgolfier, what do you know about the paper on which these letters were written?"

"Everything," said the dapper little paper manufacturer with the irritating confidence which was certain to alienate the jury. He sniffed before enlarging on his subject. "I made it. It is very simple. May I please have one of the letters in question?"

The President passed one, by way of the clerk, to the witness who was extracting a sheet of paper from his pocket. "Thank you. Now watch." He held them together and sniffed. "You will see that this sheet, which is from an exercise school-book used by Marie de Morell, is exactly the same as the paper on which this letter is written. The two sheets are identical in four respects: size, texture, colour and thickness."

"And you are sure," emphasised the President, "that you made that paper? Could it have been made by someone else?"

"Impossible. I know this paper well. It was not commercially successful, possibly because it's dull and straw-coloured. We hoped the schools would buy these books but they didn't. They bought from a better quality range, of ours naturally, so we let these go cheap to little shops."

"How can you be sure you made it," asked the President, "when the letters have no watermarks?"

"They have no watermarks because this is machine-made paper. We are still experimenting with watermarking machine paper. There is none on the market. And I can tell you more. These two pieces came from the same ream." He took out a magnifying glass and studied the edges of the

152

paper. "If you look closely at the edges you will see little chips missing in the same place on the side of each sheet. These chips are caused by imperfections in the guillotine blade which trimmed the ream."

D'Est Ange offered the jury a look at the paper with the magnifying glass and a candle. Two or three accepted. The President went on, "Is it likely that one ream would be divided so that some would be made into exercise-books and some into note-paper?"

"No," said Montgolfier. "A ream is between four hundred and fifty and five hundred sheets, so it would be uneconomical to switch production in the middle of such a small quantity."

Berryer joined in. "In the little town of Saumur, there is but one stationery shop. That shop is not only half way between the Cavalry School and the General's house, it is also on the corner of the main street and the Rue St Nicholas, where la Roncière had his lodgings."

"Where is this leading us?" asked President Férey.

"The defence contends that only Marie had access to this so-called rare paper. The prisoner had a precisely equal chance of getting it."

D'Est Ange demanded, "Why should a cavalry officer buy a child's exercise-book?"

Berryer was in no hurry. He had hoped for that question. Smiling, knowing he was scoring points, he spread his arms wide and said, "Why indeed? If he wants to implicate the girl, and that is the theme throughout this trial, what would be more natural than to use paper from an exercise-book? Where else would he buy one?"

He had made his point, and it had earned a round of applause in the public sector. The President rang his bell and asked if there were any more questions. He thanked the witness.

As Montgolfier was leaving the witness box, Maître d'Est Ange was passed a note saying that Jorry was waiting outside. He told this to the President and, for a few moments, was doubtful that Jorry would be allowed in. He had to appeal to the court on the grounds of having had so little time. The two judges approved, so there was little that could be done to keep this key witness out of the box, although Berryer muttered about contempt of court.

Jorry would have made his entrance wide-eyed with wonder had his right eye not been half-closed from the knock it had received. He was extremely self-conscious in his working clothes, shuffling in in his stockinged feet. He clutched his cap nervously and stood silently in the witness box looking around him while attempts were made to get him to take the oath.

He did this hesitantly, opening the Good Book to make sure it was really a Bible and, after his identification was over and there had been a few preliminary questions about his job and where he lived, he found himself elaborating "... so I put a new pane of glass in the dining-room window, and when I done it I had to go up to this little bedroom to put a new bit of glass in where they'd broke it."

The President asked, "Was the hole in the bedroom window large enough for a hand from the outside to go through and open the catch?"

"Yes and no, monsieur. You see, the hole was big enough for a hand to get through, but it would have been impossible to reach the catch from there if you were on the outside of the house. The hole was in the wrong place for that. Now, the reason I noticed that so well was that I'd heard about the break-in from the outside and knew at once that it was impossible. But it was none of my business so I kept it to myself until asked. Mind you, I'm not saying there was no break-in. It just couldn't have been done that way."

"I'm not interested in your opinion. Did you find much broken glass on the floor?"

"No, and I'd hoped to. But it was all outside in little bits from falling such a long way down."

"Why did you hope to find some glass?"

"When I mend a window I always take away the bigger bits of the old window as they come in handy for cutting into small squares for houses with smaller windows. I was unlucky that time."

Berryer, sensing where this was leading, wanted to destroy the credibility of the witness. "All this," he said, "happened about eight months ago. How do you remember the details so well?"

"Well, there was all that fuss and talk at the time and with me going into the actual bedroom where it happened it gave me a lot to talk about in the evenings in the café. Not that I drink. I don't, but I like a cup of coffee with my friends now and then. And another thing," said the glazier, enjoying himself and by now noticing the press writing down what he was saying, "I keep this little book" – he pulled a grubby notebook from his top pocket – "because when I work for the quality people, they don't like to pay at once, so I have to send them a note saying what they must pay. When I knew I had to come here and tell all about it, I looked it up." He stuck the book proudly back in his pocket.

Berryer asked, "You presumably have a note in your book about another window in that house?

"Yes, monsieur, I have. It was the dining-room window downstairs. That was nothing to do with the break-in. Nothing."

"Can you remember the position of the broken pane in the dining-room?

Jorry scratched his head and looked round the court. "I'm not sure. I

154

don't think there was a hole in the pane. I think it was just a diagonal crack, but I could be wrong. I might be muddling it with another house the same day. It's so long ago."

"Yes," said Berryer, raising his voice so that no one would miss a word. "You are not sure because, in your own words, it was 'so long ago'; but this was the same day you mended the bedroom window. That was just as long ago."

"Yes monsieur, but the dining-room window is not the one that all the fuss was about, if you'll forgive me saying so."

"That," said Berryer angrily, "is not for you to comment on. I am asking the questions. Tell me, think again, how was the glass in the dining-room damaged?"

"I told you. It was broken."

"I think we've all realised that by now. Was it right out?" He had raised his voice, walking over to the witness box to face the intimidated Jorry. "Was it just cracked? Had the glass fallen into the room? Was it outside on the cobbles? Was the hole big enough for an arm? A hand?" He was getting louder and faster. "Come on! Answer!"

Jorry was confused by the speed of the questions, and he was still dazed from his fall. It was hot and stuffy in the court and he wanted a drink of water. He said, "Oh dear me. That was all a long time ago. And I've told you, I might get it muddled. How could I answer all that?"

Berryer suddenly became quiet and gentle as he said, "Yes, yes, you don't have to." Jorry felt a great sense of relief and his inquisitor added in a kindly way, "It's much too long ago." Berryer turned to the bench. "I don't have to emphasise that this lapse of memory can equally be applied to Monsieur Jorry's opinion of the window in the bedroom. This poor man cannot possibly remember in detail. Thank you, Monsieur Jorry. That will be all from me." He sat down. Jorry could feel the flesh round his right eye swelling and smarting.

D'Est Ange stood up. "Monsieur le Président," he said, "I don't think any member of our noble profession would be proud of what we have just seen. It was an alarming display of bullying a witness. I am ashamed of having seen a brother advocate behave in such a way."

Berryer ignored the protest, affecting to be engaged in deep and serious conversation with Odilon Barrot. President Férey made no comment but asked the witness, "Monsieur Jorry, tell me again why you cannot remember other windows, and yet you say you remember the bedroom window in detail"

"Because it was what I talked about every day for several weeks after the scandal. They were all asking me. I couldn't possibly forget."

"Did you visit any other houses that day?"

"I expect so. They keep me busy there."

"How much glass did you see on the floor of that memorable bedroom?"

"None, monsieur, because it had all been swept up and put in the little fireplace. There was very little there. So little that I was curious, and on my way out I looked outside the house under the window and saw quite a lot."

"And what conclusions did you draw from that?"

"The window had been broken from the inside."

"Thank you. Are you considered to be a reliable man?"

"As far as I know. When I am called to mend a window, I do it as soon as I can and clean up after repairs."

"Thank you." The President sat back in his chair and turned to the jury. "This witness considers himself to be reliable man, and yet he is over two and a half hours late to give his evidence."

"Yes monsieur, you see . . ."

"This is a court of law, Monsieur Jorry, not some drinking den where you might get engaged in fisticuffs from time to time. Punctuality is essential. The reliability of a witness can be partly based on his punctuality. You do not impress me at all. I would like the jury to note that."

Maîtres Berryer and Barrot surreptitiously nodded to each other. The President, muddle-headed though he was, thought Berryer, was getting the trial back into the proper perspective.

Jorry's mind was in a turmoil. Not only was his evidence now almost discounted, but all that about his unreliability would appear in print in the papers and be read by his friends and customers. He knew he was not unreliable. He knew he has been scrupulously careful in his answers to the questions. Screwing his cap in his hands and holding it up in his distress he started, "But monsieur . . ."

He was cut short. "That will be all. You may go." The President's tone of authority silenced Jorry. His reputation had been damaged.

D'Est Ange was powerless to do anything, not knowing why Jorry had vanished. He had a strong suspicion that his absence had been arranged, but suspicion was not enough. Recalling Jorry might reveal that the glazier was late from his own stupidity. It was too big a risk to call him back and ask him outright. He made a note on his pad for a possible future trial, heading the page 'Conspiracy".

President Férey announced that the next witness, Colonel Saint-Victor, was indisposed. General de Morell had asked the Colonel to investigate the background of Emile de la Roncière and a sworn statement by the Colonel had been issued to every member of the jury, prosecution

156

and defence counsels. The President said he would not waste time reading it all out aloud.

"I draw your attention to the part that says the prisoner, Emile de la Roncière, told the Colonel that he could make the de Morells give him their daughter."

With a violence born of frustration, Emile kicked the inside of the front of the dock, and brought his fists down hard on the top of the barrier. "That's a lie!" he shouted. "I said no such thing!"

The President leaned towards Maître d'Est Ange. "Maître, if there are any more interruptions from that prisoner he must wait down in the cells, and I shall . . ."

He had no chance to finish because Emile was shouting again. "I will not hear these lies!" D'Est Ange went over to calm his client. When all was quiet again, the President looked down at the paper in his hand.

"This statement says it was the prisoner's intention to make the girl pregnant and tell her father . . ." He paused, flicking through the pages. "It goes on to say the prisoner did badly at school and, on leaving, started to associate with prostitutes, ran up debts, and on three occasions when given money by his father to settle outstanding accounts" – the President looked up – "no doubt run up at gaming-tables and in hotels, from all we've heard" – he looked back to the paper – "he dissipated it without paying his debts. Colonel Saint-Victor also says . . ."

Emile couldnot help but interrupt. "I've never even heard of Colonel Saint-Victor!" he shouted, tears streaming down his face. "What are you doing to me. Please, Maître d'Est Ange, tell them what you found!"

"Monsieur le Président," said d'Est Ange with some hesitation, because he had wanted to save this disclosure until his closing speech, "I must tell the court that I was given a copy of this report two days ago, and since then have had three people trying to discover the whereabouts of this man, or myth, called Colonel Saint-Victor. He is not in any branch of the cavalry. The lists have been most carefully checked. He is not an artillery man. He is not in the infantry. There is no man of that name stationed abroad. I have also enquired from the Quartermaster-General for such a man. No one admits to Colonel Saint-Victor."

President Férey smiled benignly at the young barrister. "You do not understand the structure of the military, maître. Every military establishment in the civilised world has to deal, from time to time, with unusual enquiries. Enquiries of this nature are made by a special branch of our noble military establishment. It is quite natural that the names of those in that branch are not listed. I deplore secrecy as much as you, but sometimes it is unavoidable, especially when we have a country that is going through an unsettled phase."

D'Est Ange looked steadily at the jury, shaking his head in a gesture of hopelessness. "My client," he said, "has denied what is written on that paper. I have tried to find this mysterious Colonel Saint-Victor, who, you will have noted, is indisposed, or so we are told. I believe this piece of evidence to be dubious. You cannot accept a written statement of that gravity without some opportunity to hear from the man who is supposed to have written it."

The President said, "You can accept this paper as reliable evidence. It carries the authority of this court." Then he added, like a pianist changing key a semi-tone upwards, "It must be about eleven o'clock. This will be a good moment to adjourn for a while until we reassemble at midnight to hear the evidence of Marie de Morell."

CHAPTER FIFTEEN

During the hour before midnight much happened.

Because General de Morell, Solange and Helen Allen were in court until eleven that night, they could not bring Marie to the court room. So one of Solange's elderly aunts had volunteered to see that Marie was suitably dressed, and to escort her to the Ile de la Cité in good time. The General's coach was waiting outside the house.

The aunt, Madame Maillat, had, at half past nine, told Marie to be ready to leave at a quarter to eleven, so it was with some surprise that the elderly aunt had found Marie lying on her bed reading a novel without having made any effort to change. However, she was not sharp with her great-niece because she knew the girl was to undergo an ordeal of consequence.

She glanced at the title of the novel and, in the way of the elderly, immediately formed the opinion that it was 'not suitable'.

As gently as possible she said, "You shouldn't be reading that sort of book at a time like this."

"Why not?" asked Marie impertinently.

"Because you should be changing."

"Plenty of time for that."

"And you should be composing your mind for the questions you will be asked tonight. Shouldn't you be considering your answers?"

"There's nothing," said Marie, sliding her feet to the floor as she sat up on the bed, "that I have to consider. I will tell the truth, and they will be satisfied."

"I expect so," said the great-aunt vaguely. She had known Marie for only two days and could not understand her, "well, you'd better get dressed."

When she reached the drawing-room on the first floor Madame Maillat was surprised to find a middle-aged, greying man soberly dressed in black and grey.

"Ah!" was all she could think of to say. She was no sophisticated Parisienne and had come up from the little village of Troyes to be near her niece and great-niece during this most difficult time.

The man shook her hand, saying, "I'm Dr Olivier. I'm a little early."

"I'm Madame Maillat, Madame de Morell's aunt. Is somebody ill?"

"Your great-niece," said the doctor.

"She looked all right just now," she answered, mildly surprised. She was quickly learning not to be surprised at what went on in Paris. "I've just come down from her bedroom. What's the matter with her?"

"They didn't tell you she has fits?"

"*Petit mal?*"

"Is there any history of that?" asked the doctor.

"Not that I know of. It was just a guess on my part. What sort of fits does she have?" Madame Maillat had not been prepared for any of this. No one had spoken to her about a doctor calling, or fits, and she had been in the house for two days. It was too bad of Solange to have said nothing.

"The fits she has have a long technical name but the outward show is not unlike *petit mal*. She sits motionless from time to time and seems to hear no one."

"How often does this happens?"

"Every day at certain hours."

Madame Maillat was openly sceptical. "I've been here for two days and I've never seen her have one."

"That's why we're all going to court at midnight tonight. She never has a fit at midnight."

"And she's not having one now. I've been talking to her."

"She'll be quite clear from midnight until two in the morning."

"Just like that?" asked the great aunt blankly.

"Yes," affirmed the doctor. "Like clockwork. I've never seen a case like it before."

Abruptly he changed the subject and, for the next twenty minutes, their conversation ranged over many things from the riots to the weather and to the construction of the railway line between St Germain and Versailles. The doctor did most of the talking because Madame Maillat was conscious of her inability to talk sensibly of anything except the weather. These Parisians, she thought, were so knowledgeable about what was going on. They were all like the doctor, and they used words that no one in Troyes had heard of. All that had ever happened at Troyes was the preservation of the relics of a pope (she was not sure which one); the fêting of Joan of Arc (she could not remember what for); and the place had given its name to the troy weight (she did not know why); and it hardly seemed worth mentioning to the important doctor with his clever words.

It was quite a relief when Marie came into the room wearing a bright red frock with an emerald green sash, her black hair and radiant face framed in a red bonnet.

"I'm ready!" she said. "This should stand out among the dull greys in that court room."

Madame Maillat may not have been a Parisienne but she had had daughters of her own in Troyes. "A man," she said, "is on trial for his life. Whatever he has done, and whatever you think of him, I am certain you should show some respect at least for the court and the people in it. You can't dress like that!"

"What do you know of a court room? Have you ever been in one?" challenged Marie.

"No," said her great-aunt, turning to the doctor for support. "Monsieur le docteur, don't you think she should be in black?"

Stomach-aches and chills, and even broken limbs he could cope with, but not two females discussing clothes.

"I — er — I —" he stammered, while Marie spun round on him like a dancer.

"You know nothing of fashion. Anyway father doesn't pay you to have opinions."

The doctor, acutely aware that he was working for one of France's richest families, swallowed his anger and his pride in one gulp and, looking at Madame Maillat, said, "There's a serious danger that Ma'mselle Marie will lose the case if she appears in court like that."

"Mama wants me to look like some dowdy widow with a black veil. Oh, all right! But Emile's guilty, you know. He's guilty. I've heard the talk about him, and I've heard what they've said about me. You'll see justice done tonight. Hell will open up and swallow him whole, not even bothering to spit out his bones!" She ran out of the room as suddenly as she had arrived.

160

Madame Maillat felt responsible for her great-niece's rudeness and was upset. "I do apologise for her," she said to the doctor. "She's under a great strain, and it seems the whole family is living in a nightmare."

Dr Olivier was understanding. He had a family of his own. "She's very young, not yet seventeen."

"I suppose," ventured the elderly lady, "that she'll come through this all right?"

"Are you talking of her health or the legal battle? I can answer for the one; I can't answer for the other."

At about the time the doctor was waiting for Marie with Madame Maillat, Maître d'Est Ange was in a cell under the Palais de Justice with the old Comte de la Roncière, Emile and Samuel. The cell was below the level of the Seine, and therefore always damp. The young barrister was arguing with the guard because he wanted to talk to Emile alone. Old la Roncière naturally offered to leave the cell.

"That is pointless if I am left with Samuel Gilieron as well as your son and the guard."

"What is it you want to say to my boy that you cannot say in front of all of us?"

D'Est Ange dropped his voice to a whisper. "Remember Descartes?"

"No," whispered the old man. "Who's he?"

"René Descartes. Cause and effect. We have the effect and I believe your son knows the cause. This may be my last chance to get it from him. Only he knows and he must tell me. It's possible that he doesn't realise that he knows. I believe in his innocence."

"He never wrote those letters," said the old man. "He never attacked a girl — any girl."

"This is why I'm looking for the cause," whispered the barrister. "There must be a cause."

"Not if he didn't do it," said the Comte.

"I don't mean that. I know he didn't do it. But somewhere there's a cause for his being accused. I have no doubt that Marie de Morell is aiming her venom at your son for a reason. This is not chance!"

"She's mad."

"Possibly. But not very mad. I have read her deposition, I've talked to people who know her well, and there is no evidence of an unbalanced mind. She knows what she is doing and she's doing it cleverly." He paused, searched in his pockets and found two Louis d'or. He rattled them in the palm of his hand and asked the Comte, "Have you any money?"

The old man found one Louis d'or. "That's all I have. Don't let Emile know, but this case is ruining me."

161

The young lawyer took the three gold coins and offered them to the guard with the instructions, "Take Samuel Gilieron and General le Comte de la Roncière to another cell. Lock me in here with the Lieutenant until I call you. Stay out of here yourself and these three coins are yours."

The guard looked contemptuously at the money, thinking at first that he was looking at three francs. The lawyer held them closer to the guard's unpleasant sallow face, realising the man to be short-sighted. The guard straightened, thinking it was a lot of money for such a small favour. For a moment he wavered in case it was a trick designed to catch him taking bribes, but the glint of gold was irresistible and he took the money.

As soon as prisoner and barrister were alone, d'Est Ange said, "I don't have to remind you that within half an hour or so we are going to meet the prime witness. You and I will be face to face with sixteen-year-old Marie de Morell."

Emile did not react as d'Est Ange hoped he would. The reminder was to cheer him, to spur him on and give him hope, but it seemed to have the opposite effect. "I know we shall see her," he said in a colourless voice, "and she'll add more fuel to the conflagration."

"Why? Why?"

The prisoner was immeasurably depressed and it showed in his voice that the strain was overwhelming him. "How do you mean?"

D'Est Ange was worried about his client's lack of fight. The spirit seemed to be going out of him. He had to act quickly to bolster him up.

"Nothing happens without a cause. Emile!" For the first time he addressed his client by his Christian name. "Emile! You alone know why this is happening. Tell me!"

"I wish to God I knew!" exclaimed an astonished Emile. "D'you think that if I understood it, I would go on deliberately putting my life at risk in this way? Do you really think I'm that stupid? Do you think I would let my father bankrupt himself with the expense of this case? Do you think I enjoy spending my nights and days in filthy cells?"

"Nothing happens without a cause."

"You've just said that. And while we're about it, I'd like you to tell me why you are not defending me strongly enough. Many times I have thought of questions I wanted to ask that corrupt parade of witnesses for the prosecution. I've been in trouble several times for being too outspoken and it's all because you don't speak up. You never ask them. You never press home obvious points. Why not? Why not?"

"I would rather forego the full examination of witnesses than an-

ticipate my closing speech to the jury. There have been many incon-
sistencies in the witnesses' evidence, and there will be many more
tonight, no doubt, from Marie; and still more tomorrow. I am noting
them and I will use them. Meanwhile, I am letting Maître Berryer waste
his ammunition while I conserve ours. I am more worried about the
silent Maître Odilon Barrot. But perhaps he says little because he has little to say. When the time comes, when I am in total command of the
court on your behalf, I will tell the jury in detail how you could not possibly have written the letters, how you could never have climbed into that
bedroom. But this is not what I want to talk to you about now. I want you
to tell me why, with so little evidence against you, that girl has managed
to persuade her father, her mother, two eminent lawyers, the press, the
original court which examined you, and a whole host of others, that you
and Samuel are in league against her."

D'Est Ange peered at Emile, searching for a glimmer of recognition
that his words might have uncovered. There was simply no reason for
this overwhelming mass of opinion against Emile. There were too many
important people involved for it to be a silly whim.

He tried again. "Emile, what is the cause for these false accusations?
You know there is one. You know it will make our task easier if you tell
me. You *must* tell me. And there are not many minutes left for you to do
so."

Emile looked blank. The barrister stopped, hoping that the silence
would extract the words he wanted to hear. It was a technique he had
used successfully before.

While Chaix d'Est Ange was desperately trying to discover the motiva-
tion behind the strange behaviour of the de Morell family towards
Emile, confined as they were in the putrid, rancid, stagnant cell below
the court room, Maître Berryer was in a mahogany-panelled, thickly
carpeted room in the same building some two storeys higher talking to an
angry General de Morell.

"So!" said the General. "You have arranged for Marie to come to this
court in spite of all we agreed!"

"I'm sorry," replied Berryer sharply, without a hint of apology in his
voice. "I did my best to keep her out of court. But public opinion might
go the wrong way if she is seen about town and yet does not appear
here."

"I don't give a damn for public opinion!"

"You may find you have to!"

General de Morell was not used to being spoken to like that. "Explain
yourself!"

"I have reports that your daughter has been seen out shopping at the very times when Dr Olivier swore she was incapable of anything except staring straight ahead. How do you want me to explain that?"

"You may not have to."

"Maître Chaix d'Est Ange may know of it and bring it up tonight or in his final speech. Then what? Eh?"

The General reacted in the way he so often did when he heard something unpleasant. He pretended he had not heard. "What is the purpose of the law," he demanded, "if it is not to uphold the people who make France what she is?"

Berryer, a strong-willed man, tried to return to the subject he had broached. "There is something you must tell me . . ."

The General refused to listen. He sensed that Berryer was about to delve too deeply. He went on angrily, "If a man of my integrity is to be impertinently questioned by some young upstart of a lawyer . . ."

"Monsieur le Général . . ."

". . . and is shown in a poor light against some irresponsible soldier who has never offered his life to the state, as I have, who has a better knowledge of the inside of a brothel than of the Nôtre Dame . . ." He pointed in the direction of the great building looming in the darkness.

"Monsieur! You are not being helpful!" Berryer was angry. This was unusual. His skill at the bar was partly based on his ability to throw others off balance while he himself remained cold, thoughtful and impersonal. In his early days of training, he had been told that to make a man angry was equivalent to making him drunk, and in that condition he would make revelations that he would not otherwise make. He was trying to make the General angry and possibly, because he was tired, he found the same being done to him.

The General was looking out towards the Nôtre Dame. He could just see the coloured light of the candles through the stained-glass windows, and he was saying something about the whole framework of society being in danger.

The advocate picked up the word 'danger'.

"You, General de Morell, you are the one in danger."

"I?" asked the General, swinging round to face the lawyer. "I am in danger?" He stressed the last word. "If I am in any danger, it is due to your extreme incompetence."

"That young upstart, as you called Maître d'Est Ange, is a very competent man. We must tread warily. He seems to do the work of ten men. He has assembled a large number of facts and witnesses in a few days that would have taken several skilled men many weeks to collect."

"Are you warning me that we might lose?"

"I don't know. If you think me as incompetent as you have just said, you are at liberty to turn the case over to someone else."

The General was worried. One of the few battles he had ever lost was one where he had sacked a colonel in the middle of it and the troops had lost faith. He took control of himself and made himself smile. "My dear maître, you must not take seriously something I said in the heat of the moment."

Berryer pressed his advantage. "If you take the case from me, I will first apply for an adjournment, and naturally, as my profession demands it, I will brief the new man with all thoroughness."

"That would put us at the same disadvantage as was contrived with such care for the defence. No, I will not allow it."

"Then, General, I must have your complete confidence."

"You have it."

"I do not!" said the lawyer sharply. "I do not have your confidence at all."

"Oh?" The General raised his eyebrows in an expression of injured astonishment.

"You're a soldier. You know the importance of surprise in attack. I have had too many surprises in that court room because you have concealed the truth from me. I must know everything that you know about this affair."

"Where do you think I have misled you? Where?"

"I'm not going to list them all. We haven't time. But I can give you two examples: one, who is Colonel Saint-Victor who wrote this extraordinary report? It was you, wasn't it? You wrote that report damning la Roncière." He did not wait for a reply. "Two, you said that the glass from the window was found on the floor of your daughter's room. Most of it was on the cobbles outside. There are a whole lot more instances. These are the reasons I can't go on with this case."

"You're serious?"

"Of course I am. How can I possibly prosecute if moments like this occur again? It's not just the case that will collapse — my reputation will go with it."

"You really are going to back out, let me down, destroy the very establishment that has helped put you where you are?" The General walked morosely to the table, pulled up a chair, sat down and laid his head on his arms on the polished table.

He thought of what Marshal Soult would say when he learned that Berryer was dropping out. He knew that such a move by France's greatest advocate could alone lose him the case. The destruction of the de Morells would be inevitable.

165

He rolled his head to one side, looked up at Berryer and asked, "What do I do now?"

Berryer answered at once and with a sting in his voice. "You can tell me the truth or ask me to pass my brief over to another. Make up your mind quickly because we're due back in court. If you pass the brief over, it will mean that Marie will not have to appear in court tonight."

"That could be to her advantage."

"Disadvantage," corrected the lawyer.

"Why?"

"Because one newspaper at least is suspicious of the whole affair and has stated that you will do anything to keep your daughter out of court. This will be seen as a ploy."

"The press is loyal to my family," asserted the General.

Berryer was bewildered by the man's naiveté. "The press is loyal only to its circulation. More copies. Bigger sales. Newspaper sales were never so high before this case. A scandal of the magnitude I foresee will more than double this morning's sales."

"The people want la Roncière to be found guilty. You know, probably better than I, that the public never read or hear anything properly. They always discount facts when their minds are made up." De Morell knew very well that the public was always on the alert for a fresh and better scandal. His experience of mixing politics with the army had shown him many times just how fickle was public opinion. Only recently he had encountered a mob jeering at the King when the jeers had been drowned by a band playing the Marseillaise. This had been followed by a rousing speech, which in turn changed the jeers to cheers. Such was the thinking ability of a mob.

"All right." The lawyer shrugged. "It's your decision."

"Wait!" The General sat up stiffly and thought for a long time. He sighed deeply. "What do you want to know in order that you may retain the brief?"

"Who wrote the letters — the ones that have caused all this trouble?"

"Don't you know?" He was trying to avoid facing up to reality.

"Yes. I want to hear it from you."

The General bit his lower lip, drew in his chin, and after fully ten seconds, relaxed and announced in a flat, colourless voice, "My daughter, Marie, wrote those letters."

"How do you know? Why should I believe you now, any more than when it seemed a foregone conclusion that la Roncière wrote them? How can I tell that you will not suddenly assault me with the unassailable fact that Madame de Morell wrote them? Or could it be that governess? Come out of this fog of surmise and give me something I can believe in. I need something to hold on to. Good God, monsieur, do you realise what you have done to your family, to the la Roncière family, to yourself?" He pulled himself up sharply as he looked down at the beaten man struggling against self-destruction. "How did you find out, and when did you find out?"

He had to wait a long time for the answers. "I found out because we had had something like them before and I had suspected my daughter. But when there appeared to be letters between d'Estouilly and la Roncière which led to a duel — and just before that, there were letters which only la Roncière appeared to have the knowledge to write — my doubts about Marie vanished. It seemed impossible that she could have done it. It was because of my uncertainty that I did not prosecute. I thought he was writing them or was in some way involved."

Berryer was aware of the enormity of the catastrophe, but he spoke gently. "Exactly. So with doubt already in your mind why did you take the risk of calling me in to prosecute someone else?"

The General looked up with a dead expression in his eyes. "Have you forgotten so soon, maître, that my wife called you in? I tried to stop it, but you had already passed the letters to the Public Prosecutor."

It was some moments before the lawyer could reply. He knew de Morell had the moral backing of the King and Marshal Soult and that if he won the case his own prestige, already at its peak, could rise even further. He walked around the polished walnut table and pulled up a chair opposite the General. He sat down with a straight back, and placed the palms of his hands flat on the table before speaking. He leaned forward so that the General would catch every word. "Do you expect me to believe that Madame de Morell didn't know what her daughter was doing?"

"That is the truth! My wife takes her social duties very seriously. She should have been closer to Marie. I am as guilty. I should have been close to both. The minute you left my house that day, I went up to Marie's room and examined her tuition books. They were of the same paper. I examined her writing and used her ink. It was the same writing except for a few amateurish flourishes to disguise it, and it was the same ink. This was my daughter. There is a close bond between my daughter and me. I blame myself. I was not close enough to my wife or daughter." He looked down at the table in shame. "Maître, are you a family man?"

"Yes. I have a wonderful wife and two sons."

"And to keep your family living at the standard they take for granted, you frequently forego your duties as a husband and father. Look! Right now, here, because of this case you have missed a whole evening with them. And to study your briefs you have missed many before. Are you, too, consumed with guilt?"

"Yes," admitted the lawyer, embarrassed by this accurate assessment of his private life. "You didn't know Emile before 1834, and yet you had strange letters in 1833. How do you explain that?"

"I didn't know those letters were by Marie. Anyway, it might not have been her. Writing anonymous letters has been a European pastime for decades, as you know. It was, as I said in court, not worth bothering about, so I threw them away."

"Have you told Madame de Morell about all this?"

"No," said the General, lowering his gaze.

"Does anyone else besides me know?"

"No. I must protect my daughter. I must protect her. You, a father, would understand that. I would die for her." His voice cracked. "Put yourself in my shoes. I can save my daughter and condemn la Roncière or I can save that whore-house fancier and condemn my daughter."

Berryer's brain had raced ahead and seen the ruin that the General would bring on himself. It also occurred to him that even if he, representing the prosecution, withdrew from the case, it would not be to his credit. It would leave a nasty smell and would not be looked upon too well by those at the top. He looked at the clock. There was so little time left, and so many questions unanswered. "And when more letters started to arrive at your house in Saumur, why didn't you tell your daughter to stop being so silly? What made you think they came from la Roncière? Didn't you recognise at once that they were from your daughter?"

"Of course I didn't! One of my officers said the writing was like that of the prisoner. I still wasn't convinced."

"You didn't think it *could* be Marie?"

"I told you, no, not at this stage."

"So," said Berryer, trying to hurry the General, "you didn't think it was Marie, but you were not convinced it was la Roncière. What made you send for him in your house?"

"Several things. He is a disgrace as a soldier. Drink, gambling, women, all that and more. That was why his father asked me to keep an eye on him."

This last statement raised a dozen questions in Berryer's mind about loyalty, friendship and trust but there was time for one question only. "You still have not given me a convincing reason for sending for la Roncière."

"It was the Cavalry School postmark on the letters. That convinced me it was la Roncière; that, together with the conviction of Ambert and d'Estouilly that la Roncière wrote them. And after that, because of the duel which la Roncière apparently set in motion, there was no doubt at all."

The General was getting too far ahead for Berryer. "How did she get them posted from the School?"

"Many of our soldiers are illiterate — I'm talking of the other ranks — and if a pretty girl like Marie gives a letter to a soldier and says, 'I think one of your officers dropped this', the man would take it into the school and, being unable to read it, he would drop it into the post box rather than own up to illiteracy. The men are very self-conscious about that. A man who cannot read will go to any lengths to disguise it so his companions don't find out. Another way she could have got them in would have been to drop them by the gates hoping that some one would see them and take them in to the post. Many must have been lost that way."

Berryer looked at the clock. It was two minutes to midnight. "You must present yourself in court." Both men got up and went to the door.

"Do you know enough to go on with the prosecution? Remember, la Roncière is not an honourable man."

"Honour," said Berryer, "seems to be a matter of comparison. We could have prevented all this if you had told me at the outset."

The General was impatient. "I didn't know at the beginning. Marshal Soult, my wife's uncle, hearing what she had done, told me that if I went on with the charges, he would help me. I told him there would be no problems."

"How would he help you?"

"The President of the court was appointed at his suggestion." They were negotiating the stone chairs down to the court.

"What else?" whispered the lawyer, trying to take the steps two at a time.

"The foreman of the jury is known to me. I think you know enough."

"I've only just begun," said Berryer, breathlessly and crossly, aware of the stink of corruption.

He just had time to ask, "Why did Marie pick on la Roncière?"

The General had opened the side door to the court room, composed himself into the distinguished soldier he liked to appear, and in measured steps of great dignity the two men crossed the arena — for that was what it had now become — to take their places for the entrance of President Férey.

CHAPTER SIXTEEN

Because of her habit of sewing sprigs of lavender into her clothes, Madame Maillat thoroughly scented the interior of the coach in which she and Marie bumped noisily over the cobblestones to the court, accompanied by Dr Olivier.

The old lady, knowing little of the case, except that Marie had received some unmentionable letters and had been assaulted, naturally thought that the young man in the dock would be some kind of monster, and took it for granted that he would have distorted features, possibly even two small lumps on his forehead, which she knew were the sign of the blood of the devil flowing in his veins.

She was not looking forward to entering the court, for, so meagre had been her education and so deeply ingrained her superstitions, that she assumed that one glance from this man's evil eye would produce in her all kinds of horrible effects from hallucinations to diabolical stigmata. She made up her mind not to look at him.

Marie, who had finally been persuaded to dress in black and also wore a black veiled hat and black gloves, was chatting inconsequentially, as merrily as any sixteen-year-old on her way to a ball. She made no mention of the case nor showed any curiosity about the questions she might have to answer, nor did she display any sign of anxiety.

Dr Olivier sat in astonished silence at her lack of concern. Psychology had been practised since the end of the seventeenth century so he knew that there was something wrong with the girl's mind. But he had never studied the science nor knew of anyone who had. His knowledge was limited to his reading of a paper by the late Anton Mesmer about the usefulness of magnets in the treatment of the mind. He had thought it was rubbish.

In the court he told a part truth when he said that there were moments when Marie would appear to see and hear nothing, when her head would flop forward and nothing would wake her.

These attacks were exceptionally rare and he had thought them to be *petit mal*, as her great-aunt had suggested. But, together with the

170

General and his wife, the doctor had agreed that the girl would be better kept away from the publicity of the court room. The doctor had no trouble in persuading Solange of this. The General's motive was far greater. He wanted Marie kept out of the box because he was afraid of what she might divulge. She could bring about the family's downfall. But the connivings of the three devious adults were in vain.

The President had insisted on her appearance and, at the back of his mind, the doctor thought this might be her salvation. He did not believe her to be guilty, as suggested by the new and terrible rumours.

The coach drew up at the steps to the courthouse and the crowd pressed forward, knowing who was in it, but saw little because the oil lamps and flares were too dim. The lamps inside the coach had been deliberately extinguished.

Dr Oliver said, "We will not open the door until a way has been cleared for us." This problem had been anticipated by the court, and two lines of officials cleared a path. A dignitary opened the coach door and helped out Madame Maillat first. She turned to help Marie.

One old woman pushed her way forward, shouting, "God bless you, my darling!" She was restrained by the officials while other cries of sympathy for Marie arose from the crowd.

So anxious were they to catch a glimpse of her that onlookers had clambered up every elevated prominence for hundreds of metres around. Some stood high on the wheels of carts, some perched precariously on statues, some even stood dangerously on the walls of the nearest bridge, but they could see nothing of Marie at all. Pick-pockets and cut-purses took advantage of the confusion and the dark.

Marie lifted her veil and smiled and waved at the crowd. Her great-aunt pulled down the veil and hurried her charge into the court. The great clock was chiming twelve.

In the court room the crowd was patchily illuminated by oil lamps and candles, making the room, already sombre by day, into a ghostly cavern of flickering lights and shadows. Key figures such as the President, the accused, the judges, the three counsel and the jury were relatively well lighted, but there was no light for the witness box or for the Press.

In the centre of the well of the court stood a comfortable armchair for Marie which had been moved into place during the last half-hour. On each side, on a plinth, stood a large oil lamp.

White-haired General de la Roncière was on his chair under the dock near to Maître d'Est Ange, while General de Morell had joined his two counsels at their table. Madame de Morell was lost in the shadows.

There was one other pool of light, not supplied by the court — a candle in a holder clipped to the drawing-board belonging to Honoré Daumier.

Next to him sat Victor Hugo, sharing the candle and making notes on a small pad. Victor Hugo had had the foresight to bring in a jug of cocoa and a mug. He filled his mug and drank from it before he realised that, as he was sharing Daumier's candle, the least he could do was to offer the artist some cocoa. He apologised for having taken the mug for himself and offered the jug. Each was aware of the stature of the other. The artist happily accepted and a friendship of mutual respect developed.

The court rose as the President and the two judges took their places. The flickering lamps, throwing light from beneath their faces, gave them unearthly countenances.

As soon as everyone was seated, the President said, "Mademoiselle Marie de Morell is about to be brought in. If there is any disturbance I shall clear the court. I hope you will restrain your natural curiosity and show the respect due to her position." He gestured at an usher who was carrying a large oil lamp. "Ask her to come in, please."

The usher went to the main double doors. Two officials flung them wide, and Marie, quite unnecessarily, it seemed, supported on the one side by Dr Olivier and on the other by her great-aunt, walked slowly up the centre of the court. A metre or so from the armchair an official took over and asked Marie to be seated. "There is no need for you to take the oath because of your age," said the President, "but you will be truthful at all times."

Marie, flicking a speck of dust from her skirt said, "Yes, I will tell the truth."

Her veil obscured her face.

"We have all heard how you received some unpleasant letters." He looked down at a paper he had before him. "In Samuel Gilieron's sworn statement he says that just after looking in vain for a letter in the drawing-room, he heard you, not many minutes later, saying that you had found a letter pinned to the wall by the staircase. Is this true?"

"Perfectly true, monsieur le Président."

"I have five separate statements from five people all unknown to each other swearing that the staircase and its surrounding walls are of a hard polished granite. Do you agree?"

"Yes. I remember Papa once saying he would like the walls faced with marble."

"How then, Ma'mselle Marie, was a pin made to pierce polished granite? It would be difficult to hammer in even a nail from a horseshoe."

Marie was silent. The question was rearranged. "How did you find a pin stuck into solid stone?" Her silence continued. "And if you did find it, how did you pull it out?" No reply. "With your bare fingers?"

172

The President did not press the point. "Several people have said these letters are in a similar hand to yours. Have you an answer to that?"

"Yes, monsieur le Président," replied Marie imperiously. "If someone is trying to implicate me, he would naturally try to imitate my writing." She added patronisingly, almost as an afterthought, "If you've seen any, you'll probably agree that they're not very good."

"We will now come to the terrible occurrence of the early hours of 23 September . . ."

Maître d'Est Ange was on his feet. "Monsieur le Président, may I ask the witness a question?"

"What is your question?"

"I have several questions about the letters. You surely don't intend to pass over them just like that?"

"We've seen the letters, and heard the evidence about them. There is no more to be said by you on the subject until your address to the jury. Please be seated."

President Férey turned back to Marie. "Tell me what happened on the night of the assault."

Marie said she had been asleep and was woken by the sound of breaking glass to see a man standing by her bed.

"Had you seen this man before?"

"Yes, monsieur le Président."

"Who was it?"

"It was Monsieur de la Roncière."

"Did he speak to you?"

"No, monsieur, not at first. I picked up the chair and tried to protect myself, he pushed it to one side, bound me with rope, stuffed a handkerchief in my mouth and took off my nightdress."

Maître d'Est Ange asked, "I would like to ask if he bound the witness with a rope and then took off her nightdress."

Marie replied instantly. "Yes, that's just what I said he did. It is exactly what he did."

"Surely," said d'Est Ange to the annoyance of the President, "it would be difficult to remove a nightdress from a person after she had been bound up?"

She replied directly, "He didn't tie my arms."

President Férey interrupted her. "Please address your answers to me."

"Yes, monsieur, he put the rope round my waist, said he'd come for revenge, hit me and kicked me. Eventually Miss Allen, who slept in the adjoining room, heard me and burst open the door. The prisoner went out the way he came in saying, 'That's enough for her. Hold tight!' "

The President looked intently at her. "Did you hear the window being broken?"

"I have just told you I did."

"Why didn't you call for help at once?"

"I was too frightened."

"What was the man wearing?"

"An overcoat and a garrison cap."

"Was he properly dressed?"

Marie looked down and hesitated before saying, "I don't know...
I..." She glanced at the jury. "I saw something when his coat fell open."

The President whispered to one of the judges. The judge nodded and the President motioned him to speak.

"What did you see when his coat fell open?"

"I don't know," said Marie in a surprisingly confident voice. "It was whitish."

There was silence. Everyone who could was looking at Marie, most could see only the back of the large chair. They all wondered what she would say next.

Somebody in the press gallery had been trying to light a candle and dropped it, breaking the shocked spell.

The President took up the thread. "Did he take off your nightdress?"

"Yes, monsieur le Président," she said with a sigh of impatience, as she flicked another imaginery speck of dust from her skirt. The tone of her voice let everyone know that she thought the President a fool.

The President closed his mouth and shuffled a little in his seat before going on. "Did he put you on the bed?"

"No, monsieur, on the floor."

"He took off his clothes?"

"No, monsieur, from what I could see, he had no need. His intentions were clear."

The other judge whispered in the President's ear.

"How did you know his intentions?"

The judge whispered again. Abruptly, the President moved on.

"Did he lie on you or beside you?"

"Neither!" Marie held her head proudly as she raised her voice. "I would not let him! I fought back!"

There was a general hubbub of approval from the onlookers. Even some members of the jury tapped the top of the barrier in front of them in recognition of this spirited defence of virginity.

The President rang his little bell. "A few moments ago," he said, "I asked that there should be no disturbance of any kind while Ma'mselle

174

de Morell gives her evidence. I call on everyone to help see that my instructions are obeyed."

There was complete silence once again. The President turned to Marie.

"When did he use a knife?"

"Just before he went."

"Did you see how he left the room?"

"No, Monsieur. I heard him shout 'Hold tight!' "

"Did you hear him say . . ."

D'Est Ange interposed to ask, "May I enquire if Ma'mselle Marie fainted because of this . . ." He paused just long enough to look round the jury as he filled his last two words with sarcasm ". . . terrifying ordeal?"

"I did not faint," said Marie.

D'Est Ange addressed the President. "Why did this witness not see how the man left the room?"

"I saw him climb on to the window-ledge. I don't know how he went from there."

The President asked d'Est Ange to sit down, then turned to Marie to ask, "When you told us he called out 'Hold tight!', who do you think he was calling to?"

"Samuel, of course, in the room above."

"Did this assault mark you?"

"Oh yes, monsieur. I still have the marks on my chest, my neck and my arms."

"If you were so badly injured, how did you manage to go to the ball on 28 September, just four days later?"

"The worst marks were on my arms and wrists so I wore long white gloves."

Marie looked around and noticed even in the gloom that she had some friends in the court room. She lifted her veil and acknowledged them with little nods and smiles.

The President tapped the bench to regain her attention. She lowered her veil.

"I'm sure you now realise the gravity of your accusation, and if proved, you know it will result in the death of Lieutenant Emile de la Roncière. Do you still say that he is the man?"

The question was answered immediately. "Yes, monsieur. There is no doubt at all."

D'Est Ange asked, "Could Ma'mselle Marie see clearly at night in her bedroom without a lamp?"

"Yes," replied Marie. "It was a bright moonlit night."

"Bright enough to see the colour of the garrison cap?"

"Certainly!" said Marie arrogantly. "It was red."

The young barrister turned to the President and asked, "May I ask the witness to repeat the colour of her assailant's cap?"

Marie answered without waiting. "It was red. I have just told you. It was red."

"Thank you," said d'Est Ange, and he repeated, "Red. Red." Before sitting down he added, "The accused was in the Lancers at the time, and the Lancers are the only regiment in France to wear blue caps. Blue, not red. Blue."

Knowing the effect of this he pretended to lose interest and fumbled with his papers while he waited for the repercussion which came, as it had to, from the President.

"What have you to say to that?" he asked. Marie made no reply. "Mademoiselle Marie de Morell, what is your answer to that?"

General de Morell, sitting close to counsel, stood up and asked, "May I be allowed to answer that?"

"No, monsieur. The question was put to your daughter."

"Can't you see that my daughter is not well? She should not have come here at all."

D'Est Ange stood up quickly and spoke fast, containing his temper and making his voice sound cold. He started quietly. "Monsieur le Général de Morell, when I asked questions of your charming wife, I was asked to sit down. She was gracious but, as you saw, I found out very little. Monsieur, I am not blaming madame, or you, for this. It was not your doing. Madame was courtesy itself. Now I question your daughter who, I hear, is very beautiful, though I am denied the pleasure of seeing her face. Again, her manners are beyond reproach. She is, you will agree, the centrepiece of this most dreadful affair and in addition she has said things once or twice which appear to condemn her. I am sure there is good reason for this and that is why I ask the indulgence of the court so that I can clear up any errors she may have made. Would you, monsieur, agree that it would be better for me to ask the questions that every man on the jury would like asked, rather than let her character appear smirched? For that is how it looks to me."

For all d'Est Ange's outward show of manners, the General knew at once what he was doing and was furious. He raised his voice at the President. "Who does this man think he is?"

The President asked the General to be seated. He would not sit; instead, scarlet in the face, and with a hand out-stretched to d'Est Ange, he continued. "That man is without a sense of propriety! He disgraces an honourable profession!"

"That is enough!" barked the President.

"No, monsieur le Président. It is not enough . . ."

D'Est Ange hoped he had correctly judged the mood of the court when he said, "I assume that Monsieur le Président will reprimand General de Morell as he reprimanded my client. Both disturbed the order of the court with outbursts. There is no difference."

The General had controlled his temper and turned on the barrister. "The difference, maître, is that I am not on trial!"

D'Est Ange looked straight at President Férey and asked quietly, "Is he not, Monsieur le Président? Is he not?"

The President rang his bell. "Gentlemen, gentlemen, please sit down."

D'Est Ange sat down, having made his point. But the General remained standing and said, "My daughter's health is at stake. Hasn't she suffered enough?"

"The prisoners have also suffered," said the President, "and it is not la Roncière's health which is at stake. It is his life."

Maitre Odilon Barrot rose and with his sheer solemnity of expression and the gravity of his bearing brought the proceedings back to the question which had sparked the disorganisation.

"I would stress," he said with his deep booming voice, and putting one hand on General de Morell's shoulder to reassure him, "that it is not for Ma'mselle Marie to divine the quirks of this prisoner. This is a man who admits to having served in many regiments. There is no reason that I can think of that he should not have worn a red cap on that particular night. And you must consider too," he went on ponderously, "that he had good motive for wanting to disguise himself. A red cap would be a great help to a man normally seen wearing a blue cap." He signalled that he had finished his oration by an outward twist of his palms in the manner of a conjuror who had just made a rabbit disappear and wanted to prove it by showing his empty hands. Even Barrot's manner of reseating himself was a performance of consequence to be observed by all the lesser lights of the court room.

The President thanked Maître Odilon Barrot for his advice, and said that for the sake of the witness's health it might be better to adjourn for a few minutes.

Marie protested that she was quite all right.

"Very well," said the President. "Now if this man was partly disguised by his red cap, and I see from your statement that his face was covered with a black handkerchief, how did you know it was the prisoner?"

This time the pause was so long that Odilon Barrot rose again only to

177

receive a signal from the President to sit and wait. The question was repeated.

Marie answered simply. "By his voice. I knew him by his voice."

The President turned to Emile. "Monsieur de la Roncière, what have you to say to that?"

"She's making it all up."

"What's the reason behind it?"

"I don't know! I don't know! I can't understand why she's doing it."

"Has the family anything against you?"

Emile shook his head from side to side and spread his arms in a gesture of despair. "I've never done them any harm, so why should they want to harm me?" Tears started to run down his cheeks. He had no control over his voice.

His counsel had the strange feeling that while he knew his client was innocent, the cause of the charges might now be revealed. He tried to remember everything Descartes had written on cause and effect and he could think of nothing that applied to this case.

Emile was shouting at the witness. "Marie! Marie! What have I done that you should behave in such a spiteful way? Worse than spiteful. What is it all for? Your father, your mother, everyone against me, and for what? For what?"

The President was ringing his bell. "I will not have these outbursts. They do not further your case. Each time I ask you a question as a reasonable man, you start behaving like this. You should . . ."

Emile would not be quiet. "The whole thing is an invention," he cried "She has made it up!"

"Will you be quiet!"

"Ask her why!" shouted Emile, kicking at the inside of the dock.

"Silence! You make it impossible for anyone to help you."

D'Est Ange had moved over to the dock with old General de la Roncière to try to quieten Emile, but he went on, "I beg of you ask her why she has chosen me. Why me? Why must I be executed for no reason?"

Between them, d'Est Ange and Emile's father persuaded him that it would be better to keep quiet for a while. When d'Est Ange was reasonably sure of his client's silence, he walked over to Marie and stood barely a metre and a half from her large armchair.

"Can you see me through your veil?"

As Marie had had very little idea of what to expect in court, this behaviour did not surprise her.

"Yes," she said. The President was curious so he said nothing.

D'Est Ange spoke in a subdued voice, "Marie, never in all my experience have I met an accused man who is, not only on the evidence obviously innocent, but does protest his innocence so forcibly. You know as well as I, that the wrong person is in that dock." Everyone had forgotten Samuel. "So I give you this one last chance to admit the possibility that you could be mistaken, and that it was not the accused in your room that night."

The firmness of her voice was touched with arrogance. "There is no mistake."

D'Est Ange went back to his table and sat down in silence.

The President asked, "Did he disguise his voice?"

"He talked in a low voice, it was not a disguise."

"A low voice is a kind of disguise."

"Monsieur!" replied Marie, her temper rising, to the surprise of all present. "I have sat next to the accused at dinner more than once. He visited the house several times, so I don't see how you are in any position to say whether or not I would recognise him. I know that was the man. You were not there, so what can you say about it? I know what he did to me! I knew him at once!"

"Ma'mselle Marie," said d'Est Ange sharply. He felt she needed a verbal slap in the face. "This court will not permit that!"

The President frowned. "I will say what is, and what is not, permitted in this court!"

"Yes, monsieur le Président, of course, naturally, please pardon me; but Miss Allen's statement says that Ma'mselle Marie was not sure at first who it was ..."

Marie's temper was mounting. "Miss Allen was wrong."

"And," added the young barrister, feeling things were going his way again, after this outburst, "in Ma'mselle Marie's written statement too, she also says she was unsure at first."

"If that is so," said Marie furiously, "then that statement too is wrong! I would know Emile anywhere!"

The President whispered to each of the judges before turning his attention to Marie.

"Ma'mselle Marie de Morell," he enunciated slowly, "with so many young cavalry officers visiting your house, and all in similar uniforms, it is possible that you may have confused one with another. So will Emile de la Roncière please stand."

Emile, looking and feeling frightened, rose and stared, unseeing, straight ahead of him. He stood at attention with his arms at his sides. The muscle started to twitch in the right side of his face. He hoped it would not show.

President Férey looked from Marie to Emile, and back again to Marie.

179

His expression seemed to carry all the weight of the law as he said, "Look at this man, and tell me if you recognise him."

Marie came slowly to her feet. She took off her hat and veil, revealing her face. The lights were near enough for those who were in front of her to see her small, white, even teeth, her red lips, her dark blue eyes. Her pale skin was emphasised by her black, wavy hair which framed her face and which had been brushed so much that it shone, catching the light of the candles and lamps around her. She took her time turning to Emile. Her hat and veil were in her left hand at her side. She raised her right hand to point at the frightened man standing in the dock.

"Yes," she said. "I recognise him. He is the man."

While Maîtres Berryer and Barrot congratulated themselves, Maîtres d'Est Ange concerned himself with one question. Twice during the evening Marie and Emile had referred to each other by their first names. He wondered if he could be getting nearer to the cause.

CHAPTER SEVENTEEN

Breakfast in the de Morell household next morning was a sombre affair. Solange took croissants and coffee in bed while the General, who was not hungry, drank coffee in his adjoining dressing-room sitting in front of his looking-glass and surrounded by polished mahogany wardrobes on top of which stood dozens of pairs of riding boots.

It was ten o'clock, and they had been awake since nine, yet not a word had passed between them. Solange, for all her sociable ways in society, was not able to communicate easily with her husband. There had been a time when they were young when they had been able to chat freely; but now they had exchanged all the trivia they intended to exchange, and when there were serious matters to discuss, matters that needed talking out, Solange was often afraid to start because her husband would immediately withdraw into long, worrying silences.

From his point of view, he did not consider that women should be drawn into discussions of serious matters like politics or the military. It was his duty, he thought, to protect his wife from such things; a woman's mind, he assumed, should only be occupied with fashion, etiquette, and social values. He had his duties, she had hers; and he knew that she was a most capable hostess, and as such she furthered his career. There were times when her intellect showed to his detriment. If she started to discuss music or literature in front of guests, he would slide the subject gently into some other sphere where he could hold his own. She was careful not to let him see that she had more brain than he, but even so, she had once accidentally revealed that she knew more about the cross-breeding of Arab horses than he did. Up until that moment he had felt that the subject of horses was a good safe one in any company. Everyone had a horse. Everything he knew about them was from experience. But she had read about them as well. He had been careful that evening not to show his feelings, but he had to admit to himself that in all subjects she was better read than he.

Because she was so well-read and such a good listener she knew that those who had power in Paris had more power than strong men in other capitals of the world. She was aware that the French capital led the country in everything from fashion to philosophy, from literature to haute cuisine. Provincials, from whatever station in life, were, through no fault of their own, out of touch and consequently inferior.

She knew that the weakness of old General le Comte de la Roncière, Emile's father, was not in his character, nor in his rank, nor in his ability, and certainly not in his position in society; it was in the inescapable fact that he was a provincial. He lived and worked where he had always lived and worked, in Boulogne, except when campaigning in days now long since gone. Socially, he was the equal of the de Morells but he did not have the ear of any powerful man in the capital, whence all ideas sprung.

It was for two reasons that General de Morell was dressing hurriedly that day, when the court was not to reassemble until after lunch.

He suspected that Maître Berryer might want to continue their conversation and de Morell did not want to discuss anything with him He had issued the order, albeit unwillingly, 'Prosecute la Roncière'. That was the strategy; the tactics were up to the professional lawyer. It was not for a military man to interfere with or alarm his legal champion with an unpalatable truth that would become demoralising in battle. He would be out if Berryer called.

His other reason for speed was that he was concerned that his case might collapse unless he took bold steps to shore it up, and strategy being more important at this stage than tactics, he was going to see Marshal Soult.

He had no reason to mention this to Solange, who was reading the newspaper accounts of the earlier part of the trial. The midnight session had been too late for the first edition.

He told Solange that he would be back for lunch, and, as she had long since given up asking where he was going, he left the room unquestioned. He said a curt 'good morning' to the servants he passed on his way to the stables, sending a boy running ahead of him to saddle his horse.

He arrived at the stables before the saddling was complete, just as the boy was having trouble with the girth; the General's impatience made him nervous and this communicated itself to the horse.

"That's not my horse. That's Chiffon, madame's horse."

"I'm sorry, monsieur, but Noix has a loose shoe."

"When did you find that out?"

"At six o'clock this morning."

The General asked why Noix has not been properly shod at once and did not bother to listen to the reply.

He was so distracted that he mounted from the right as was his custom, forgetting that almost every horse, except Noix, expected to be mounted from the left. Chiffon was already showing signs of worry, and the odd way of mounting unnerved her even more so that she started to prance around the slippery, cobbled confines of the yard.

The General understood horses. He relaxed until she had calmed down and was under his command. The slight movement of his heels against her flanks and his hands lightly on the reins reassuring the mare, he spoke gently to her, and together they made their way over to Marshal Soult's house a few kilometres away, due south in the Bois de Meudon.

Chiffon wanted to canter, but the General did not, immersing himself in one of the oldest problems in the world: getting his own way and choosing between the carrot and the stick. For Berryer he knew what the stick would be. He could see to it, via the society grapevine, that Berryer would win no good briefs in future. The carrot would be harder because direct bribery was out of the question. Reduced to military terms the problem resolved itself without difficulty. Promotion would be his if he won the case. The present Minister of Justice, he remembered, would have to retire in about five years' time. To get that job for Berryer would place him in the most coveted position in the French legal world. This was the strategy.

This would mean admitting to Marshal Soult that the case was not quite the simple affair that the Marshal had been led to believe, and time was short. Doubts, like scurrying clouds on a stormy night, ran through his head in bewildering variety. He wondered if Soult would be at home. If he were at home he hoped he would be able to see him. If he saw Soult he hoped he would not be too curious about the timing of the

182

visit. He would surely wonder why and what had gone wrong. The General did not like his uncle-by-marriage and was afraid of him. Marshal Soult could, and did, desert members of his own family when it suited him. The position of Minister of Justice, the carrot for Berryer, might have already been promised to some more worthy man, or worse, promised to a barrister who had been pushed successfully against his conscience.

After lunch Berryer was due to sum up for the prosecution. This was to be followed by d'Est Ange for the defence. D'Est Ange worried the General too; at first when he saw his youthful, inexperienced face he had not realised that it concealed a good brain and a lightning grasp of facts. He was alarmingly quick at grabbing weaknesses in the prosecution's argument. He was also a showman, a consummate actor whom the jury liked. He showed one weakness in the prosecution's favour by letting the cards in his hand be seen before he reached the summing up. The General thought again about that; it could be that he was playing small cards to upset the prosecution and was holding a bunch of aces up his sleeve.

They would almost certainly adjourn for the night after the speeches for the prosecution and defence to allow President Férey time to plan his address to the jury.

The President worried him too. He was to have put a slant on the evidence, yet he was the one who had extracted from the glazier that most of the glass from the bedroom window was found on the cobbles outside the house. He was the one who had demanded the Marie give her own evidence and not have it read from the deposition.

There had been too many moments like that for comfort. President Férey had been protecting himself more and more as the evidence was presented. Perhaps he could sense the possibility of a previously unexpected verdict and was guarding his future. The General wondered who was left whom he could trust.

It was a hot morning, but he was sweating from fear; fear of ridicule, fear of losing face, fear of disgrace, of being cast out from his own, of losing his possessions.

He allowed Chiffon to canter and the movement hid the shaking hands of General le Baron de Morell. He broke into a gallop and the gallop was not from high spirits, but from a feeling that speed was an escape. Only Chiffon enjoyed it.

The General was not alone in his fear. Old General de la Roncière had been incapable of sleep that night, and was dressed and out early. He walked round to d'Est Ange's room, where he found the barrister surrounded with papers having prepared his speech for the defence.

D'Est Ange had been up early too – not from worry, but from excitement. His speech was ready. He would not read it, but the writing of it had cleared his mind, and fastened him to important points. These he had reduced to single words written on a small card he would hold in court in the palm of his hand as an aide-memoire. He had never believed in speeches being read.

His excitement was from his conviction that the chances of winning were now in his favour.

To win this case would mean a brilliant future. He knew that every word of his final speech would be reported in the press and so, not only would he win, but he would at the same time save the character of Emile. His attitude to justice was not only seen through the eyes of a lawyer. His ability to distinguish right from wrong was highly developed.

D'Est Ange was sufficiently experienced to temper his enthusiasm with the knowledge that a jury can be unpredictable. They forgot salient points. He wanted to use a brief example of a near miscarriage of justice to demonstrate that possibility to the jury. He mentioned it to General de la Roncière, who promptly asked the lawyer to tell it to him first. D'Est Ange accepted, and recounted a case, almost parallel to this one, in which a servant girl was on trial for dragging her mistress, Countess de la Palisse, from a sofa. She was said to have laid her on the floor and forced her to drink a mixture of turpentine and other noxious substances. Next day, three letters were found in the servant's room which made it clear that the girl had planned and carried out the assault. In spite of the doubts raised by the defence, as was proper and expected, there was a line in the speech from the President of the court in which he said, "I will not prosecute this child with the full and awesome weight of the law, because there is an area of grave doubt, and this doubt has been mentioned even by the prosecution."

The jury had heard enough long dreary speeches, or they had been drawn from a group of singularly illiterate people, because they missed, ignored, or did not understand the implications of the President's warning. They brought in a verdict of 'Guilty' thus forcing the President to sentence the girl to death.

Fortunately, before the sentence was carried out, proof was found that this woman of high social rank had tied herself up, drunk the poisonous liquid, blackened her lips and breasts, and in what she intended to be thought her last words, although she was completely recovered the next day, she accused the servant of attempting to murder her.

At the re-trial of the servant, a verdict of 'not guilty' was quickly reached.

The reasons for the Countess's remarkable and by no means unique behaviour, were never discovered.

D'Est Ange went on to bring considerable relief to the Comte's mental anguish by running swiftly over the evidence given by Marie during the night, showing where she undoubtedly lied, and emphasising the absurdity of President Férey's asking Emile to stand up so that Marie could identify him.

He did not mention to the Comte that it would be difficult to draw the attention of the jury to this idiotic form of identification without incurring the anger of the President, whose speech was to be the last and usually best remembered by the jury. He too was aware that genuflecting to superiors was not to be ignored.

As he outlined to the Comte, even the story of the Countess, the listing of the lies by Marie, the value of the glazier's evidence, the totally false character reference by the fictitious Colonel Saint-Victor, the hand-writing evidence and other as yet unrevealed aces for the defence, were not enough without the key to the whole frightening affair — the cause. He must find it, and quickly.

Now that he had seen Marie in court and heard her speak, he realised that this was no plain girl trying to draw attention to herself. She was so exceptionally and outstandingly beautiful that she would be surrounded by admirers. He had also seen that this was not a demented girl living in a world of fantasy. Her lies were transparent because she lacked experience, but they did not lack intelligence and had been, with one or two exceptions, carefully planned. He prided himself that he could spot a primed and rehearsed witness, and this girl was neither; otherwise she would never have claimed, among other things, that she had been bound before her nightdress was removed. She would not have said the rope was round her waist and then let it be known that her hands were tied behind her back when Helen found her.

Each of these statements was absurd — attempted rape could have taken place simply by lifting the hem of her nightdress.

"Monsieur," said d'Est Ange, using the old man more as a sounding box than as an adviser, "I have considered that governess, Helen Allen, with great care. What is she? Twenty-three or four at the most? From what I know of girls, they must have discussed all this, over and over again, for the last eight months. It is impossible that there could be a more important topic to them. So I am certain that whatever Marie knows, the governess knows too."

"Agreed," said the Comte. "Their way of living would prevent them having secrets from each other."

"Had the lie of this attempted rape," said the lawyer half to himself,

185

"been planned, one or other of them would have seen the absurdity of it. A rope," he repeated, "round the waist of a girl in a nightdress is ridiculous, and it takes no brains to understand that! Now then" — he lifted a finger to make a point — "this means that this eight months of discussion between the two girls, technically both women — and remember that — could only have been about the cause which, to them, was more vital than how to lie their way round it. It's the cause that I have to discover."

"Maître, we both know that Emile is falsely accused, but the more I hear, the more certain I am that the girl is evil without reason. I don't think there is a cause any more than there is a cause for the occasional armed soldier to go mad and shoot his brothers in arms. You and I know this happens. You and I know there is no reason except that he is mad. This girl is mad, and like so many mad people, she is cunning and conceals her madness."

"No, there must be a cause for it all. How else could her father bring in so many to speak for her?"

"It's a father's duty. My son is innocent, but had he been guilty, do you think I would have deserted him? No! I would have defended him with my life, right or wrong. Every father would do the same, and especially for his only son. The meaning of the holy phrase 'everlasting life' is no reference to waking up in Heaven. It's about the continuation of our seed in our children, and through them to their children. There is no death for a man and woman with fruitful children. This is why a father will die for his son."

D'Est Ange had no desire to wander into an old man's philosophy, and brought him back by saying, "Your son, Emile, knows the cause. Of that I am certain. Even with his life in the balance he won't reveal it to us. Could it be that he doesn't understand, and that is why he's not told us?"

"I have told you," said the old general, "the girl is mad, and that's enough for you to stop bothering your head about this so-called 'cause'. You'll be trying to catch shadows if you try to catch that. Get down to what you know already and set my boy free."

"My speech for the defence is ready. If I keep going over it, it will sound practised and too polished. Let's go to see your boy. I think I may have stumbled on it. If I ask him outright, he may tell me."

"Ask him what?"

"We'll see when we get there."

"If you think you've found the cause, then surely Maître Berryer will have found it too."

D'Est Ange remembered that during the examination of Marie,

Berryer had spoken once only, and his attitude had changed. He wondered if it was because he had found out the cause.

"He may have accidentally stumbled on it, and, unlike me, he can't use it. Now let's get a cab."

That same morning, Marie had woken cheerful and refreshed. In Paris too she had an adjoining room next to Helen whom she sent down to the kitchen to bring her coffee, three croissants, some apricot jam, a lightly boiled egg and the newspaper.

When Helen came back some twenty minutes later, Marie was still in her nightdress and sitting on her bed.

"Put the tray there," she said, pointing to the chair, "and go back to your room. But leave the door open so we can talk. Where's the newspaper?"

"The footman says that your mother still has it."

"Go and ask her for it."

"I wouldn't dare!"

"Oh, you are silly! You wouldn't say 'Boo'. She won't eat you. She'll either give you the paper or say she's not finished with it."

"You know she doesn't like you reading the papers while all this wretched business is going on."

"Newspapers were always boring until this. I don't want to miss a word, not a word. I wonder what they said about me last night. You should have been there."

"Your mother told me to go to bed because her aunt would look after you."

"My great-aunt's a silly creature, one foot in the grave, no idea what's going on. You know the kind. And the smell! What a terrible smell of lavender! I think she stuffs her knickers with it. I heard that the scent factory in Grasse makes you choke when you're in it. It must be like sharing a coach with great-aunt. Can't do anything right while she's around. She said I was reading rubbish when she found me reading that novel there, and later she told me not to wear that lovely red and green frock. She made me go to court in black after asking silly old Olivier. As if he'd know a frock from a bandage!"

"Tell me what they asked you in court."

"Nothing I didn't expect. I think you'll find that the papers say I did better in court than you did. They hardly mentioned you. They'll print everything I said, I'm certain of that."

Helen ignored Marie's egotism and asked, "What was said about what happened in your bedroom at Saumur?"

"Hardly anything. They didn't mention you. I don't want to talk about it. Forget it."

Marie and Helen were the only two in the world, as far as Helen knew, who could tell the truth. Neither would ever mention it to a living soul, so there was no chance of anyone finding out. There was no proof, there was no witness, and the evidence had gone for ever.

Helen needed to talk about it. It lay heavy on her heart and conscience. That the truth was safe was Helen's only comfort; and at the same time the safety of the truth was the reason she would cry into her pillow nearly every night. She wished she was not so afraid of Madame de Morell. She would have liked someone in whom she could confide her secret.

She had make up her mind one Sunday to tell her priest at confession, but she never did. Instead, and probably more wisely, she had taken a coach to Mass in a village just outside Paris, and told the strange priest there. It made her feel better for a while. There was no penance that could cleanse her soul. Ave Marias and Paternosters ran endlessly through her fingers. Hail Marys were said interminably to no effect. She felt unclean all the time and found herself wishing it had all come out in court, but from the evidence so far, it was apparent that no one had guessed the obvious.

If it came out in court the entire case would be over in twenty minutes, and she could go back to her beloved father in Kent. She thought of her family and how appalled they would be if they knew of the unbreakable bond between her and Marie.

She could not tell the secret even to her mother. Her mother was one of those people to whom one could only say obvious things such as "The honeysuckle smells lovely this year," or "There was a frost last Christmas." One could ask her no questions except ones like "How is old Mrs Robinson's leg?" or "Do you think the village shop will have crumpets in October again?"

It was that life that made her take the job of governess to Marie. Cavalry officers, Saumur, Paris, high society, the excitement – they were all so different from the village in Kent. Excitement! Yes, it *was* excitement, and far, far away and beyond her imagination. It was excitement that was too much for her.

The post of governess was not quite what she had thought it would be. It seemed that Marie would study only when she felt like it. There was no way of imposing discipline, and she had not thought she might also have to be a lady's maid and sweep out her room. Hers too was the business of preparing Marie's clothes, ensuring that they were ironed, pressed, darned and put away. Marie never looked after her things, not because she was untidy, but because she had been brought up to expect someone else to do it for her.

Helen considered herself upper-middle class, several stages above the shop-keeper's daughter, and one stage below the squire's daughter. Here in France she was not quite sure where she stood. Certainly she was above the servants — there was no fraternising with them, and they did not expect it. She was not accepted by the family as an equal either, often taking meals alone except when she would pass unnoticed at a large dinner party or a musical soirée.

Marie's voice broke in on her musing. "What have you prepared for me to wear for the summing-up this afternoon?"

"You know very well that your mother has said that none of us except your father will be there."

"I want to be there for the verdict."

"You won't be. Your mother says you will not go to the court again, and she was very upset that you had to be there last night, especially as we'd been told you wouldn't be called. The summing-up isn't this afternoon. Maître Berryer will speak for the prosecution and address the jury."

"And they'll go out and convict Emile and sentence him to death."

"Of course not. The defence has to talk to the jury next."

"Can't think why he'll bother. The defence knows nothing about it. They shouldn't let him speak."

"And after him, the President sums up the whole thing so he can guide the jury to their verdict."

"Which will be guilty!" said Marie, half to herself and with relish. "It'll serve him right. He'll learn a lesson he'll remember for the rest of his life." She laughed. "It'll be a very short life after the verdict." She waited for the shocked reply from Helen but there was only silence. "I said he'll only have a short life after the verdict." Still there was no reply, so Marie jumped up and looked round Helen's door to see her kneeling before her crucifix, running her rosary through her fingers. She stopped at a large bead and started intoning the Gloria Patri. "You haven't heard anything I've been saying."

Helen looked up at her, stopped her prayer, and said, "You've no shame. You've no soul. You've no conscience. If my soul is damned, yours is doubly damned."

CHAPTER EIGHTEEN

That afternoon General le Comte de la Roncière took his customary place at the table he shared with Maître d'Est Ange under the dock, and there must have been few members of the public who did not feel a touch of sorrow at seeing the veteran hero of the Napoleonic wars wearing his full regalia of medals, his empty right sleeve tucked into his jacket as he stared straight ahead of him.

A few seconds later General le Baron de Morell came in with Solange and sat waiting for their two legal advisers, who followed almost immediately. Maître Berryer sat with Maître Odilon Barrot on his right.

General de Morell had been correct when he guessed that Berryer might call on him to discuss further the implications of the letters having been written by Marie. He had been wise to go out. But there, he thought, perhaps his wisdom finished. He had ridden to Soult's house only to be subjected to a most distressing interview by the Marshal who, beyond expressing surprise that any kind of help was needed, gave no hint as to what action, if any, he would take. When de Morell had taken leave of his all-powerful uncle-by-marriage he had a feeling that he was being dismissed, and he had left his house humiliated and frightened. He considered that the visit alone had damaged his professional life, and regretted going. All the fear of the humiliation of early retirement was overshadowed by the possibility that he might now lose this case, and with it his daughter, his possessions, his position in society and his wife. Should this happen he wondered if he would have the courage to put a pistol in his mouth.

He remembered having to identify a soldier who had done just that, and was interested to note that his features were almost unaltered, yet the back of his head had been blown off.

When Solange had received Maître Berryer she was curious to find out what it was he wanted, but he would not discuss it with her. She offered him coffee which he refused, but he stayed for about half an hour when she said she had no idea where her husband was or how long he would be. She was irritated with the lawyer because he would not confide in her. When she tried to talk about the case, he changed the subject almost rudely. She thought it was because she was a woman and supposed that he, like her husband, did not think it proper to talk of serious matters to her.

President Férey was the last to arrive that afternoon, and simultaneously Emile and Samuel took their places in the dock.

Immediately after taking his seat and without any preliminaries, the President said, "I now ask Maître Berryer to speak for the prosecution, and while he does so we must have complete silence. The ushers will let no one in or out unless I give the order." He nodded to Berryer who stood. It seemed that the whole court room was holding its breath. He looked around him slowly to make sure he had the attention of everyone. When he spoke, he did so quietly and with no dramatics.

"Monsieur le Président, gentlemen of the jury, one of the greatest generals from one of the most honourable families in this country has accused a man of writing obscene letters, of attempted rape, of assault, and of causing severe injury to his daughter." He waited, deliberately giving the jury time to absorb the gravity of the four accusations. All eyes were on him. All ears were waiting to hear the next words.

"The man who faces these four accusations is a man of evil repute, a man known for bad company and debauchery, a man who was unpardonably rude to Mademoiselle de Morell under her own roof while a guest at dinner." He passed his right hand over his hair. He had kept his voice down to make everyone listen with care. He now considered it time to give them a jolt and so he spoke loudly and as fast as he said, "My mind is made up! I have no doubts! No uncertainties! I am profoundly convinced that Emile de la Roncière and he alone" – he dropped his voice again – "is guilty." He looked round the court.

Samuel's sigh of relief could be heard by everyone. There was a faint murmur among the crowd. The President did not ring his bell to call for order, but he merely tapped his fingers on his desk. There was silence again.

"The defence has more than once asked what I think his motives could be. Is it possible that this question is intended to cloud my judgement? Am I," he asked, slapping the palms of his hands on his chest, "am I expected to tell the jury the reasons behind this man's behaviour?" He spread his arms wide. "I hope not! Some minds move in a way I am proud not to be able to understand. There is wickedness I can believe, but not conceive." He glanced up at the press gallery to be sure that they had all recorded that last statement. "It has been suggested that all this is in the imagination of Mademoiselle Marie de Morell. Imagination can't produce bites, bruises, scratches and weals on her body. The defence has accused me of bending the evidence of the hand-writing experts to my own purposes as if I have some motive outside that of pure justice." He looked puzzled and hurt as he spoke and again smoothed back his thinning grey hair. "It is well-known that the authorship of writing can't be discovered by looking at the shapes of the letters. It can only be revealed by looking at the contents of the message. It is just not possible that these letters were conceived by a cloistered girl, a girl of gentle birth and education." D'Est Ange was making copious notes while the President seemed absorbed in his own daydreams. "She was only just sixteen. Her birthday was on the fifteenth of August, just a month before. We are talking of an innocent child!"

There were nods of approval from some members of the jury. The President closed his mouth and, having caught the last sentence, nodded and made a note on his papers. Members of the press were glad to write down Marie's birthday because there had been much speculation as to her age.

"A man," said Berryer, "who has lead a debased life could write such letters. So unless expert testimony is accompanied by proof from a different source, you must ignore that testimony."

He paused to let the jury accept what he had said, and then turned to face and point at General and Madame de Morell. "There sit a mother and father!" All eyes turned to look. The General was staring unblinkingly at Emile in the dock, while Solange looked down at her hands folded in her lap. "What must their feelings have been when they were forced to conceal the shame put upon their daughter? To hide it, they had to continue entertaining, go on receiving people, go on laughing and joking so that society would not suspect the horror below the surface." D'Est Ange was wondering if Berryer could get back to any form of evidence that attacked Emile. So far, he considered, Berryer had produced no acceptable facts. This was not worthy of being called a prosecution speech. "And finally," said Berryer, "when the father thought he had silenced this man and had honourably and generously permitted him to resume his duties in Toulon, how did la Roncière repay him?" He leaned forward to the jury and raised his voice. "How? By allowing his family a brief period of peace before sending them another letter, this time threatening to expose to the whole world the monstrous lie of their daughter's pregnancy."

He went over to the dock and stared at Emile in the face. Emile did not look away. "Yes, you! Emile de la Roncière! You did that! It was you!"

Emile suddenly shocked the court by shouting, "I didn't write that letter then!" He stopped abruptly because he had confused himself, and started again. "I mean that letter was not from me. The letter I wrote was written after I had been arrested. Don't you see why I had to write it? Does no one understand why it seemed to me that the family was attacking me for no reason?"

The President rang his bell. "Silence! Maître Berryer is speaking!"

Emile countered with, "There are only half truths!"

"If you speak once more," said the President, "you will be taken to your cell below."

Maître d'Est Ange rose. "May I speak to my client for a moment?"

The President nodded. "Be brief."

"Listen," said d'Est Ange, "if you do this once more you'll lose your case. This part of the trial is not evidence."

"It's certainly not the truth. You're right!"

"I shall be answering soon, and you're making it difficult for me."

Maître Berryer walked over to the bench. "Monsieur le Président, if you please, is it usual in your court for counsel to be stopped like this?"

"I'll have the prisoner removed," replied the President.

Chaix d'Est Ange made a final appeal to the bench for his client to remain by promising there would be no more outbursts.

"Very well," said the President. "Let the prisoner remain. Now then, maître, if you feel that your argument has in any way been harmed by that interruption, I am quite prepared to adjourn."

"On the contrary," smiled Berryer. "It has served as a perfect illustration of the man. The jury can be in no doubt now as to the type of person with whom we are having to deal."

After a short pause to gather his thoughts, he went on. "Much has been made of the silence of Marie and her governess on the night of the assault. Just because they were upset and bewildered, this can't be held against them.

"What else were they supposed to do? Their silence is conclusive proof of the crime and their truthfulness. Had it been an invention, then they would have shouted to create a great disturbance, trusting to the darkness to conceal a trick."

The speech for the prosecution went on in this vein for an hour, placing emphasis alternately on the innocence and virginity of Marie, and on the black and horrifying character of Emile. Berryer's skill as an orator carried everyone with him. D'Est Ange watched the jury closely as they hung excitedly on each word that came from France's greatest orator. But Berryer's mistake was in trying to present all the flaws he thought he saw in the defence, and to present all the goodness he saw in the de Morell family; and d'Est Ange, watching the jury closely, saw their attention starting to wander. First one member looked around the court room, another man yawned, another fidgeted on the hard bench while yet another started to cough.

The rot had set in. With every minute that went by d'Est Ange became more delighted, as the after-lunch sleepiness dulled the reception of the speech. This, he thought, would make the brevity of his own speech more telling.

By sounding unemotional, Berryer was deserting facts in order to play on the sensitivities of the jury. D'Est Ange planned to present facts only, and in an emotional way.

At long last Berryer finished by saying, "If you acquit this man, France will ask you this question. 'What use will it be ever again to love and uphold justice, righteousness and honour?' " He sat down.

General de Morell was relieved. Evidently Marshal Soult must have spoken to Berryer. Berryer's speech had been strong, he thought, not having noticed the drowsy jury.

There was silence as President Férey made some notes on the pad in front of him, and put down his pen.

"It is not necessary for me to ask you for the deepest silence and concentration. The first principle of freedom is for the defence to be heard without interruption. So you must understand no one is to show any sign of approval or disapproval. We will now hear from Maître d'Est Ange."

"Monsieur le Président," began d'Est Ange, "gentlemen of the jury, I defend a man who is unjustly accused by one of the most powerful families in France. He is at the same time unjustly condemned by blind passions. We have discovered him to be an irresponsible man, but his behaviour is much the same as many other young cavalry officers, and we can't condemn them all!

"Madame la Baronne de Morell is an accomplished hostess and leader of fashionable society. Is it likely she would seat a man next to her daughter if she believed him to be a vile creature? This makes it appear she is not capable of the most elementary precautions."

He dealt with the previous letters of November 1833, written before Emile knew the family, and so carelessly thrown away by the General. The fact that they were admittedly in the same hand-writing alone showed the innocence of Emile.

"I believe the General said this to alleviate his own conscience. Or could there be a simpler reason? That I sprung it on him unexpectedly and he had forgotten the date on which he first met the accused."

He dwelt briefly with rumours that Emile had tried to force his attentions on Marie and asked the jury to reconcile this with his writing to say she was dull and stupid.

194

"But did he write this? When I first applied to the de Morell family for a sample of her writing and paper, the General sent a message in his own writing which I will read." He pulled a letter from his breast. " 'And so we must refuse your request because one does not ask for proof from me. Mine is the word of an honourable man.' "

D'Est Ange held the letter above his head so that all could see it. He took it over to where General de Morell was sitting and dropped it contemptuously in his lap. The General brushed it to the floor.

"Every obstacle was put in my way. Ask yourself why, and the answer is tied inextricably with the accused's innocence. Here are four reasons my client did not write the letters. One: no motive. Two: he could not have found and paid so many accomplices to distribute them. Three: experts have shown Marie wrote them herself. Four: the letters have fewer grammatical and spelling mistakes than are natural to my less literate client."

He mentioned the character reference by the elusive and illusive Colonel Saint-Victor. "Each of the five trails I have had time to follow has led me to the same man." Again he walked over to General de Morell, stood in front of him and pointed at him. "This is the man who wrote that reference, and I am told it is an impertinence to question him."

As he walked back to his table, the General jumped up in anger. "Monsieur le Président. I . . ."

The President rang his bell. "In all my experience . . ." He broke off, not knowing what to say. D'Est Ange filled in quickly for him.

"I hope, Monsieur le Président, that you will offer General de Morell the hospitality of the cell below this court that you offered to the accused."

The General, still on his feet, said, "This man has no respect!"

"I have," said d'Est Ange, "but it is for justice."

The President recovered himself sufficiently to say, "There is no precedent for these interruptions. First the prisoner, now the General. If there is one more such occurrence I will clear the entire court except for the press and the jury, so we can continue thoughtfully with the proceedings. Now, maître, would you like to continue?"

"Thank you. Unlike my learned colleague, I have no need to demean my argument by taking advantage of the interruption because it will not serve the course of justice."

He went quickly through the flaws in the prosecution argument, singling out instance after instance of factual evidence. For example, the architect who said it would need a forty-foot long ladder to reach Marie's room and the fact that it would be impossible to carry one even with help on a bright moonlit night without either of the guards on the bridge noticing. He reminded the jury that there were no marks left by any hooks above the room either on the roof on from Samuel's window, and such marks would be visible if a rope ladder had been used.

He took everyone by surprise when he turned and addressed Berryer, knowing that such an action was almost unprecedented. "Maître," he said icily, "you should be aware that no prosecuting counsel can stand up in court and say he is at a loss to explain anything."

Berryer was astonished. He knew that during the speech for the defence any interruption would be unpardonable. There was nothing he could do except sit still and listen with a look of contempt on his face. D'Est Ange was pleased with the effect he was having on the jury, and continued in the same cold way. "You stood here and said 'Some minds move in a way I am proud not to understand'. You implied that you are too honest a man to comprehend. Do you think that your honesty excuses you from proving anything? Because you are a man of integrity, is the jury supposed to take your word for the prisoner's guilt? I ask you time and again for proof, and all you say is 'The accused is guilty; accept my word as an honest man and convict him.' Oh no!" he protested, turning again to the jury. "Before a man is executed there must be proof. Here there is none; and there is plenty of evidence for Ma'mselle Marie de Morell having invented it all. The word of that chief witness has already been shown to be so unreliable that it cannot be used to convict Emile de la Roncière of an unreasonable, unlikely, improbable, cowardly, vile and atrocious crime. Therefore you can only say that Emile de la Roncière is innocent."

He sat down, happy in the knowledge that the jury had paid close attention to him and had shown him no antagonism. He noticed Emile smiling for the first time. General de Morell looked white. General de la Roncière watched the President closely as he made his notes. Everybody wondered what form the summing-up would take, and in which direction it would lean, so it was with some disappointment that they heard the President say, "This case is of unparalleled consequence and it is most important that I have the evening and the best part of the night in which to consider every point for each side. I have missed nothing, but the brevity of the case makes it all the more important that great care is taken to see justice done. I will begin to sum up for the jury at ten tomorrow morning. We will adjourn until then."

As soon as the President had left, d'Est Ange went over to Emile. "I'm sorry," he said. "I was hoping we would sit late. Then it might just have been possible to get in both the summing-up and the verdict and so save you another night in the cells."

"Are you that certain?" asked Emile, hopefully.

"No lawyer is ever certain of anything, but you can sleep tonight knowing that the opinion of the jury is moving in your direction. What could be better than have them go to bed with the speech for the defence to sleep on? It is an unexpected bonus for us."

General de la Roncière shook the young barrister's hand. He did not sound as optimistic as the barrister when he said, "Thank you, maître, you put up a brave and spirited show. Bravery helps win battles, but it is not just a tragic coincidence that all the bravest of my friends have been killed."

General de Morell crossed the floor to thank Berryer, but the lawyer turned his back on him. He swept his papers into his case and, engaged in deep conversation with Odilon Barrot, hurried from the court.

General de Morell went uncomfortably back to Solange and together they left by a side door. Their coach was waiting outside. The mood of the crowd, which had daily haunted the steps of the Palais de Justice, was antagonistic. They had seen the papers which had printed Marie's evidence in full and their disapproval was apparent from the occasional boo and hiss. Several people waved the headlines at the de Morells as they climbed into their coach.

They rattled over the cobblestones without speaking to each other until they were outside their house when Solange said, "I won't come to court tomorrow. I'd rather wait at home for you to come back and tell me what is to be done with la Roncière."

"He's guilty," said the General without much conviction. "He'll die."

Solange had not noticed his changed mood, and with remarkable naiveté asked, "Who pays for all this? It must be very expensive."

"The loser. It will run into thousands."

"That will mean the end of old General de la Roncière. Pity. He looks a charming man."

CHAPTER NINETEEN

The President of the court was to sum up the next morning without Emile having any idea what it was all about. He did not understand the broken bedroom window, the assault, the letters, the duel with the strange, willowy lieutenant Octave d'Estouilly, nor any of the nightmare that had been happening to him. He did not know why he had been chosen for this ghastly role, when it must be plain to everyone that he was not involved.

Breakfast was at the usual time in the de Morell household that morning, and the General had sat through it silent and morose. He looked in wonder at his daughter who chattered away and seemed not to have a care for anything. He felt he was at the gates of destruction, able to share his fears with no one. He suspected Solange knew nothing of the truth, while he himself thought he knew it all.

It was customary for Helen Allen to breakfast with the family. She, silent as usual, glanced at the General and wondered how much he knew. She suspected that he knew most, if not all, of the reasons behind the letters, because he had trebled her salary, telling her it was an inducement to stay in the country and that it was some slight compensation for the trouble she must endure. She did not believe this. She thought it was more of a bribe. The whole affair now stank of corruption.

The General finished his breakfast, and without speaking, left for the court, calling for Lieutenant Octave d'Estouilly on the way so that he could have Solange's seat.

Marie's incessant, bright, idle chatter irritated her mother, who said to Helen, "When today is over, and I don't minimise the strain it is having on all of us, I think the sooner you get back to a work schedule for Marie, the better. She needs something to occupy her."

Marie looked up and said disrespectfully, "Oh, thank you, Mama." Solange's habit of talking about Marie as if she were not in the room was annoying. "So you don't think this trial has been enough to occupy my little mind?"

"You know what I mean, Miss Allen," said Solange as she smiled patronisingly at her daughter.

Helen made no reply, her eyes filled with tears and she hurried out of the room.

"Oh, that girl!" said Solange. "Go after her and find out what's the matter."

"No, Mama. I think she should be sent back to England as soon as possible. I know you think nothing of her, so I can't understand why you and Papa hired her to teach me. That wasn't very sensible, was it?"

"Her academic ability, and her qualifications to teach you and look after your clothes are not affected by her bursting into tears all the time."

Marie started to look around the dining-room. She got up and looked under cushions and behind curtains. "Where's the paper?"

"I've stopped them being delivered until this case is over."

"Very well. I'll go out and get some."

"You will not leave this house until we hear the verdict!"

Marie jumped up and ran from the room. Solange followed her daughter but was not quick enough. Solange went straight to the main door of the house, down the short drive and into the street to look for her. There was no sign of her. Marie had gone straight to the kitchen quarters where she found the cook reading the paper she wanted. "Give it to me!"

"Yes, ma'amselle." The grey-haired, ruddy-faced woman hand it over. "There's a lovely drawing of you, and it says you're ever so pretty."

Marie found the page, which not only included the previous day's proceedings but also the midnight examination which had been too late for the early edition of the previous day.

The ownership of the paper was no concern of Marie who left the kitchen, taking a croissant as she went, and disappeared up to her room to read it carefully. She read it over many times, delighted at the stand the press had taken against la Roncière. She did not know that not all the papers had taken the same stance.

She was quite half an hour reading and re-reading the reports, during which time President Férey was engaged in summing up for the jury in an absent-minded way shown first by his opening remarks at ten o'clock when he said:

"This case is so full of emotion that I shall take great care to be dispassionate in my evaluation. Two highly respectable families are involved, and one of them therefore is bound to emerge disgraced.

"You are not here to judge simply between two individuals, you are here to judge between two great and honourable families . . ."

The irrelevance of the last sentence delighted General de Morell. So, much later on, did President Férey's five reasons which he claimed proved that Emile wrote the letters, even though he tripped up badly on the first.

"One: the hand-writing proves it." At this, d'Est Ange went over to Emile. This was seen with irritation by the President, who continued as if he had not noticed. "Two: there are expressions in them used only by the accused. Three: the letters were posted from the Cavalry School." D'Est Ange was picking up the errors made by the President. He knew that not all the letters had originated in the Cavalry School, but the jury was being told that they were. "Four: the prisoner boasted of copying the writing of many other people." Wrong again, thought the young barrister — he had boasted only of copying one man's writing. "Five:" said the President, glancing at the prisoner talking to counsel, "he confessed to the forgeries."

By this time Férey was unable to endure the whispering any longer. "You have no business to hold a conversation while I am summing up."

Maître Berryer interrupted, "Must we be subjected without restraint telling my client of an unintentional error on your part."

"Where am I in error?"

"I can make it grounds for a new trial."

Maître Berryer interrupted "Must we be subjected without restraint to this continuous harangue from the defence?"

"Maître Berryer," replied the President, "learned counsel for the defence is saying I am misdirecting the jury. If this is so, it is to the advantage of all to put it right; if it is not so, then Maître d'Est Ange knows that this is a most improper moment to interrupt and may be laying himself open to disbarment." He looked at d'Est Ange. "Do you still persist?"

"Yes, Monsieur le Président. You gave five reasons for the prosecution saying that the prisoner wrote the letters. Your first reason – 'the hand-writing proves it' – is fiction. The prosecution made much of stressing that hand-writing in itself proves nothing."

The point was conceded by the prosecution and the President told the jury to 'eradicate it from your minds'.

From there the President drew attention to evidence both for and against Emile, being weighty for the prosecution and verging on the sarcastic when speaking for the defence.

Meanwhile, Solange had found Marie reading the paper and had taken it back to the drawing-room where she rang for the cook to come and claim her property, at the same time advising her not to buy papers and leave them lying about so that Marie could get them.

Marie lay on her bed and sulked. She thought she heard someone muttering. Guessing what it might be, she jumped off it and opened the adjoining door to Helen's room to find her kneeling on the floor.

"Oh, for God's sake! What are you praying for now?"

Helen crossed herself quickly and looked up at the bright face of Marie. "You!" she said, and about to say more, she started to cry, just managing to get out, "And for myself."

The President finished his summing-up in less than three-quarters of an hour, and after formally directing the jury to find Samuel Gilieron not guilty, he sent them to their deliberations with these words. "Your conscience is your guide. It is not moved by passion. It will not allow for doubt. Your conscience will rely on truth drawn from incontestable proof. It is from these conditions alone that you can make the law stand for justice.

"Society has put into your hands its gravest, most sacred interests. Your heritage is such that if an accused man, who is innocent, comes before you, he may stand there without trembling, and with complete confidence in his own acquittal. Now you may retire."

General de Morell worried about the penultimate sentence.

The members of the jury looked about them, unsure what to do, and slowly shuffled off. One man, like most of the others, could scarcely read or write. He had come from a café half a kilometre away where he was employed as a kitchen hand to wash dishes. He was worried because both of the gentlemen who had done most of the arguing appeared to be right. He thought that Maître Berryer had been most convincing and was a man of authority too. He had used a few long words which were unusual. Then there was that other man with the difficult name who kept saying the prisoner was innocent, he was believable too. The café hand turned to the man next to him as they found their way into the jury room. "What d'you make of it?" he asked.

"Oooh! I don't think we should say much. These are all grand people. How could chaps like you and me say what was going on? There was something though. But I dunno what."

The jury sat at the sides of a long table and for a half a minute or so chatted amongst themselves. One man stood up. He had a voice of authority when he announced, "We must now appoint a foreman." He looked around him and chose the worst dressed of those present, and pointed at him. "Would you like to be foreman?"

The poor man was at a loss to answer. He did not know what 'foreman' meant, and had no idea of his duties. He shook his head without replying. "In that case," said the man of authority, "unless there is strong disagreement by at least five of you, I'll do it. I've done it before." He did not stop to take a vote but walked to the head of the table and sat himself in the chair there.

He took command at once and went over the case as he saw it. Most of the others were grateful to him.

Using convoluted sentences, he now and then asked for a show of hands. Few were quite sure what he meant, but as they did not want to appear ignorant, they followed the lead he gave with gratitude. There seemed to be one or two awkward jurymen who did not agree with the leader.

Solange was sure of the outcome of the trial, so sure that she had had time to discuss lunch with the cook and order a cold buffet because she did not know when or how many would be coming. Perhaps, she thought, the verdict would come well after lunch, so there would be just three for the meal.

There were three for lunch: Solange, Marie and Helen. They received a message that the jury had retired shortly before eleven, and at half-past one they sat down to eat. Marie and Solange ate with their usual appetites, Helen hardly touched her food. Every move by a servant on the stairs or in the hall she thought might be a messenger with the verdict.

As soon as Solange had left the room, Marie and Helen went into the General's study, a little room filled with books and still called the library. It was normally used by the General for reading his newspapers and writing military reports.

"I can't make you out," said Helen. "I'm so afraid, and you don't seem to care at all."

"Why should I? I've done nothing."

"But you must know what you did! If you think it's so obvious that Emile did it, why didn't the jury come back after a few minutes and say so?"

"And if you're so frightened that they'll understand, why haven't they come back and said 'Not Guilty'?" Marie laughed and went on. "I'll tell you why!" She was getting excited. "They'll no more understand what's happened than a duck understands why a fox can take it when it feels like it. Like the ducks, they can sense something is wrong. They know that Emile is involved or what the hell is he doing in the dock? That's why they'll find him guilty!"

Helen gave a sad shake of her head, picked up an old newspaper, threw it down again and said, "Everyone in the world must know by now that you wrote the letters."

Marie stopped her. "Have you forgotten what you did?"

Helen ignored the interruption and turned on Marie. "Everyone knows except your mother and that dolt of an artist, Octave d'Estouilly. They must be quite blind to the facts."

"No!" said Marie with a little laugh. "They'll be proved right. You'll see!"

Helen sat down suddenly in the big shiny leather armchair. "Suppose," she said, "just suppose I tell what I know."

"You wouldn't dare."

"Why not?"

"You'd be arrested for one thing or another."

"How do you mean?"

Marie's smile turned to a laugh as she explained, "You see, if you prove anything different from your evidence in court, you'll be arrested for perjury. That would means several years in gaol. If you tell the papers after the verdict and they don't believe you, or you tell the court, but they think it's nonsense, they'll say you're trouble-making against my family. Papa is an officer under the crown and so you could be arrested for treason. Which will you take, treason or perjury?"

"A verdict of not guilty will ruin your father and mother through no fault of theirs."

"And you and I are the only ones in the world to know why; who know the reason, the real reason."

"You can still save your soul," said Helen, "by telling the truth before the verdict is announced."

Marie laughed again, and picked up a stiletto that her father used as a paper-knife. "I've just realised what all this is about! I know! It was the President when he said the noise of the window breaking in my room should have woken you! Otherwise, as he said, you wouldn't have woken for the low voices later. That's what it is. You're scared that they'll find out that you broke the window. You're scared! That's why you want to give it all away." She tapped the blade of the stiletto on the palm of her left hand. "You won't get the chance to spoil it all. You won't get the chance!"

"Does the truth mean nothing to you?" asked Helen, not noticing the stiletto. "Don't you know that God watches your every move?" She was deep in the shiny armchair and Marie was standing over her.

"All this piety is fright. You're scared!"

"I'm frightened because I'm alone. I've no one to talk to about it all."

Marie was waving the point of the stiletto at Helen. There was a look in Marie's eyes that she had never seen before that alerted her. Marie said, "You can talk to me about it all. Any time you like. I wouldn't like to think of you talking to anyone else. Of course, you can talk to God about it as long as you do it silently so no one else can hear. You've very close to God. And at this minute you've never been closer."

The shiny armchair had high arms and a tall back with large wings which made it a trap.

"What are you going to do?" asked Helen.

Marie did not reply.

"What are you going to do?"

The door opened and Solange came into the room. Helen got up and dodged past her.

"What's the matter with her now?" asked Solange.

"Nothing," said Marie vaguely, the almost hysterical excitement dissipating. "She gets funny ideas, that's all."

"What have you been saying to her?"

"I've just told you — nothing." Marie flopped down into the arm-chair. "Oh well, we were talking about the newspapers, and they hadn't said much about her, so she didn't like it when they said I looked pretty."

"I wish the newspapers would leave us alone."

"Did you see the drawings of me by that cartoonist? They were very good. So good that people outside recognise me."

"You've not been out alone."

"No, but yesterday afternoon Helen and I went for a walk in the Bois and as we crossed the road a knot of people — there were some newspaper men among them — recognised me. One of them shouted, 'There she is, that's Marie, the one it's all about!' and one or two in the Bois recognised me too. Helen got cross because I waved back to them. She even got cross about the glass."

"What glass?"

"You know perfectly well, Mama. The glass that fell into the bedroom. The glass that the glazier said he found outside."

"That man was just a peasant, he couldn't be expected to be exact. He'd forgotten, that's all."

"I know that!" asserted Marie. "But suppose, just suppose, that Helen had also forgotten whether the glass had fallen inside or outside the window . . ."

"Well?"

"It would have looked so bad for you and Papa, wouldn't it? So would that Colonel Saint-Victor thing. I suppose Papa really has met this colonel?"

"Most certainly. He was here one evening, I think it was last Wednesday."

"Mama," said Marie, looking sideways at her mother, "did you see him yourself?"

"No, Papa saw him in this room. It was quite late at night."

"Just before you went to bed?"

"Yes, why?"

"I thought so! I thought so!" exclaimed Marie "That wasn't a colonel. That was a man called Monsieur Lefevre."

"That's not what your Papa told me. Anyway, what makes you think so?"

"I heard him announced, and I listened over the staircase as he went. I heard Papa say to him, 'Thank you, Monsieur Lefevre, and I'll see you get the full amount when it's over!'"

"When what's over?"

"I didn't know then. But I had a pretty good guess when I saw him again in the middle of the night in court."

"Why? What is this all about?"

"Monsieur Lefevre was sitting on the jury."

At that moment there was a knock on the door and Helen came back looking quite composed. "I'm sorry I ran out just now. I thought I heard someone come into the house."

"No," said Solange. "I keep thinking someone has come back with the verdict too. Perhaps we should all go back to the drawing-room and wait there. I don't want you to be alone at a time like this."

"Neither do I," said Helen looking at Marie. "I certainly don't want to be alone."

They crossed the hall, and went into the drawing-room to sit and wait. When Solange left to speak to the cook about supper, Helen told Marie that she had written it all out so that if anything happened to her, someone would find it and know what Marie had done. Helen said she would leave the house for ever as soon as possible and she would take the damning paper with her.

"What's written on it?"

"Everything you want kept secret, including your threatening me. You're quite safe, Marie, provided I leave this house as soon as is reasonably possible."

Solange came back and the three sat and waited for the verdict. They waited an hour, two hours, three, longer. There was no conversation.

In the boulevards, the cafés, the restaurants, the multitudes of work-rooms, the farms and the houses all over France, people waited. Everywhere there was argument for and against Emile as all the papers were bought and read and re-read. The mood of those who had read all the reports so far was shifting in favour of Emile. But news travelled slowly, so this change of mind was around Paris only.

As the afternoon changed subtly into the gold light of the evening, the old men came out to drink coffee or wine, and play boules. Nothing was done for its own sake. It was done to fill in the time until the verdict was announced.

Slogans were chalked up. Some said, "Death to la Roncière — Rapist!" Others said, "Death to Marie — Liar!"

There were a lot of people who said openly that it was a put-up case by the government to distract the people from the agitation of the republicans fed by the rising labour discontent, and that there were no such people as Marie and Emile, merely an actress and an actor paid to give substance to the lie, and a focal point for the fictitious trial.

Many of the Paris theatres were empty because the patrons were afraid they might miss the verdict. Several of the more enterprising of these places put out placards saying that when known, the verdict would be announced from the stage.

As darkness fell, Solange became worried about the verdict for the first time. She was still sitting with Helen and Marie, and said, "The verdict must come tonight? Mustn't it?"

"I don't know," said Marie. Helen did not speak.

"I can't stand this terrible waiting." No one responded. "I don't see why we have to wait. He's already confessed. You two have no doubts, have you?" She waited. "Have you?"

Helen ventured, "That he's guilty, or that they'll find him guilty?"

"It's the same thing," replied Solange, but as Helen stared unblinking at her she hesitated. "Isn't it?"

"He's not guilty," said Helen.

Marie jumped to her feet, and shouted, "Shut up!"

"Don't talk to Miss Allen like that! What is it that you two know? There's something you haven't told me. Isn't there? Isn't there?"

At that moment two horses could be heard galloping up the short driveway. Two men dismounted. All three women in the drawing-room stood and stared at the door.

General de Morell strode in, followed by Lieutenant Octave d'Estouilly.

CHAPTER TWENTY

The General, with Octave a couple of paces behind him, stood in the doorway and looked at his daughter. Slowly his gaze moved to Helen, who thought she was going to faint. He looked hard and long at his wife. For a few seconds no one spoke.

Octave d'Estouilly quietly closed the door behind him.

"Emile de la Roncière," said General de Morell, "has been found guilty on all four charges."

Solange whispered, "Thank God!"

The General turned and jerked the gold, silver and red ornamented bell pull.

Marie asked very softly, "When do they guillotine him? Or will he be shot?"

"Neither," said her father. "He will not be executed."

Solange protested. "But that kind of assault is a capital offence."

"Surely, Papa . . ." but that was as far as she got when her father spoke over her.

"He will not be executed." At that moment a man-servant came into the room in answer to the bell. The General ordered, "You will close all the shutters to this house, and you will see that all doors leading into the house are locked and bolted. No outer door will be opened except on my orders. Whatever anyone else is doing, stop them, and get help so that we are sealed off as quickly as possible until daylight at least. Start on the ground floor. I will look after this room myself. Use the minimum of light. There is no need for alarm. I have detailed a contingent of infantry men to guard this house, and they will be here within the hour."

"Yes, monsieur," said the servant with astonishing calm and he went out to obey his orders.

"What on earth are you doing?" demanded Solange.

At that moment Marie went to the window and looked out. "Mama! Papa! There's a crowd of people crossing the road and coming to the house."

"Close the curtains," ordered the General.

"But they've come to cheer me," said Marie.

"I said close the curtains. Miss Allen, put out all the lights except for that little oil lamp on the table in the corner."

Helen went round and blew out the lamps helped by Solange.

"Marie!" said her father. "I told you to close the curtains and come away from the window."

"They're going to cheer me! Listen to them!" said Marie.

Helen went over to the window and drew the curtains saying, "No! That's not cheering. Listen again." At that moment the strange sound of the multitude mumbling in discontent could be heard.

Solange was at a loss to understand, and said so. Helen said the verdict of guilty was an unpopular one, and therefore they must expect trouble.

Marie rounded on her and suggested she went to bed. Solange ignored Marie's rudeness and asked, "Surely now that they've found him guilty, our troubles are over?"

"This," said her husband, "is the beginning of trouble, not the end."

She looked at him in wonder. "That's what Madame Jardinier said last week. It can't be true. How can it be true? I wish those terrible people would go away. They're making me nervous."

Marie had another peep through the curtains, closing them quickly after her. "They're right in our driveway!" There was another upsurge of discontented murmuring from the crowd.

Just as Marie stepped back from the window there was the crash of glass behind the curtains, and with a great thud a brick, halted briefly by the heavy curtain, rolled noisily under it and across the polished parquet to come to rest on a Chinese carpet.

The General ordered his family to move close to the fireplace. He took the small oil lamp from the table and pulling back the curtains, opened the French window and walked out on to the large balcony, the waist-high ornate wrought-iron railings offering no protection from the crowd. He was followed by a nervous Octave d'Estouilly, and the crowd booed loudly.

"Silence!" he shouted. "Silence!" And the accustomed authority in his voice quelled the noise. A small pebble struck the masonry above his head to rattle harmlessly on to the balcony. There was a three-quarters moon so he could be seen as clearly by the crowd as he could see the people below. He held the lamp close to his face to be seen the better.

"Go home!" he ordered.

The crowd booed.

"You weren't in court to hear the evidence."

The crowd booed again, this time not so loudly because they knew he was going to say more and did not want to miss it.

"If you didn't hear the evidence, how can you say what the verdict should be?"

There was a stronger wave of shouted vulgarities and cat-calls.

"All right, then! If you have a leader, let me talk to him. I am willing to talk to any two of you. Two only because it is impossible to talk to a crowd. Who will come forward?"

There was no reply. A large stone just missed the General and struck Octave d'Estouilly in the chest, doing him no harm short of a bruise and a dust patch on his uniform.

"Will no one come forward?" The mass was silent. "Then go to your homes. All of you!" Another stone was thrown, breaking more of the already damaged window. "Within five minutes a contingent of infantrymen will be here. They will put you down if you're still in this mood. I advise you, for your own safety, to go home."

He spotted a woman with a small boy on her shoulders. "You! Woman!" He pointed at her and the crowd turned to see whom he had singled out. "What are you doing here with a child? Do you want him killed? Take him home at once."

The message got through to the mob and slowly they dispersed, melting into the shadows of the trees of the Bois. The General lingered

208

on the balcony peering into the gloom of the night. Faintly at first, he could hear the tramp of marching feet. Not until he could hear the orders being given and see the soldiers for himself did he come back into the house, closing the windows and curtains behind him.

"Put the lights on again," he said as he sank into an armchair. "It's all right. We have our guard."

Octave picked up the large brick and wandered uselessly about the room with it, wondering what should be done. He thought of putting it in the fireplace, changed his mind and put it behind the curtains with the broken glass.

Slowly the room grew bright as lamp after lamp was lighted. Solange offered Octave a chair, and he sat next to Marie who was flushed with excitement. Helen sat at one end of the large sofa. Solange perched on the harpsichord stool, and after a long silence said, "If la Roncière is guilty of assault I don't understand why he will not be punished."

"I didn't say that," said the General. "I said he will not be executed."

"Why not?" asked Marie having difficulty controlling her voice.

"Because," said her father, "the court has made a special ruling."

"Why should they?" asked Solange.

"We must not question their methods. There were extenuating circumstances, or so they said."

"Papa, what does that mean?"

"Deportation for ten years."

Solange was curious, but knowing she would get no more from her husband, turned to Octave d'Estouilly. "Did the President announce this?"

"Yes, madame. It was originally a recommendation from the jury which the President said he was glad to accept 'under the circumstances'."

"What circumstances?"

"That's what I don't know. He didn't enlarge on it. He made it sound as though there is some excuse for la Roncière's outrageous behaviour. What possible excuse can there be?"

The General was frowning. He wanted to stop the conversation. "This is not the time to discuss it."

"But monsieur," said Octave, "I'm sure you understand that this puts your family in a very bad light."

Both men had been barracked as they left the court and some women had spat at the General.

"Other people," said Solange, "will think there is something strange if you leave it as it is. There must be some . . ."

The General held up his hand patiently to stop her. "My dear," he

209

said, "you must see it is something we cannot discuss now. Honour is satisfied."

"It is not!" argued Solange, quite insensitive to her husband's humiliation. "It can't be allowed to rest here. I for one," she said, clenching her fists, "will not allow it. You, Lieutenant d'Estouilly, can see my point!"

Octave, too, for all his artistry, was incapable of sensing the mood of others, but he had a feeling that something was wrong and he was embarrassed at being drawn in. He looked to his general for a reply.

"You must let me do what I think best," said the General quietly to Solange who ignored him and said to Marie, "Take Miss Allen and Lieutenant d'Estouilly into the dining-room. There's a cold supper for you." She wanted to be rid of them so she could talk to her husband alone.

As soon as the door had closed behind them she started. "Of course you can't let it rest with la Roncière being deported for ten years." Her temper was rising and she was having difficulty in keeping her voice subdued. "I will go tomorrow and ask the President what I can do. It's our name now that will suffer if I don't."

He was on his feet in a second and now he did not bother to control his temper. "Haven't you done enough damage for one life-time! We would never have reached this point if you hadn't driven me to prosecute!"

"I did what? Drove you?"

"Yes. There would have been no prosecution if you had kept the letters to yourself. Now the whole of Europe knows of something which would have died a natural death if the problem had been left to solve itself, and burn itself out."

"What are you talking about? Solve itself! How could it?"

The General was loath to tell Solange what he knew. She kept impatiently tapping the back of her right hand in the palm of her left, while her husband stared blankly ahead of him and said nothing.

There was the sound of raised voices from the dining-room. Marie was trying to get Octave to tell her why Emile had not been given the death sentence.

"And why did they let Samuel go?"

Helen was desperately thinking how she could get away from the house that night. The idea of a room with an adjoining door to Marie's room terrified her. Somehow she must contrive a way of seeing the General alone because he knew all the secrets of his daughter except this new secret, the pent-up violence which would explode if she was not given her own way. The sentence on Emile was not death, and so, she reasoned, Marie could become vicious with frustration. She turned her back on Octave to face Marie. "Isn't it enough that Emile is being deported?" she asked. "What else do you want on your conscience?"

"Why," asked the astonished Octave, "should anything be on her conscience?"

"All right!" said Marie to Octave. "Think this out! If they've let Samuel off, then he could not be the one to put Emile's letters round the house. And," she said as she turned to look at Helen, "if he didn't do it, it must have been someone else."

"Oh, stop that," protested Helen, remembering thankfully that she had packed her travelling box a couple of days ago and was living in clothes that were taken from the top tray. If she could get a coach, she had only to close the lid, get the servants to carry it downstairs to the drive and she would be away.

Marie would not stop. "Who else could write such well-phrased letters? Remember, they said they were well-spelt, good grammar, and so on. She's a governess, she uses the English letter 'V' and the exercise-book paper . . ." She stopped and ran out of the room back to the drawing-room to open the door just as her father was saying, "Emile did not write those letters."

She heard it and without hesitation said, "No, Helen Allen wrote them, and had them posted from the Cavalry School by Emile. Didn't you know they were lovers? The others she put round the house herself. Samuel helped her, naturally."

"But they let him go," said her mother. "And why would Miss Allen do a thing like that?"

"Remember what they said?" Marie did not wait for an answer. "One said I was ugly and dull. Only another woman, a jealous woman at that, could write such a sentence. It was because I was getting all the attention from the officers. She, dull little mouse, got none. She was envious."

The General said nothing. He was biting his lower lip. Her mother asked, "But if you are right in saying that Miss Allen was having an affair with la Roncière, she had no reason to be envious of you. She was getting his attention."

"She wanted more! More! More! She hated any man looking at me. And we are rich while she is poor." Marie paused and like a cat spitting said, "She had every reason for envy, spite, jealousy, hate." She searched frustratedly for more odium and was momentarily silent.

The General put a restraining hand on her arm. "Don't go on, please, my darling. Stop."

She sprang away from him. "All this trouble has been caused by that governess and her beloved Emile! The lengths they went to just to upset us all. Letters in the hall, letters from the Cavalry School, letters . . ."

"Please stop!" said the General, terrified that she would give herself away.

She went on. "Found in the music-room, they were all over the place. There was even one in a new cigar box . . ."

"How did you know about that one?" asked her mother.

"Of course I knew. Samuel had put it there, and you Papa, questioned him about it. He told me."

"Please, my darling . . ." said her father doing his best to halt this outburst.

She was not to be stopped. "I think the bit in one of them about you, Mama, having a lover was going too far, don't you?"

"How long have you known about Miss Allen, and why have you never mentioned her before?"

"I thought it would all come out in court."

Solange knew her daughter well enough to know there was something more than strange about her manner. Perhaps, she thought, it was the relief at the trial being over. It had been a strain on all of them. She thought back over the horrible experience she had had when she opened the iron box and read all those letters. They had been foul and they had all been reproduced in court. She had not had a lover as was written in the letter Marie had just mentioned. She remembered — that letter was not copied out for the court. It was not among those she took to the Préfecture. She asked, "What happened to that dreadful letter saying I had a lover? It was never read in court."

The General knew, and was afraid his wife might recall it was the one found in the cigar-box.

"Oh yes," said Solange at her husband. "You burned it, of course. I'm so glad you did. It would have started another line of gossip if it had been read out."

The General tried to steer her away from it by saying, "La Roncière is sentenced and that is enough."

Solange's mind went back to the Saumur drawing-room and like a picture in her head she could see her husband burning the letter, crushing the ashes and sweeping them behind the flower vase in the fireplace. Very softly she said to Marie, "If Emile or Miss Allen wrote that one, how do you know what was in it?"

Marie stared at her mother. "You're mistaken. It was with the others. I read it in the papers."

"Enough is enough!" said her father.

Helen and Octave had just come into the room behind Solange so she did not notice them. "That letter was burned at once, Marie, so how do you know what was in it?"

Marie had seen them both come in; her father and mother followed her eyes and saw them too.

"Say how you knew," demanded Helen, not knowing to which letter they were referring but knowing this would expose her. "Tell them. Go on!"

Octave stood there wondering what was happening. The silence was broken only by the shouts from the infantrymen guarding the house. A dog barked in the distance. Octave closed the door behind him. The General turned his back on the other four and gripped the high mantelpiece with both hands while he stared at the flowers in the chimneyplace. A late cab clattered over the cobbles of the road but it was some time before the silence in the room was broken.

Without looking up, the General said, "Lieutenant d'Estouilly, I wanted you to go before this happened. Now it is too late. I must speak to you, so please wait. Solange, take Marie to her room."

Solange, now standing by the harpsichord, turned away from her daughter. She made no other movement. The General turned to Helen. "Miss Allen, you will take Marie to her room."

This was a moment she dreaded. Marie was staring at her and making her feel trapped again. She summoned up all her courage because what she was wanting to say seemed impossible. The General was waiting for Helen to carry out his order.

Instead she said, "Monsieur, as I can't do as you tell me, you must consider" — she searched frantically for the right words — "you must consider my employment in your household at an end."

The General looked unbelievingly at her. "But Miss Allen . . ."

"I would like you to arrange for a coach, please, to take me to a hotel in Paris for the night, and tomorrow I will make arrangements from there to go home to England. My travelling box is already packed, because I knew I had to leave as soon as the trial finished. You know why this is so."

The General looked at the ground. "Yes, I know, but you can stay until the morning surely . . ."

"I must leave at once. I want no kind of association with Ma'mselle Marie, not even for a minute, so I will wait down in the kitchen with the servants and ask one of them to go up to my room to fetch my box for me. Can you spare me a coach, please?"

Looking away from her and in a scarcely audible voice the General spoke. "Yes, of course. Tell the coachman to take you to an hotel. When he comes back he can tell me where you are and I will send on what money is owing to you."

Marie was looking very angry. Helen turned to Solange. "Good night,

213

Madame de Morell, and goodbye, Monsieur, goodbye." She nodded to Octave and left the room.

The General turned to Solange. "Please, my dear, please take Marie to her room."

"Very well."

"No," said Marie, "I don't want her." She walked over to her mother. "Goodnight, Mama." She kissed her, but there was no response. Turning to Octave, she said "Goodnight, monsieur." to which the embarrassed man replied, "I — er — goodnight, Ma'mselle Marie."

She went over to her father. "Goodnight, Papa." She hugged him and he kissed her, saying, "Goodnight, my little girl. Don't worry. Leave it to me." He put his arms round her and held her close as she started to cry and sob. "Oh Papa! Papa! Papa!"

She let him go and, with her mother, she went out and up to her room, leaving her father alone with Octave, who was ill-at-ease, mystified and badly shaken.

"Lieutenant d'Estouilly," said the General as soon as the door was closed. "Remember this well."

"Monsieur?"

"If anyone discusses my family, he will instantly be dismissed the service."

"Is it right that an innocent man . . ."

"That will be all!"

"The letters?" asked Octave, still unsure.

"No, he didn't write the letters. It is as you heard. My daughter wrote them all."

"Oh dear," said Octave feeling as inadequate as his comment. He wanted to ask questions about his wretched duel and many other things. Instead he repeated himself and said, "Oh dear."

"La Roncière did not write the letters but that is not sufficient reason for me to sacrifice my daughter, my name, my position, my considerable contribution to this country. It would mean the end of all we stand for if I had to sacrifice my child. With her would go a way of life respected by all who love order."

"But, monsieur . . ."

"Put yourself in my position. Here I am, one of the most respected generals. When there is trouble, who do they send for? Me. Never once, mark you, never once have I let a riot get out of control. If what you now know were to be made public, the state would lose a valuable servant in me. And what is the loss of la Roncière? Nothing!" The General could see that Octave was shaken. "Of course, it is not right that the man should have to suffer like this, but life is cruel. The older you get the

214

crueller you realise life is. There are also some matters that ..." He
stopped, feeling he had made his point.

Octave felt sick and wanted to leave, but the General had his back to
the door, and there was no escape. He was appalled at his own foolish-
ness at having sat through all the evidence in court, having wondered
again and again about the parts that did not fit, and only now was he beginning to see beyond his own short-sightedness.

The General was talking again. "There are times when for the sake of
honour it is expedient to come to one conclusion. So I want your word as
an officer and an honourable man that you will never speak of this
again."

Octave looked at the General and saw a simple man driven by something he could not understand; yet this same man was talking of respect,
of love and of honour.

"If I don't have your word, I must assume you will talk of what you
know. If you do, I shall have to bring an action for slander against you.
The prosecution will be conducted by that most able Maître Berryer,
and your past will be presented in court on a sworn statement by Colonel
Saint-Victor. Now, monsieur, your word!"

Octave wondered if this were not a nightmare. In front of him stood
General le Baron de Morell, a great and loved man whose administrative
genius allowed for any contingency, a man who banished fear with his
left hand and held the key to respect in his right, a man who with a single
speech could rally cowards to startling acts of bravery for the sake of patriotism, a man who would march at the head of his men, ignoring and
laughing at the possibility of death, a man who gave wise counsel to Marshal Soult and the King. He was a man for whom, only that day, Octave
would have laid down his life had he been asked, and now he saw that he
had not heard beyond that compelling voice, not seen beyond that uniform. He saw the man for the first time.

"A charge of slander," said the General, "is a serious matter, and you
could not hope for promotion after that. As things are," went on the
voice from the uniform in front of him, and in the tones that had always
commanded attention, "you have very good prospects." The stink of
corruption was unendurable.

To his surprise, Octave felt himself suddenly relax. He could not explain to himself why he no longer felt nervous, ill at ease and in awe of
the man before him who was now asking, "Would you deliberately jeop-
ardise your future? Will you deny France the right to a fine officer for
that debauched prisoner? Think clearly where your duty lies."

Octave looked his general straight in the eyes and moved closer to him.
"Mon Général, you have my word."

"Thank you. Good night." The General stepped to one side to allow Octave out of the room.

Octave did not go at once. Instead he turned and said, "You have my word that I will not gossip about you or your family. Not because I am afraid. My personal loyalty to you has exceeded my duty. The whole of France will know by tomorrow what you have done. I shan't tell them. I shall not need to."

"What do you mean by that?"

"You, general, have abused your rank. You have abused my trust. You have abused your country. You have corrupted its servants. I must resign my commission, and I am sure other officers under your command will follow my example."

"How dare you! Why should they?"

Octave opened the door. "Because you can no longer inspire loyalty. I can find my own way out, thank you."

The General sat down wearily in the big armchair and stared at his boots. It seemed that in winning, he had lost everything except the one he loved most of all, Marie. He remembered there was food and wine in the dining-room set out for a celebration. He did not want any of it. He could hear the contingent outside guarding the house and considered that too might have been a mistake. There might be questions about it. Marshal Soult was sure to find out.

Eventually Solange came down from seeing Marie to bed. She was alone, and the first thing she said was, "Why didn't you tell me everything?"

Almost too exhausted to reply he said, "I thought you knew."

"You've never been close enough to tell me."

"And you were not close enough to Marie to find out," he said.

"This is not the time for recriminations. When did you know?"

"There wasn't an exact moment. It was possible that Marie was writing the letters until they came from the Cavalry School. I had no way of telling that she must have written dozens and either left them in the road for some soldier to pick up and post or give them to illiterate soldiers who posted them anyway."

"But what was it all about? It wasn't just letters. There was the assault, and the blood on the floor to prove it."

"Miss Allen and Marie broke the window. I don't know which one did it. It had to look like an assault because of the blood and the pain Marie was in . . ."

"But what was it?" she asked.

He was not sure where to begin. It seemed extraordinary that his wife did not know even that much about her own daughter. There had been

216

moments when he was certain that Solange knew what was the matter with her, but it had not been discussed because of mutual embarrassment. He had to share it with her now if only to get it off his own chest. "Now then," he started bluntly and promptly changed his mind. It was too aggressive an approach to a difficult subject. Very carefully he began again. "Do you remember the time when you were afraid that Marie had somehow become . . ." Again he could not bring himself to say it.

She said it for him. "I thought she was pregnant twice. I never forgave myself for that. It was an obscene thought."

"But," he said very quietly, "you were right. She was pregnant the first time. Not the second."

She stood motionless for a few seconds. "What makes you say that? How could she possibly get into such a condition without my knowledge?"

He looked at her and for the first time in his life thought her naive. "Many girls get into that state without their mothers knowing."

"But how do you know?" Solange was angry.

"Do you remember," he asked, "that I found a letter in her room early that morning when you were comforting her?"

"Yes, yes. Just another filthy one." She was still not used to the idea that Marie had written them.

"No," he said, "it was not quite like the others, because the last line said something about 'you can be happy if you command Marie to marry me'." From there he told his shocked wife how their daughter had had a lover. He told how she had miscarried, and in her pain and distress she had called for Helen Allen.

"Why didn't she call for me?" asked Solange.

"Because neither you nor I have ever been close enough to her to gain her confidence." He explained that there had been a lot of blood. The floor-washing and Marie's debility from the miscarriage of a pregnancy not many weeks old had used up the missing four hours. He said that somehow Miss Allen had managed to contain the real evidence in Marie's nightdress and it had been hidden until the evening of 25 September. It was during that afternoon that Emile de la Roncière was told to get the coach to Tours and thence to Toulon. That evening the General had been looking from a window high up in the house and had seen Miss Allen throw something white into the river. From where she was she could see it drift away but he could see it catch in some reeds a little further downstream. Suspicious, he waited until nightfall and with a lantern and a stick he went down to investigate the bundle. That, he explained, was how he knew it had been a short pregnancy. His wife put her hands over her ears at that point.

He waited patiently for her to listen to him again, and he explained that the letter on her table was to get them to compel Emile to marry her.

Almost to herself, terrified even to ask, Solange had to find out. "So la Roncière would have been the father?"

"No. They had never met except in this house and under our protection. He had been here so often that they were naturally on Christian name terms."

"Who would have been the . . ." She could not bring herself to say "father" again.

"She's never said. It may have been someone of lowly station, or of inadequate means or possibly . . ." His distorted, strained mind discovered this was a way of punishing his wife. She had let him down; she had foolishly passed the papers over to a lawyer; and she had been a disinterested mother caught up in the social whirl at such a cost to both Marie and himself that Marie had had to find affection elsewhere. "Or possibly," he repeated, "she had had several lovers and did not know who it was." He said it firmly and it was enough. Solange was numbed by it. "She also knew that I had taken on the personal care of Emile, son of my old friend. She knows that Emile is of good family. She was a desperate girl, a beautiful one; yet he ignored her when she needed to marry someone quickly. Even after her problem was solved she was still furious that he ignored her. Don't blame her too much for this."

She looked up in astonishment. "Don't blame her? I want to know why you went so far to see him ruined."

"Once the case had started, I had to go on with it to protect our family name, and to protect Marie. I love her."

"Love! This is not a father's love of his daughter! This is an obscene, jealous passion. This is not anger that she had an affair or two. This is fury from within you." She was surprised at her own words. "My poor little Marie!" The General noticed that this seemed to be first sign of compassion his wife had shown in years. "My poor little Marie!" she repeated. "Why didn't she come to me?"

"Because you live in a different world. In the back of your mind you knew the truth as well as I, and probably sooner. Remember the next morning when you couldn't find Marie's nightdress? You searched for a while and then, almost relieved that it was missing, you gave up. You did not want to know what was wrapped in it."

"I thought it was lost."

"But if it had been torn, with a little blood from the assault, it would have been excellent evidence. No! You didn't want to know. You've always been able to push unpleasant things out of your mind. This time I'll see you don't. You're face to face with it."

She closed her eyes to shut it out. "Please stop. I've had enough. You went on with the case after you knew that la Roncière was innocent."

"I had to," he said weakly.

"Why? Why? Why?"

"As soon as I saw that bundle I knew there'd been no attempted rape or break-in, but I had thrown out la Roncière that night because I was not sure, but I thought he *could* be writing the letters. I didn't want to take a chance. Remember, I never asked him to confess to any kind of assault." He was defending himself against the indefensible, and knew it.

"When did you find it out?"

"I had a thorough look at Marie's exercise-book paper, her writing and her ink." He stopped and looked angrily at his wife. "If you had taken enough interest in your own daughter to recognise her paper and ink you would never have been taken in! She had no reason to write to you so you didn't know her writing, but you were so bored by her education that you had never bothered to see if she was learning anything!"

"Don't you talk to me like that! It was you who bullied that man into a confession. So, in the next few days you found out . . ."

"Yes, and I got Marie to tell me everything." Another kind of jealousy was now flooding over Solange. She was angry that he had had Marie's confidence and had not told his own wife. She asked him why.

"Because I told her that it would be kept from you, but I had to know the truth."

"And even then you didn't bother to write to la Roncière and apologise . . ."

"How could I? He would never have kept it to himself. He would have ruined me, and after you passed the papers over the journals were full of it. We had the witnesses, the evidence. Berryer assured me of a conviction because we held the trump card, the confession."

"Yet, even knowing that Marie had forged the letters, it was still your choice to go on."

He did not reply at once. "Choice?" he echoed "Choice? In our way of life is there a choice about anything? Decisions are made in accordance with standards laid down before we are born. To observe these standards becomes a matter of self-respect."

"Don't defend yourself. I'm not attacking you. It's my fault too." She started to cry. There were no sobs, no hysterics — the tears just rolled down her cheeks and she made no effort to stem them with a handkerchief.

He walked over to her and took her hand, which she withdrew at once. She turned away.

He felt deserted, alone, and empty of all emotion. He wanted to sleep and sleep for ever. Sleep might shut this out.

Even with tears streaming down her face, Solange's voice was controlled. "Go to Marie," she said. "She needs you." And as he hesitated she added, "I don't need you."

General le Baron Charles Paul de Morell left the room slowly and climbed the stairs to his daughter's simple room at the top of the house.

The dog in the distance barked again. Another carriage rattled by. One of his own carriages went slowly down the drive with Helen and her box. Subdued orders to the guard outside penetrated the walls of the house. An owl perched in a plane tree in the Bois de Boulogne hooted. A fox taking advantage of the shadow seized a duck from among its kind and for a few minutes there was a great disturbance of quacking and flapping. But it all died down and a blanket of darkness and silence at last hid everything.

EPILOGUE

At the beginning of the following week Solange made arrangements to go to live with her sister in Versailles. Somehow she managed to get back into the society she loved so much; but it was never quite the same.

People would stop talking as soon as they saw her come into the room, and conversation would take a little while to resume its normal buzz. Returning invitations too was difficult as she was no longer living with her husband.

Helen Allen left the Paris hotel as soon as she had been paid, and carefully destroyed the incriminating letter she had written. She had no intention of doing or saying anything that might delay her return to her father's house in Kent.

After Louis-Napoleon's attempted coup of 1840 had failed, he was defended by Maître Berryer, whose support of religious liberty brought him into collision with the leader of the left centrists, Adolphe Thiers. Despite his defence of Louis-Napoleon, Berryer was firm in his denunciation of the *coup d'état* the following year and was accordingly imprisoned for a short salutary time only. On his release he returned to the law and in 1855 became a member of the French Academy. He was elected to the Legislative Assembly as an adversary of the empire of 1863, and died five years later, never having become Minister of Justice.

Maître Chaix d'Est Ange never achieved the distinction he deserved at the bar, and never discovered the 'cause' of Marie's anger. If he had known that Marie had had designs on Emile, and if he had also known that an unknown person had made her pregnant, he would have quickly grasped that a 'respectable' marriage would have solved all. He had realised that she had an unstable nature but he had not discovered that she felt herself snubbed by Emile and thought herself to be 'a woman scorned'. D'Est Ange made a reasonable living at his chosen profession, having the necessary brains, the ambition and the ability; but he was denied the heights because he lacked ruthlessness.

Samuel Gilieron, a good footman, was taken back into the home of Solange's mother, whence he had come.

Lieutenant Octave d'Estouilly resigned his commission, kept his vow of silence on the la Roncière affair in a drastic way by joining a silent order of monks, and died some thirty-five years later in the monastery.

General de Morell tried hard to entertain in his Paris house with Marie at his side. Few invitations were accepted, none returned. Even Marshal Soult was otherwise engaged when asked on three occasions to dine.

Old General de la Roncière, with Maître Chaix d'Est Ange, appealed at the Court of Cassation, but the appeal failed, and was seen by both men as a totally incomprehensible blow. The old general did not spare himself in trying to clear his son's name. He wrote to London, to Lord Abinger, Chief Baron of the Court of the Exchequer and asked his opinion.

Lord Abinger said that the confession, having been extracted by threats, had no judicial weight at all. He confirmed that Emile had not written the letters. He wrote to the old general saying that it was appalling that the evidence of Marie was given under circumstances deliberately contrived for dramatic effect, and that proper cross-examination was forbidden. He told General de la Roncière to take some comfort in the certainty of his son's innocence.

This declaration from Abinger back-fired and was thought in high French circles to be an impertinence by an English foreigner who had no right to publicly question French justice.

It is on record that President Férey said after the trial, "I would have cut off my right arm rather than sign that judgement." It is not on record that he removed his right arm. He had qualms about Emile's sentence to the extent that he went back on the deportation order and had him gaoled in France within reasonable distance of his father. This brought a little comfort to the old man, who did not live to see his son released but was given free access to visit him whenever he liked.

Maître Berryer was also reported to have said, "I have always regretted that verdict. I am now filled with remorse."

Marshal Soult strenuously prevented any review of the case, although the clamour was noisy at first.

King Louis-Philippe in 1843, sensing that an undercurrent relating to the case might well up against him, lopped two years off Emile's sentence.

In 1849, when the July Monarchy had fallen, it was Odilon Barrot who was Minister of Justice, not Berryer. Barrot, who had never mentioned the case in public after leaving the court, instigated a full enquiry, as a result of which, Emile, who had now been out of gaol for six years, was made a Commandant in the National Guard. He retired in 1869 with the celebrated cross showing him to be a commander of the Legion of Honour and died in 1874.

In her nineteenth year, Marie fell in love with and married a well-known Belgian diplomat, the Marquis d'Eyrargues. They retired to Normandy where she became the mother of three children.

Later, she was to become a regular patient of the then-famous mental specialist, Jean-Martin Charcot. Marie was never known to speak of Emile, and on the two or three occasions on which his name was mentioned in her presence, she had either forgotten who he was, or pretended she had.

General le Baron de Morell became a social outcast, even losing the one he loved more than himself and his possesions, Marie. He was not invited to her wedding. He had no friends, and was so continuously and mercilessly snubbed that he resigned his posts, left Paris and went to live in the south of France in Hyères, where the story had travelled ahead of him. As far as is known he knew no rest from the scandal until his death in 1865.

Emile's own diary is so revealing about his sexual appetite that it must be assumed to tell the truth. He listed the girls he slept with in spite of having a real love for his mistress, Melanie Lair, a girl he had met in Paris, who followed him to Saumur and paid for her own lodgings to be close to him. The letters exchanged between Emile and Melanie show that he had an affectionate and gentle nature. He mentions Marie only once, and then as being 'unattainable' because she was his general's daughter.

Should you go to the Cavalry School in Saumur, you will see a polished oak rectangle on the wall in the officers' mess. In gold paint are the names of all the generals who had charge of the school since Marshal Soult rebuilt it in 1814. The years 1833, 1834 and 1835 have been obliterated by sand-papering and the board has been revarnished. I doubt that anyone will be able to tell you why this has happened, nor who that general was, unless it is someone who has read this book.